A Handbook for Teaching African Literature

Elizabeth Gunner
Lecturer in Commonwealth Literature,
University of London
formerly Teacher Fellow, Extramural Division,
School of Oriental and African Studies,
University of London

HEINEMANN

in association with
the Extramural Division
of the
School of Oriental and African Studies

Heinemann International Literature & Textbooks
A division of Heinemann Educational Books Ltd.,
Halley Court, Jordan Hill, Oxford OX2 8EJ

PMB 5205, Ibadan · PO Box 45314, Nairobi
PO Box 10103, Village Post Office, Gaborone

OXFORD LONDON EDINBURGH
MADRID PARIS ATHENS BOLOGNA
MELBOURNE SYDNEY AUCKLAND
IBADAN NAIROBI GABORONE HARARE
PORTSMOUTH NH (USA)
SINGAPORE TOKYO

Heinemann Educational Books Inc.
371 Hanover Street, Portsmouth,
New Hampshire 03801, USA

British Library Cataloguing in Publication Data
Gunner, Elizabeth
A handbook for teaching African literature.
  1. African literature—study and teaching
  (Secondary)—Great Britain
  I. 1. Title
809′.896′871241 PO 8004

ISBN 0-435-92260-2

Set in 10/11 pt Sabon by Oxprint Ltd, Oxford
Printed in Great Britain by
Thomson Litho Ltd, East Kilbride, Scotland

91 92 93 94 10 9 8 7 6

Contents

Preface

This is one of a series of publications of the School of Oriental and African Studies' Extramural Division, designed to support teachers who wish to introduce or extend one or more aspects of Asian and African Studies. We think it is a substantial and practical contribution which will be of interest particularly to teachers of English and also to those teaching social studies or general studies, wherever their schools are situated.

Elizabeth Gunner is particularly well qualified to make this contribution as she has taught English in Britain and in West Africa and South Africa, has held a SOAS Teaching Fellowship and has also undertaken research at SOAS in African Oral Literature. Dr Gunner has also tested much of the material with the help of teachers in a number of schools and through participation in in-service courses for teachers.

E. O'Connor
Organizer of Extramural Studies

The author and publishers have made every effort to trace copyright holders, but if any have been overlooked they will be glad to make the necessary arrangements at the first opportunity.

Introduction

There is a greater need now than ever before to look critically and carefully at the range of texts taught in English courses in British secondary schools. We need to ask ourselves whether pupils are being exposed, through class texts, to the real range of what is available. There are many reasons why African authors writing in English should be increasingly recognized as having a central rather than a marginal place in our cultural life. For one thing – the essentially multi-cultural, multi-racial character of late twentieth-century British society needs to be reflected in the range of cultural experience which literature can provide. Books do not only shape reading habits, they also shape habits of thinking on issues such as race, culture and social values. Texts by African writers often provide an alternative view of history, or illuminate an aspect of history and individual experience previously not available to a particular pupil or group of pupils. Family relations, the sense of identity, the interplay of personal and political roles may all appear in a vivid and forceful new light in a work by a writer who uses English, yet comes from a very different society from his or her British reader. That is the essence of the books brought together for study in this *Handbook*. They constantly present the reader – and in this case I am thinking mainly of the British secondary pupil – with new and challenging images of experience. Thus the texts constantly demolish stereotypes, challenge and disturb complacent images of distant, static black societies. By their vitality, their joy and sometimes the pain they depict, these texts provide an antidote to aggressive or arrogant racist responses to black people. They should encourage children to feel more deeply in touch with those in other societies, and should encourage them to address more firmly the social and political issues which provide the wider context of any literary text.

For some British children, particularly those of Afro-Caribbean descent, texts by African authors may provide an opportunity to explore further, aspects of their own past, and present, in a particularly meaningful way. Such explorations may do much to lessen the tensions generated by a diet of literature – and much media coverage – that makes no effort to include a wider sense of contemporary British culture, or to provide a wider sense of the past beyond a narrowly British past.

The texts included in Section One of the *Handbook* could all be used in the work of a lively and forward-looking English Department. Only the first, by the Guinean writer, Camara Laye, is in translation from the French. All the others were written in English, although in some cases, particularly in the two novels by Chinua Achebe, there is a distinct sense of the idiom and images of another language being worked into the English. In other words, English is made, in a most skilful way, to become a window into another culture and another language. Camara Laye's text, *The African Child*, is part of the large and important genre of autobiographical writing, and focuses, as the title indicates, on the author's early, formative years, firstly in northern Guinea and later in the coastal capital of Conakry. A second, powerful contributor to the same genre is Peter Abrahams' *Tell Freedom* which provides an intense and painful insider's account of childhood and youth in South Africa in the late 1920s and 1930s. The two texts by Camara Laye and Abrahams provide contrasting accounts of childhood in an African context and could be taught together or included as part of a wider study of British, Caribbean or Commonwealth autobiographies of childhood.

A text which relates closely in cultural terms to *The African Child* is Niane's edition of *Sundiata, An Epic of Old Mali*. Sundiata was the first king of the thirteenth century West African kingdom of Mali, located in the same part of the upper Niger as that where Camara Laye lived some seven centuries later. The epic of Sundiata is still sung by travelling poets who use Mandinka or Bambara to sing of the exploits of the famous Sundiata. Indeed, even London has lately been fortunate enough to hear the Mandinka griots who have made several performances in the capital and other centres, singing of Sundiata and other heroes and accompanied by the music of the elegant, harplike kora. The text of Niane's *Sundiata* provides a unique insight into an African epic rich in history and rich, too, in its literary motifs of qualities relating to the hero, themes such as loss and exile, and the struggle to recover an inheritance. The two texts included from the works of the Kenyan novelist Ngugi wa Thiong'o focus on various kinds of conflict in the lives of young people growing up in independent Kenya. *Weep Not, Child* shows a young Kenyan boy living through the years of 'Mau Mau', the independence struggle by the Land and Freedom Army against British colonial rule in Kenya. The boy's family life is destroyed and the pain and disruption caused by living in the midst of violence and confrontation are portrayed with persuasive skill by Ngugi. In *The River Between* Ngugi, drawing from a slightly earlier period of colonial rule in Kenya, again depicts young people caught in a situation of deep conflict where there is no easy choice when it comes to deciding between love and wider community loyalties. The two novels by the celebrated Nigerian novelist Chinua Achebe which are included in the *Handbook* bring into sharp perspective the wide and important area of culture clash. *Things Fall Apart* deals subtly and powerfully with violent change within a society because of the intrusion of a more powerful force which brings with it British colonial rule, and Christianity. *No Longer At Ease*, set in contemporary Nigeria, addresses the same problem of a clash of cultures and its effect on the individual's personal and public life. The same key problem of the uneasy dialogue between very different cultures is examined in a fairly light-hearted way in the play *The Lion and The Jewel* by Wole Soyinka. This early work by the 1986 Nobel Literature Prize winner draws effortlessly on the resources of his richly poetic mother tongue, Yoruba. Yet it shows too, the influence of Shakespearean drama, as Soyinka studied at Leeds under the Shakespearean critic, Wilson Knight, and has often acknowledged his debt to him. A writer whose work is receiving increasing recognition is the South African Bessie Head, who did so much to celebrate and explore social and personal life, and particularly the lives of women, in Botswana, her adopted home. Head's *When Rainclouds Gather* takes the reader into rural community politics, and weaves in the themes of love, family life, and a haunting account of the challenges and dangers for a child in rural Botswana.

A very different but equally powerful insight into Southern African life comes from the play by Athol Fugard, John Kani and Winston Ntshona, *Sizwe Bansi is Dead*. The play takes the reader into the heart of political oppression by showing the typical dilemmas facing black workers in Port Elizabeth, one of South Africa's major industrial centres on the south east coast near the 'independent' Transkei. The play poses basic questions about individual freedom, identity, work, and family life in a dramatic style that relates to European dramatists such as Brecht and Ionesco but is still distinctively South African in its cultural resonances. The third play included in the *Handbook* is by the Ghanaian writer Ama Ata Aidoo. She turns to the history of her own Fante people to explore personal and public themes. She shows the dilemma of a young woman, Anowa, who marries against her family's wishes only to discover that her handsome husband, in his quest for easy money, is willing to buy and sell human beings and become one of the richest of the coastal slave traders. The sorrow of a barren, spoilt marriage, and the disgrace of conniving – however indirectly – in slavery, thus form the themes of this very accessible play which courageously focuses on a painful era in the history of Europe, Africa and the New World. The appreciation of a play such as *Anowa* is greatly increased if there is access to information about the cultural and political context in which it is set. The same is true for virtually all the texts included in Section I of the *Handbook* and for that reason I have included in each unit brief points relating to the cultural, social and political contexts of the particular text.

The units of oral and written poetry in Section 1 are intended to provide teachers with new material both in English and in translation from African languages and to provide some insight into the techniques and themes of African poets working in both the oral and written modes. Fortunately there are now also excellent working anthologies for schools which include African poets within a broad sweep of world writers in English. A very recent and extremely useful publication is Rhodri Jones' *One World Poets* (Heinemann Educational Books, 1986).

Section 2, 'Themes from African Literature', draws on a range of texts many of which fall outside those covered in Section 1. These should prove useful for group or individual work around a particular theme (an approach now included as an optional part of the new GCSE syllabuses). Passages and poems in Section 2 could also serve as points of departure for further reading, leading pupils – and teachers – to explore in more depth work by a particular writer, or the literature of a particular country. For instance in the important thematic section, The Land, the first extract, from a novel by the prolific Nigerian writer John Munonye, shows a farmer shifting – in the face of family opposition – away from the traditional, but unprofitable, and backbreaking practice of yam growing to the innovative and potentially more profitable practice of trading in palm-oil. In the extract entitled 'The Barren Land' the Zimbabwean writer Charles Mungoshi relentlessly depicts the arrogant youth,

Lucifer, his head filled with an education and aspirations that take him away from his people. Yet he also shows the reader that the land is barren because it has been neglected by those in power – the land, like the people is 'waiting for the rain', waiting for change. Passages in Section 2, therefore, could be used to link into wider development issues such as the discussion of rural poverty in Africa, and its causes. Classes could also discuss possible ways out of the cycle of urban and rural impoverishment, or the role of education in the Third World: for instance, is the expensive, often elitist model of western education appropriate, or is the type of 'dialogic' education advocated by the Brazilian educationist Paolo Freire (*Pedagogy of the Oppressed*, 1972) more appropriate? Section 2, therefore, is intended to be multi-functional and should both serve as a resource in itself, and as a catalyst for ideas and for further research.

African literature, British syllabuses and examination boards

There is now (in 1987) no excuse for any teacher-training institute or university education department anywhere in Britain not to have texts by African authors in its lists. African literature in English is a distinctive part of the wider body of world literature written in English and as such must be taken on board by all but the most myopically ethnocentric of Education and English departments. This shift away from a narrow definition of what constitutes 'English literature' has been recognised by those responsible for laying down the new national guidelines for the GCSE English Literature syllabuses, exams for which will be taken for the first time in 1987. Thus under the heading 'Content' the GCSE National Guidelines document states:

Examining groups may extend the scope of what is traditionally regarded as the canon of English Literature in recognition that awareness of the riches of cultural diversity is one of the rewards of the study of litera-ture. The majority of the works must be literary texts originally written in English which may, for example, include American and Commonwealth writing, but works in translation may also be included.

The second point made as regards content is also relevant for teachers wishing to use this *Handbook*. Boards are recommended to allow teachers a great deal of initiative over the selection and grouping of texts:

The works for detailed study need not be prescribed in a set texts syllabus of a traditional kind. For example, a wider personal choice may be offered in recommended reading of authors, themes, periods or genres.
(GCSE *National Criteria for English*, p. 5)

A glance at the syllabus of the London and East Anglia Group (LEAG), one of the five new GCSE Boards, gives some indication of how the guidelines have been translated into the recommendations of a particular Board. The LEAG's 'Aims' mentions the need to allow pupils 'to explore through literature the cultures of their own and other societies'. The syllabus contains an 'Advisory Book List' with the rider that, 'Where it is desired to use a text not in the advisory list care should be taken to ensure that it is of a comparable quality and demand'. Clearly this is no realm for the timid, but exciting territory for the determined and the resourceful, and teachers who, singly or as a group, wish to suggest their own texts need to be armed with evidence of 'comparable quality'. A *Handbook* such as this can provide tangible evidence of such quality. It can also provide pointers for the more open-ended, imaginative treatment of texts, an approach that is now recognised as relevant, alongside the older, more tightly critical approach to a text.

The great amount of teachers' option which the LEAG and the other four GCSE Exam Boards now allow, throws the onus for inno-vation and careful, informed grouping of texts, neatly onto the teacher and thus allows

for greater scope for the use of texts such as those in Section 1 of this *Handbook*, and indeed, Section 2. For instance, the LEAG in its Open Study unit (Section 1 is 'Drama and Open Study') suggests as one of the possible topics, 'Study of a place or region, for example literature which has a strong geographic and/or social context'. Although Africa, or regions of Africa are not mentioned, there is an obvious possibility here for building a group of texts either on an Africa-wide basis or regionally, round, say, Kenya, Southern Africa, Nigeria, or, more broadly, West Africa. Texts covered in this *Handbook* are possible ones to start with in working out such groupings. Again in the LEAG's optional Section 3, 'Poetry and Prose Course Work' whch is the study of a theme or topic, the Handbook's Sections 1 and 2 each provide possibilities for working out how African texts could be integrated into broader studies. It is at present largely in the area of teachers' own choices that African writing in English will find its place in the literature syllabus in British schools. The LEAG's Advisory Booklist does not reveal any great advance as far as work by African writers is concerned. Of the 117 texts listed for 1987–88 only three – texts by Achebe, Emecheta and Paton – could be called African although there is a welcome sprinkling of texts by Caribbean, Asian and Black British writers. Evidence from some London schools, the Midlands and some Northern centres suggests that teachers are in fact taking advantage of the new possi-bilities for flexibility in the GCSE syllabuses, and African texts are in this way finding a place at GCSE level. There is however still much need for informed dialogue among teachers, English teaching organisations, Heads of Department, multi-cultural advisers and parents.

Surprisingly, it is the A-level Boards which have shown the most responsiveness to the pressure of groups such as NATE, NAME and ATCAL, multi-cultural advisers and head teachers in the call for greater multi-cultural diversity in English syllabuses. For 1987 the Associate Examining Board has Ngugi's epic novel of post-independence Kenya, *Petals of Blood* as one of its optional texts and the Cambridge Examinations Board includes Bessie Head's *Maru* on its Modern Writers paper (as well as a text by the Jamaican, Roger Mais). The University of London Examination Board includes Chinua Achebe's *Arrow of God* as a 1987 text, and also a text by Roger Mais.

Texts on booklists of public examination syllabuses lend much needed official backing to the voices calling for commitment to a multi-cultural approach to the teaching of literature. But that alone is not enough and could on its own soon become little more than window dressing. There must be momentum for continuity and growth in this area. The thrust to achieve real confidence on the part of successive generations of teachers must come from teacher-based organizations, parents and community pressure groups, heads and multi-cultural advisers. Moreover those working in teacher-training colleges and in university and polytechnic education departments, and in libraries, have a special responsibility in educating future generations of teachers. There are clear signs of an increasing interest in African, Caribbean and, more broadly, Commonwealth writing in a number of universities and polytechnics in the country. The universities of Exeter, Edinburgh, Leeds, Sheffield, Hull, York, Kent, Reading, Sussex and London all offer some component of African, Caribbean or Commonwealth literature in undergraduate or post-graduate courses, and the University of Kent has for several years offered a degree in African and Caribbean Studies in its Humanities faculty. The polytechnics of Hatfield, Bristol, Portsmouth and North London, and Humberside College of Higher Education also have strong interests in the area of African and Caribbean literatures. The inclusion of African writing at secondary level is not, therefore, an isolated event, but, together with much excellent work at primary level, is part of a broad move towards recognising the value of diversifying and extending our notion both of 'English literature' and of British culture.

The question of levels

This edition has been written especially with British schools in mind but teachers in a number of countries where there is a growing interest in African literature and an awareness of its potential for the classroom may well want to use the handbook. For this reason each of the first eleven units of Section 1 includes a suggested *age range* in its *Level of use* section in addition to mentioning the British form which seems most appropriate. This I hope will make the units and levels accessible to teachers working in educational systems in some cases very different from the British one. So, for instance, age 15–16 in *Level of use* would be the equivalent of:

Standard 9 (or pre-Matriculation) in South Africa
Grade 4 in Zimbabwe
Years 10–11 in Australia
5th form in New Zealand
Grade 12 in Canada
and Grades 10–11 in the United States of America.

The age ranges given and the suggested forms are, of course, only relative. Colleges of Further Education and Adult Education Classes may also wish to use selected units from Section 1 with groups of varying ages. After all, *The African Child* was declared a 'minor masterpiece' not by French teachers but by French critics who were writing with the general public in mind, not schoolgoers.

The Thematic Anthology which makes up Section 2 is by design adaptable for use at various levels of secondary or high school. In a number of cases a passage or poem chosen can be used for study at different age levels depending on the specific needs of the class and the intentions of the individual teacher. Section 2 should also have much to offer those working in Colleges of Further Education and in Adult Education. The thematically grouped sections could be used for intensive oral and written work in language classes as well as in work on wider topics connected with North–South relations, colonialism and independence and identity in the Third World.

In short, in Sections 1 and 2 I have aimed to be both precise and wide-ranging, specific and versatile. In this way I hope that a subject which I consider of great educational importance will be introduced to as wide an audience as possible.

How to use the *Handbook*

Section 1

There are 13 units in this section and the first 11, each dealing with a single work, all follow a similar layout:

Level of use and scope gives a brief critical account of the work.
The author and *The setting* provide background information.

Classroom use includes:

> *Level of use*
> *Points for focus and emphasis*
> *Teaching suggestions:*
> (a) questions on the text
> (b) questions involving creative writing, dramatization and so on
> (c) questions which attempt to link aspects of the book with work in other subjects.
> *Topics and passages* lists themes in the work and a few passages for reading aloud.

Teaching aids covers:

> *Audio-visual aids*
> *Background reading*
> *Reading links.* Here I have listed, sometimes rather optimistically, other books by African and non-African authors which could be used and referred to along with the text under discussion.

Most teachers will of course want to work out their own approach to the novel, autobiography or play being studied and will use only a few of the questions I have supplied in *Teaching suggestions*. Nevertheless I have included a fair number in the hope that too much is preferable to too little. In some units I have

marked questions suited to group work **G**. **D** indicates a question that is suitable for dramatization.

The final two units, on poetry, attempt to give the briefest of introductions to both oral and written poetry and to suggest some poems for use. Here I have given no specific questions on poems but have suggested possible approaches and outlined possible difficulties.

Section 2

This grew out of a rather smaller anthology compiled for use during a day conference on African literature and African history held at Haringey Teachers' Centre in November 1979 and organized by the Haringey Multi-cultural Curriculum Support Group. It is a thematic anthology. Teachers should be able to integrate the material into other already established thematic units such as Childhood, treat sections as separate entities, or take a number of themes in sequence (see *The question of levels* p.xi).

Section 3

This is a resource section. Though by no means exhaustive, it aims to give a general coverage of the audio-visual materials available in Britain and to provide suggestions for texts available for classroom study. General resources such as museums, associations and bookshops are also included.

I would like to thank the following people for assistance in the course of preparing the *Handbook*: Kenyan and Nigerian friends based in Reading or London patiently answered my many questions about the cultural, social and political background to particular texts and I am very grateful to them. Rachel Funke Faluyi (now a Registrar at Ondo State University, Ado-Ekiti, Nigeria) was particularly helpful with the Nigerian texts, and Margaret Baffour-Awuah from Cape Coast gave me much illuminating information about the Fante coastal region and people, as background for *Anowa*. She also provided helpful details about the play's author, Ama Ata

Aidoo. Meeting the late Bessie Head very briefly in London while I was working on the book was an added impetus and inspiration for the unit on *When Rainclouds Gather*. Dr Tony Burgess and Professor Henry Widdowson of the Institute of Education gave advice in the early stages of planning the book and H. L. B. Moody suggested ways of expanding the original outline of the *Handbook*. Moira Mechem, Gillian Dorman-Smith and Janet Inglis commented on an early version of Unit 1. Stephen Wicks sent me his comments on teaching *A Man of the People*, and made enquiries about resources in the West Country. Rosalind Walker read and commented on several units of Section 1. Mike Convey of the English Department at Newman College commented on several early units and gave much valuable advice. Dr Francis Burns, Head of English at Newman College, gave advice at all stages, and I am particularly grateful to him. Peter Rogers at the Newman College Centre for Asian and African resources also gave advice and provided a useful forum for discussion with teachers on African texts. Professor Andrew Gurr of Reading University made suggestions for East African material, Professor Gordon Innes helped with material on *Sundiata* and Dennis Walder with material on Athol Fugard. John Picton of SOAS advised for the note on masks and masquerading and Tony Humphries helped with the drama, in the light of his own teaching experience in Nigeria. My thanks also to Elizabeth Marvin who sent material from Hampstead Hall School, Birmingham and to Liz Gerschel of ILEA for allowing me to use material from her *Fourth Form Approaches to 'The African Child'*. Thanks also to Richard Tames who gave generously of his time and advice.

Finally I would like to thank my husband Mike for assistance with Section 3 and, as always, for general moral support; also my mother, Pearl Tucker, who took charge of the children in long school holidays, thus enabling me to complete this and several other projects.

E. G., 1987

Classroom comments

The African Child

*From Hampstead Hall School,
Birmingham*

The following comments came from a fourth-year 'O' level class who had just finished *Pride and Prejudice* and Durrell's *My Family and other Animals*.

The class read *The African Child* at home and spent only a few periods on it. Yet their range of response is interesting. Some stress the shared areas of experience in the book: school, father—son relationships, friendships. Others are interested in the carefully controlled transition to adulthood. There are also negative comments, suggesting that the strangeness of the names and customs remained a barrier to enjoyment.

1 Even though this was written in another country with people of different cultures it showed that people are the same – the bullying of the younger children at school, his possessive mother and his relationship with Fanta and Marie. This could have happened in England. (Amanda, 15)

2 Although I didn't enjoy the book much, I was curious to know how the author's career was going to turn out in the end . . . Before the ritual the author considered himself as just another one of the boys, but after the ritual he was a man, proud and strong, and most of all he was an individual. He was given his own house, men's clothes and was on his own, free to do whatever he wished and to lead his own life. (Lesley, 14)

3 I didn't know how to pronounce them, so I just had to shorten the names to something I could understand. The book took me longer to read. I was less interested in it.
(Helen S., 15)

4 I couldn't get into the book and it didn't interest me. (Helen G., 15)

5 It was expressive, but not as dramatic as *Pride and Prejudice*. The description in *The African Child* was tremendous as you could easily imagine the way of life. It was easier to read than Jane Austen's classical novel. The story content did not stay at the same high quality throughout the book. The middle of the book seemed the most interesting.
(Geraldine, 14)

6 To understand it was easy enough but you had to concentrate on it all the time, if not you would find yourself lost. The story was immensely vivid. You can almost imagine yourself on the coast of Conakry just watching the rushing waves and the fishermen in their small boats ready to catch unwary fish.
(Malcolm, 15)

7 The story content on the whole was interesting and explained the author's childhood vividly. I think I would like to read more books written by African authors because in this way we can also learn about different religions, different superstitions and a different way of life in other countries.

I thought the most interesting part of this book was about the author's education. I liked this because it explained how he was taught, the discipline and how the older boys treated the younger ones. Also how the teachers refused to be aware of what was going on in schools outside lesson time.
(Surbjit, 14)

8 One of the most interesting parts of the book in my view is when Camara tells us of how the older boys of his school used to tease and pinch things from the younger ones. His friend's father heard about this cruelty and decided to invite one of the older

boys over to supper one night. The older boy came because he thought he would get an enormous meal, but when he came his father kicked him out of the family's compound. Also when Camara's father got to hear about the same cruelty towards the younger boys, he thought he might go and have a word with the headmaster. They met each other in the centre of the playground and got into an argument. His father hit the headmaster which I really enjoyed because the headmaster comes over as a cruel character.

(Paul, 14)

A fifth-year CSE class at Hampstead Hall School also studied the book and extracts from their writing follow.

In two separate essays on the book, Jasmine, 15, first compares Camara Laye's schooling with her own, and in the second essay tackles the difficult topic of the black snake, mystically described by Camara Laye's father as 'the guiding spirit of our race.'

(a) Parents agreed to almost anything that went on in the village school, but did object, very strongly, about the bigger boys beating the younger ones. One of the boy's parents went to see the headmaster about this situation but the headmaster told him everything in the school was all right and told the man to mind his business and gave the man a thump. 'And he hit out with his fists.' Teachers now are not allowed to hit our parents in any way. They talk things out together if they don't agree to anything that is going on in schools. Although the system in Africa was different pupils are much the same as those today. They all do the same kind of tricks and childish pranks such as pulling hair. 'We liked to tease the girls and pull their hair.' I would prefer the education we get today because we have more privileges to do things. Our school buildings have changed over the years and got better. We have better books, rulers and pens. We also are able to say what we feel and the teachers don't object.

(b) The snake was important to the villagers for several reasons. The snake selected someone as a leader, whom all the rest of the tribe could respect and rely on. This leader had authority over all the others in the tribe. The passing on of power, by the snake to different leaders, continued from one generation to another; this gave stability. The snake was like a religion to all the people, they had a great faith in the snake to do anything, the most impossible things that they thought he wouldn't be able to do. The faith they had in the snake is just like Christians because they have a religion and believe in someone who they think is great and mighty. The snake also formed a protection for the tribe because it gave them warning of future events, and so this gave them their guiding decisions.

From Parliament Hill Girls' School, London

This fourth-year class spent four weeks on *The African Child* and besides dramatization and creative writing based on the book, small groups recorded their discussions on tape. Liz Gerschel's interesting study, *Fourth Form Approaches to The African Child* (unpub. typescript, 1981) shows the way in which members of the class moved through the issues, among them, child–parent relationships, and the change from childhood to adulthood, which Laye explores. In A below she describes the class and her approach to the book. Extracts **B** and **C** are transcriptions of taped discussions between small groups and **D** is written work by a class member.

A The class included some people whose families are of Cypriot, Asian and Caribbean origin, and many of the girls knew themselves the strain of culture conflicts. One of the most interesting effects of reading *The African Child* was the sharing of experiences, as the class moved towards a greater awareness and understanding of each other and of their parents. Through their discussions of the differing reactions of Laye's mother and father to his going to school, the girls were able to understand the reactions of their own parents to the changing cultural patterns around them – and this was true of the whole class and not only of the minority ethnic groups within it.

B A discussion on Chapters 1 and 2.
  C: The mother and the father ... they wanted him to live the life they had.
  A: Yeah, I see. Also they didn't have many luxuries ... it was quite primitive.
  C: It's supposed to be 1924, but I thought it was much earlier ...
  C: It seemed very early.
  A: Yeah, I see what you mean.
  S: I didn't really think it seemed like a tribe.
  E: There weren't enough people there.
  S: You know, when you think of a tribe you think of real Africa.
  C: They used 'compound' a lot, though. They said it was a compound, didn't they?
  A: Yes, but it was very very close.
  C: That's what I thought, yes.
  A: Also nobody hurried anywhere. They had a dignity all of their own which was interesting, you know ... he said further back that no one hurried anywhere. They seemed to take everything quite slowly and in their stride.
  A: The main thing about Chapter 2 is the gold ...
    (General agreement)
  A: (with animation): Also, you know, yeah, the ritual of putting the liquids on his body – I thought that was interesting.
  S: Yes, what were they? They looked like pots, weren't they, and if they, like ...
  E: What did they do? Ward off evilness?
  A: I think so – something like that ...
  S: Wiped it on his body, didn't they?
  A: Different oils for different things ...
  C: Like oils ... to protect ... like ritual washing because they – oh, I know – was it because they were Muslims?
  E: But where did they get the oil from?

C A discussion of Camara's transition to manhood and his changed relationship with his mother; the role of his mother (Chapters 5, 7 and 8):

  A: She's *not* put down, she's *not* put down ...
  N: It's because they're going into adulthood.
  A: You know boys are meant to be separated.
  N: They're not going to be with their mother any more.
  A: I don't think we're meant to be talking about this, but we're talking about customs and traditions which maybe has got part of the sense that Camara is separated from his mother, but that's kind of the male unity, the whole part of the ... not the male dominance, but the whole sense of the tribe. I think Debbie was wrong in saying the mother was put to the back of the mind. She's not, the mother is so important ... but also there's another part of their lives. He's realizing that he's coming into adulthood and taking women seriously, where before he didn't. You know, he didn't know how to treat this girl, he just pissed around when he was young, but now he's going to take it seriously, 'cos it's important ...
  K: Yeah, but he does later on with Marie when he's staying with his uncle.
  N: Even in England, even in Britain, right in this modern day even now, if you're still tied to your mother's strings, so to speak, then you're often thought of as not being particularly an adult if you're still living with your mother in the same house and all that ...
  A: But why, why is it?
  N: I don't know, I don't know ....
  A: But you've thought that if your string's attached to your father ...
  N: But wait a minute, the point is that's what they're doing now in there, because he's becoming an adult, or so they say, and so they're trying to cut him ... to show him that he does not need his mother any more ... and he *doesn't* need his mother, because his mother has a particularly – what's it called – parental or whatever it is ... she has it

more in her. It is a *fact* that she has it more in her than the father — I don't know why, probably because she's carried it and she's fed it, etc.

A: It? Camara.

N: Yeah, well, any child — you see the mother's always got more feeling — almost always — got more feeling for the child.

A: That's 'cos of the society they've been brought up in.

N: No, no, she's gone through much more. . .

K: The mother has the more dominant part, hasn't she, from the beginning when the child's born . . .

N: Yes, she's carried it, she's gone through with all the pain.

D An extract from an essay on becoming an adult, with reference to *The African Child:*

These [i.e. for a boy, growing a beard and having your voice break] are only a few aspects of growing into an adult, the one that I normally think of is when you have responsibilities like a family. Many men are the bread-winners of the family. Some people think that we have been put into stereotype positions in society. In some ways I agree but not in others. For example, the daily routine of a man may be going to work, coming home, having his dinner, then going to the pub or something like that. In the discussion we had, many didn't agree with this, but if men didn't want to go to the pub they wouldn't just because society has said that this is the thing for a man to do. When I say this it does not involve all men. Most people tend to think of a man being brave and strong and him being the one that the son will look up to, and want to be like when he grows up. Some people do not like to see a man with a built-up body with great big muscles, but if you had to choose between a puny white skeleton of a man or a bronzed muscle-man who would you choose? Well, it's obvious to me.

In the book they had certain rituals that showed that they were growing up, e.g. circumcision and the lions. The only thing today

which is similar is the Jewish boys have their barmitzvah. It is a kind of bravery when they have to go on a platform and read from the Koran [sic]. Nobody can really tell when you become an adult as it depends on the individual. I think that once you have left school and have got a job you do become more adult.

I think that women have a much harder role in life, mentally they are more grown up than boys anyway. I think that this is why girls often think when they are little that they would like to be boys because they have more freedom and get away with a lot more. Especially when they have children because they have to devote much more time to them than has the father. This may be the cause of many break-ups because the woman cannot stand the strain of looking after the child, this could also lead to child-battering. Many men do not realize how hard it is to look after children for hours.

Some women have a much better life than others especially when they are single as they can do as they please and are not tied down in any way. They are also independent as they have their own job and money coming in.

(Stephanie, 14)

Teachers' comments

What was gained then, by having chosen *The African Child* rather than any other book in the stock cupboard? There were some specific benefits in terms of both literary and social awareness:

1 The point was made that an African novel may be included in the CSE/'O' Level English work as successfully as a more traditional English novel. This may not seem much of a point to make, but I think it is important to state the obvious.

2 Links were made in the minds of the students between West African childhood and their own experiences, especially as regards parental expectations and relationships, taking adult responsibilities, etc.

3 There was an appreciably larger demand for 'more books about Africa' and an increased

pressure on my library and on the main school library to stock a wider and better African section. The inadequacy of much of the available material was deplored.

4 Some of the stereotypes and assumptions the girls had brought with them were questioned and rejected, thus it was positive anti-racist teaching.

5 Links between the African novel and European works were introduced naturally, on a literary level and in terms of the colonial influence and heritage.

6 There was a sense of greater understanding of each other in the class. It may not last, but it certainly arose from the sharing of experiences prompted by comparison with Camara Laye's experiences.

7 There may have been spin-offs into other subjects. I heard later that the French teacher had been questioned about Francophone Africa – perhaps too the girls' understanding of history and geography will be a little broader than it might otherwise have been.

Gerschel, *Fourth Form Approaches to The African Child*, p.12

A Man of the People [1]

We usually choose one 'challenging' 'A' level text each year, and the Cambridge Board offers some good ones in its 'Literature Since 1900' paper. I had not read this novel (nor any other Achebe), but having done so felt sure it was a good one to do, though it seemed slight on first impression. The pidgin was an obvious problem, so I joined ATCAL! This proved crucial, because at the 1980 Conference I met Tuks Pearse, who agreed to come and talk to my Sixth Form students, and said we could make a tape of his talk.[2]

Before Tuks' visit, my students had simply read the book once, and at that stage we had not even discussed it. His talk, principally about pidgin generally and specifically, but full of valuable anecdote, affection and humour,

ensured my students' acceptance of the text, and provided the first stage in our discoveries of what lay behind the deceptively slight surface. Tuks also gave me a first class bibliography of manageable proportions.

The students all acknowledge early difficulties in coming to terms with a novel from an alien culture, and a historical context with which they were entirely unfamiliar. One or two think its remoteness from 'Britain in the 80s' discounts its value, but most now speak of coping with the problem as enjoyable and of the cultural insights and sense of common humanity gained as what good literature can offer. The novel also makes them laugh a lot! They like, and can understand the slightly picaresque narrator/hero, and the way in which his chauvinism is feelingly modified by events is not too remote from their own experience. Achebe's lack of technical assurance in developing and deploying his women characters offers a test appropriate to my students' critical maturity. Probably what they find hardest to grasp is the equivocal position of an Achebe/Odili character, involved in and troubled by the forms of autonomy in Africa, and both attracted and repelled by western values and opportunities.

Both they and I like the technical interest of the author/hero/narrator's insight into and comments on his multiple role. It is something that Achebe brings up in a really unpretentious way. Altogether we have found *A Man of the People* exactly the sort of middle-weight novel that gives a gifted 'A' level student a pleasant break, and the less able student a chance to talk and write with pleasure and confidence.

Stephen Wicks,
Camborne School, Cornwall.

[1]This appeared first in the ATCAL Newsletter No.7, August 1982.
[2]Adetokunbo Pearse's tape on *A Man of the People* is now held by the National Sound Archive (see Resources p.141). Copies are available for teachers at a reasonable price.

Section 1 Selected Texts for Classroom Use

Chief Alimani Seku II of Sierra Leone at a memorial ceremony for his father and grandfather (Mike Gunner)

Unit 1 *The African Child*

Camara Laye

Level of use and scope

Camara Laye's *The African Child* is a vivid and poetic evocation of the author's childhood in the Mandinka region of northern Guinea, and of his gradual movement into the world of western education and alien values. He wrote the autobiography when he was studying and working in Paris, thousands of miles from his home. He was, he admits, isolated and lonely: 'I was living alone, in my poor student's room, and I would write. I remember I would write as if in a dream. I would write for my pleasure, and it was an extraordinary pleasure, one that the heart never tired of.' (quoted in Zell, Bundy and Coulon eds, *A New Reader's Guide to African Literature*, Heinemann, 1983, p.404). Laye writes of his close relationship with his parents – his father, the respected goldsmith and blacksmith, and his dignified and loving mother. He does not shirk from exploring the mystical and spiritual aspects of their times: his father's belief in the black snake, 'the guiding spirit of our race', his ritual incantations and the smearing of ointments to ward off evil; his mother's safety from crocodiles because it was the totem of her clan. Here, as in the Manding epic *Sundiata*, old religious beliefs and the teachings of Islam co-exist.

The culture of the French colonial power is encountered through education. Camara attends a Muslim school, and then later a French-speaking school, studying at first in his own village and then later in the distant coastal capital of Conakry. He describes his experiences of school in Kouroussa and recounts also the important stage in his life when childhood was left behind and he became a man. Many African societies mark this transition symbolically with a set of ceremonies which often call for endurance and the acquisition of special knowledge by the new initiates into manhood or womanhood. Once he is circumcised and has passed through the ceremonies of initiation Camara is treated as a man – he has his own hut, new adult clothes, and his once intensely close relationship with his mother becomes more distanced.

Camara's success at school moves him increasingly further away from the sure boundaries of his family life and his own Mandinka culture. He has to leave Kouroussa and makes a 400-mile journey to the coast to attend technical college. The parting, first of all from his parents and then at the station from his brothers, sisters and friends is one of the most moving sections of the book (pp.115–20). He hopes the train will be late: 'Sometimes it was late; perhaps it would be late today. I looked at the clock. It *was* late! But suddenly it appeared and I had to let go of their hands and leave their gentle pressure behind, as if it was the whole of my life' (p.119).

Parting and separation are underlying themes throughout the book. Camara Laye emphasizes, quietly, that it is education which brings this about. Even when he is on holiday with his grandmother in Tindican he is different from the others. As he works with his uncle harvesting rice he asks:

'Won't you let me reap for a while?'
'What would your grandmother say? A sickle is not a plaything: you have no idea how sharp it is!'
'Yes I do.'
'Now it isn't your job to cut rice. I shouldn't think it ever will be: later on . . .' (p.49)

The African Child, Camara Laye. First published in French by Librarie Plon, 1954. English edition, Fontana Paperbacks, 1955, translated by James Kirkup.

The author stresses that his knowledge of his father's work and of his beliefs is incomplete because of the increasing amount of time he spends at school. His mother regrets that he was ever sent to school and bitterly opposes his eventual plans to study in France:

'Do they imagine I'm going to live my whole life apart from my son? Die with him far away?' (p.155)

His father's response is quieter but equally agonized:

'Promise me that you will come back?'
'I shall come back,' I said.
'These distant lands,' he whispered slowly. (p.153)

The book therefore evokes Camara's family life, his community and culture with great immediacy; yet it shows also his separation from that way of life and his struggle to define his new identity.

On its publication in 1954 *L'Enfant Noir* received a mixed reception; it was called 'a minor masterpiece' by some critics and 'a colonialist potboiler' by others, chiefly African nationalists who felt that the book lacked political commitment. Zell and Silver remark that the book is still 'the subject of heated literary discussion'.

The written and spoken responses to the novel which have been quoted (pp.xiv–xviii) show that in British schools the book is likely to be read and discussed with varying degrees of enthusiasm and interest. There is much in the autobiography which should interest classes. Teachers using only extracts from the book have found the school passages in Chapter 6 successful even with first formers (11 year-olds who are perhaps more conscious of what it means to be bullied than those in higher classes!). The mystical and spiritual aspects of the book, touching on both the doctrines of Islam and the respect for the ancestors and other supernatural powers could lead to a discussion of ritual and religious belief and

their part in our lives. Teachers could explore, as Liz Gerschel did with her fourth-year class (14–15 year-olds), the different ways in which the move from puberty to adulthood is marked in Camara Laye's society and in our own. Camara's relationship with his family, particularly with his mother and father would also interest classes. It would give the opportunity to compare experiences and to relate the book as a whole to other novels and autobiographies. The topic of education, from the early Koranic school to the Technical College and after, could lead to discussion contrasting home and school education. Classes might like to discuss the success and failure of education, what makes education worthwhile. Perhaps the last word about what can be gained from reading *The African Child* as a class text should come from a Birmingham schoolgirl, Ashita Patel:

I think I would read more books by African authors because I'm interested in reading about other people's lives as many people in this world of ours do interesting things, their customs, rituals [are] complicated. . . Camara in his young days was surrounded by rituals and customs. I find these enthralling. Superstitions, magical ceremonies, the gay singing and the joyous dancing all made up the mystical atmosphere this book brings alive.

The author

Camara Laye returned to his home country after his years in France. However, he became disillusioned with what he regarded as the intolerant and doctrinaire regime of Sékou Touré. From 1965 he lived in exile in Senegal under the protection of the Senegalese poet-president, Léopold Sédar Senghor. His wife Marie (the girl-friend of his student days in Conakry) spent seven years in jail in Guinea but subsequently joined her husband in Senegal. Other works by Camara Laye include *A Dream of Africa* (1966; Fontana, 1970) and the celebrated allegorical novel *The Radiance of the King* (1956; Fontana, 1965). Camara Laye died in Senegal in 1980.

The setting

Guinea

Guinea gained its independence from France in 1958, led by President Ahmed Sékou Touré. Guinea's colonial relations with France began in the nineteenth century. In the 1860s the French began to gain influence and establish control over the coastal regions. By 1883 the southern part of the country was being ruled as a French colony. Only by 1911, however, was the whole of what is now Guinea under French control (Colin Legum, (ed.) *Africa Handbook*, Penguin, 1969, p.357). One of the most famous opposers of the French was the nineteenth-century Mandinka warrior leader, Samori Touré. Praises for him are still composed and performed for large audiences or played over Radio Guinea.

Guinea is mountainous, the Futa Jalon mountains (mentioned in *The African Child* and in *Sundiata*) being the most famous. The country is rich in minerals, especially bauxite. There are also iron reserves in the Nimba mountains on the borders of Guinea and Liberia. It shares borders with a number of other African countries: the Gambia, Senegal, Mali, Ivory Coast and Sierra Leone. The Mandinka, or Manding-speaking people, among whom Camara grew up in Northern Guinea, are spread over several countries: the Gambia, Upper Volta, Mali and Senegal. Mandinka is one of the major languages of Guinea; another is Fulani (or 'Peuhl' as it is called in the text). The official language is French.

The praise singers or 'griots'

These poets or bards feature in *The African Child* and it is they who perform the *Sundiata* epic in its many versions. Such poets have to be able to adapt their praises to a variety of occasions, as they do in the book, praising Camara's father as he works, and later the boy himself as he leaves for Conakry.

Classroom use

Level of use

As a whole: fourth or fifth year GCSE.
Age 14–16.
In parts: the sections dealing with his school life in Kouroussa and his father's workshop could be read with first or second years (age 11–13) or used in a topic on work with fourth years. The initiation ceremonies: the mysterious roaring being Konden Diara and later circumcision could be read with fourth or fifth years, perhaps with other passages on 'Growing-up' or 'Change'.

Teaching resources are listed at the end of the unit.

Points for focus and emphasis

1 *The author's experience at school in Kouroussa* (Chapter 6):
   the strictness of the teacher
   their unpleasant (and unjust) punishments
   the bully and his downfall
2 *His visits to the farming area of Tindican* (Chapters 3 and 4):
   his uncles and his doting grandmother
   his young companions
   harvesting the rice
3 *His friendships* (Chapters 6, 7, 10 and 11):
   with Fanta (Chapters 6 and 9)
   with Kouyate (Chapters 6, 7 and 11)
   with Check (Chapter 11)
   with Marie in Conakry (Chapter 10)
4 *The preparations for the final move to manhood* (Chapters 7 and 8):
   the fearsome and mythical 'monster' Konden Diara
   the more painful and more important rite of circumcision
5 *His parents*:
   his mother (cf. esp. Chapters 1, 2, 7, 8 and 10)
   his father (cf. esp. Chapters 1, 2, 7, 8 and 12)
6 *The importance of music, poetry, dancing and song* (Chapters 2, 7, 8 and 9):
   the praise-singer
   the drummers and dancers at Ramadan

the dancing and song before and after circumcision

7 *The mystical and spiritual aspects of his life* (Chapters 2, 5, 7, 9 and 10):
the black snake
his mother's and father's magical powers
the consultation of the marabouts
the prayers to the ancestors
the presence of Islam

Teaching suggestions

(a) Interpretation and appreciation

1 'we lived in constant fear of being sent out to the blackboard.' (p.64) Write a description of a very strict teacher you have known.

2 Which of the three punishments, sweeping the school yard, working in the kitchen garden or taking out the school herd of cattle, sounds the worst? Do you think any of these are good punishments? Can you suggest three punishments to put in their place?

3 '"Get all that swept up!" the headmaster would tell us. "I want the whole place cleaned up at once!"' (p.68) What does the author's father do to the headmaster? Why did he do it? Who was in the right? What qualities do you think a good headmaster or headmistress needs?

4 Read from '"Do you know what's been going on in school?"' (p.76) to '"Look! That's the schoolboy whose father went and beat up the headmaster in his own school yard!"' Write this episode up as a news report for the local paper. A suitable heading might be 'Headmaster in school brawl' or 'Headmaster falsely accused'.

5 '"My father is most anxious to meet the boy who has been kindest to me in the top class, and I thought of you at once. Can you come and share our dinner this evening?" "You bet I can!" answered Himoursana, who was as stupid as he was brutal . . .' Do a drawing or a set of cartoon drawings with words to illustrate 'The Bully's Downfall'.

6 Read from '"You've never seen as many birds as there are in the fields this year!"' (p.40) to '"in any case our shouts and our singing were generally sufficient to keep the birds away, even the millet eaters that used to descend in dense flocks on the fields."' (p.41) Draw or paint a picture to illustrate what you have read.
Other suggestions for drawing: the interior of his grandmother's hut (p.39); harvesting the rice (pp.46–53).

7 'My little playmates were very kind to me. They were really wonderful friends . . .' (p.41) List the different things the boys did and then put them in order from most enjoyable to least enjoyable (pp.35–44).

8 'Konden Diara, that terrible bogeyman, that lion that eats up little boys.' What happens to the young Camara Laye the night he joins 'the society of the uninitiated'? (pp.78–86)

9 Read Chapters 7 and 8 and discuss the value of the two initiation ceremonies which Laye passed through. Is there anything similar to these in western society? G

10 'Black woman, woman of Africa, O my mother, I am thinking of you . . .' Read the dedication poem to Camara Laye's mother at the beginning of the book. What evidence have we in the book of the close relationship between mother and son?

11 '"My father, what is that little snake that comes to visit you?" "What snake do you mean?" "Why, the little snake that my mother forbids us to kill." "Ah!" he said.' (p.17) Why is the little black snake so important?

12 Camara Laye singles out two girls for special mention, Fanta (pp.63–5, 119–20 and 144) and Marie (Chapter 10). Think about the ways in which they might be different and what qualities in each girl appeal to him.

13 Read the section from pp.120–30, his departure from Kouroussa and his first year at Conakry. How do his uncle's views on education differ from his own? Laye writes that 'By a strange coincidence that I

cannot explain, the ending of the school year coincided with my return to health'. List the things you think he would have missed and which would have made him homesick whilst he was in Conakry.

14 '"Father!... Father!..." I kept repeating it. "Father, what must I do, what is the right thing to do?" And I wept quietly, and weeping I fell asleep.' (p.21) What are the choices the author is faced with at various stages of his early life?

15 'I knew quite well that one day you would leave us. I knew it the very first day you set foot in school.' (p.152)
How important a part does education play in Laye's life?

16 'Then suddenly my father said in a broken voice: "Promise me that you will come back?"' (p. 153)
Describe Laye's relations with his father in the book as a whole.

17 How important a part do the teachings of Islam play in Laye's life a) at Kouroussa? b) at Conakry?

18 'My little playmates would be there waiting for me.
"So you've come back?" they would say.
"I've come back."' (p. 40)
What does the Tindican section (Chapters 3 and 4) add a) to your understanding of Camara Laye? b) to your overall appreciation of the book?

(b) Creative

1 Camara Laye writes of his mother, '... she always used to hold herself very straight and so appeared taller than she really was. I seemed to see her walking along the dusty road, her dress falling in noble folds, her waistband neatly tied, her hair carefully plaited and drawn back on the nape of her neck.' (p.111) Think about a close relation or a friend whom you have not seen recently and write a short description of him or her.

2 Write about – or speak about – a time when you were bullied.

3 'The women and girls would come running to the gates of the compounds to watch us go by; then they would follow closely on our heels, decked in their holiday finery. The tom-tom would throb and we would dance in the square until we were ready to drop.' (p.94) Describe a fair, a festival or a carnival which you have seen or taken part in.

4 What seem to you to be the main differences between growing up in Camara Laye's Guinea and growing up in your own community?

5 Compare Camara Laye's relations with his mother and father with child–parent relations in this country. Draw on your own experience and the experience of your friends.

6 'in our December, the whole world is in flower and the air is sweet: everything is young and fresh ...' (p.46) Read Camara Laye's description of December in Tindican then read this extract from Claude McKay's poem about Jamaica, 'Flame Heart':

So much I have forgotten in ten years,
So much in ten brief years! I have forgot
What time the purple apple comes to juice,
And what month brings the shy forget-me-not.
I have forgot the special, startling season
Of the pimento's flowering and fruiting:
What time of year the ground doves brown the fields
And fill the noonday with their curious fluting.
I have forgotten much, but still remember
The poinsettia's red, blood-red, in warm December.

I still recall the honey-fever grass.
But cannot recollect the high days when
We rooted them out of the ping-wing path
To stop the mad bees in the rabbit pen.
I often try to think in what sweet month
The languid painted ladies used to dapple
The yellow by-road mazing from the main,
Sweet with the golden threads of the rose-apple.
I have forgotten – strange – but quite remember
The poinsettia's red, blood-red, in warm December.

(from 'Flame Heart', in *Selected Poems of Claude McKay*, Harcourt Brace Jovanovich: New York and London, 1953, p.13)

What do the Tindican and Jamaica December have in common? How much does an English December differ? Write your own poem (or prose piece) about December in any country you know.

(c) Curriculum-linked

1 Make a map of the author's journey by rail from Kouroussa to Conakry. Mark in if you can the changing terrain and also the different languages of the regions he travels through (Chapter 9).
2 Make a list of the kinds of poetry, music and dancing mentioned in the book and say when they are used. Try to find out more about two musical instruments, the kora and the balaphone (wooden xylophone) and about the praise singers or 'griots' as they are often called.
3 Find out what you can about the famous nineteenth-century Guinean leader Samori Touré.

4 'The Niger flows slowly and abundantly' – make a map tracing the river from its source near the author's home town of Kouroussa to its estuary in south-eastern Nigeria. What journeys did the nineteenth-century explorer Mungo Park make along the Niger?
5 Find out about the history of Guinea. List the good and bad effects that the influence of the French colonizers might have had on a community such as Camara Laye's. Bear in mind the reactions of Laye and his parents: when people write of their own experiences this is called 'primary evidence' and is very important to historians.

Topics

Schools and education
Family relationships
Work
Growing up/puberty
Two cultures
Ritual and religious belief

Passages for reading

See Section 2 for extracts from *The African Child*

Teaching aids

Audio-visual   Any of the following would be useful introductions to the book:

Films   *Bozo Daily Life*
Time: 16 mins   Colour   Distributor: Edward Patterson   Hire: £9.50
Everyday life on the banks of the Niger. Not about Mandinka society but shows people's dependence on the river. Links with Camara's reference to his mother drawing water from the Niger; also his village Kouroussa is on the Niger.

After the Drought
Time: 30 mins each   Distributor: Concord   Hire: £11.20 each
Three films about Upper Volta. Two relevant to *The African Child*:
1 A peasant family in West Africa
2 An urban family in West Africa

Emitai (Lord of the Sky)
Time: 15 mins each   Colour   Distributor: BFI   Hire: £3 each
Director: Sembène Ousmane

Two extracts from the full length film which is set in Senegal during the Second World War. The Diola (Manding-speaking) people of Senegal resisted the heavy rice tax imposed by the French. Shows people's reliance on spiritual beings unrelated to teachings of Islam. Could link with Camara's father's beliefs and sense in book of co-existence of Islam with the older religions. See also *Emitai* Resources p.138.

Taaw
Time: 26 mins   Colour   Distributor: The Other Cinema   Hire: £15
Director: Ousmane Sembene
A day in the life of a 20-year old youth who cannot find a job and quarrels with his family. Could extend sense of school, work and city life in latter part of *The African Child*.

Gambia: River of the Ancestors
Time: 15 mins   Colour   Distributor: Concord   Hire: £4
Filmed in Juffereh, the Mandinka-speaking village of Alex Haley's *Roots*. Explores the village's past and present. Excellent for giving reader's a sense of the setting of *The African Child* and *Sundiata*.

Slide sets

A School in Kenya
CWDE £5.50 + VAT
Twenty slides plus detailed notes. Would help in discussing Kenyan school-children's experience in relation to Camara's and to readers' own experience.

Resource wallet

The Manding of West Africa
Section 3 of Unit 3, 'Living Together', Schools Council Integrated Studies Project, Oxford University Press, 1974.
1 Pupils' and Teachers' Notes; topics covered: geography, history, daily life, music, art, towns and markets, education. Simply written, pictures and maps; also an extract from Alex Haley's *Roots*.
2 Tape to accompany above contains folk tales and music.
See also *Music* in Teaching aids, Unit 2 (p.16).

Background reading

See references in Teaching aids, Unit 2, also:
David Killingray, *Samori Touré, Warrior King*, Hulton (Round the World History), 1973.
Richard Tames, *Mungo Park*, Shire, 1973. Illustrated. *Approaches to World Religions: Islam*, John Murray, 1982.

Reading links

Camara Laye, *The Radiance of the King*, Fontana, 1956, 1980. An allegorical novel describing the search of a white man, Clarence, for an understanding of the spiritual in African terms. Sixth form. Age 16–18.
Gordon Innes, *Sunjata: Three Mandinka Versions*, School of Oriental and African Studies, University of London, 1974. Contains some war passages which would be good for reading aloud – dramatic and fast-moving.

D.T. Niane, *Sundiata: An Epic of Old Mali* (see Unit 2).

Léopold Sédar Senghor, poems in, for example, J. Reed and C. Wake (eds) *A Book of African Verse*, Heinemann (African Writers Series 8), 1964, pp.72–80. One of the founders of the francophone aesthetic and political movement 'negritude'; his poems attempt to define an African identity and often express the longing of an exile for Africa.

V.S. Reid, *The Young Warriors*, Longman 1967, Longman (Horizons), 1979. A story of the young Maroons in Jamaica. Enjoyed up to fourth year. Age 11–14.

Other auto-
biographies or
novels of
childhood

Peter Abrahams, *Tell Freedom* (see Unit 4)

Danny Abse, *Ash on a Young Man's Sleeve*, Penguin (King Penguin Series), 1982. A Welsh boyhood.

Michael Anthony, *Green Days by the River*, Heinemann (Caribbean Writers Series 9) 1973.

Bernard Dadié, *Climbié*, translated from the French by Karen Chapman, Heinemann (African Writers Series 87), 1971. An account of a child growing up on the Ivory Coast.

Nafissatou Diallo, *A Dakar Childhood*, translated from the French by Dorothy Blair, Longman (Drumbeat 48) 1982. A quiet but vivid account of a young girl growing up in a Muslim household.

Charles Dickens, *Great Expectations*, Heinemann Educational, 1977.

Zee Edgell, *Beka Lamb*, Heinemann (Caribbean Writers Series 26) 1982. An account of the school and family life of a young girl in Belize. A sensitive portrayal of adolescence in the Caribbean.

Merle Hodge, *Crick Crack Monkey*, Heinemann (Caribbean Writers Series 24) 1980.

James Kirkup, *The Only Child*, Pergamon, 1970.

Ngugi wa Thiong'o, *Weep Not, Child* (see Unit 3)

Wole Soyinka, *Aké: The Years of Childhood*, Rex Collings, 1981. An autobiographical account of childhood by the continent's major dramatist. Highly recommended.

Richard Wright, *Black Boy*, Nelson (Panafrica Library), 1980. A childhood and youth in the Southern states of America.

Short stories

Doris Lessing, *Nine African Stories*, Longman Imprint, 1968.

Sam Selvon, *A Brighter Sun*, Longman (Drumbeat 4) 1979.

Critical

Adele King, *The Writings of Camara Laye*, Heinemann Educational, 1980.

Unit 2 *Sundiata: An Epic of Old Mali*

D.T. Niane

Level of use and scope

This oral epic tells the story of Sundiata, founder of the kingdom of Mali. Versions of *Sundiata* still circulate today in Manding-speaking regions of West Africa, particularly in Guinea, Upper Volta, Mali, Senegal and the Gambia. The epic is related to local audiences by travelling bards known as 'griots', with the accompaniment of a harp-like instrument called the *Kora* and, less frequently, a xylophone.

Although Djeli Mamadou Kouyate, the griot from whom Niane obtained this version of the epic, claims that 'by my mouth you will learn the history of Mali' (p.1), the relation of the epic to historical events is vague. Certainly there was a Manding empire of Mali which flourished in the Western Sudan during the period known to Europeans as the Middle Ages. Its rise is associated with the Keita prince Sundiata, also known as Mari Djata, the Lion Prince. The defeat of the Sosso King, Soumaoro, at the battle of Kirina (or Krina as Niane calls it) is set at 1235. Apart from this bare historical outline though, the epic takes its own course, remaining 'true to the facts of the moral and social life of the Mandinka' (Innes, 1974, p.30) rather than to details of history.

At the centre of the epic is the heroic figure of Sundiata. Sundiata at first seems an unlikely candidate for greatness. His birth is accompanied by prophecies of high destiny, yet he proves a disappointment and lags far behind his playmates in development. At seven he cannot even walk. When his father dies the kingship passes to Sundiata's older half-brother

Sundiata: An Epic of Old Mali, D.T. Niane. First published in French by Présence Africaine, 1960. English edition, Longman, 1965; Longman (Drumbeat 15), 1979, translated by G.D. Pickett.

who is like putty in the hands of his scheming and ambitious mother, Sassouma Berete. Yet, suddenly and miraculously, Sundiata proves that he combines almost superhuman strength and the qualities of leadership. Overnight he becomes the popular hunter prince. When his stepmother's jealousy leads to voluntary exile, he, his mother, Sogolon, his sisters and his half-brother Manding Bory wander from court to court, in some cases making valuable allies for the future. The enemy he has to overcome in order to gain his kingdom is not his weak half-brother but the powerful magician King Soumaoro Kante who rules from his fortress city of Sosso. When victory is at last achieved Sundiata, the Lion King, rules his wide dominions not as a despot but with the co-operation of his allies and his government is wise and just.

The epic can be read and enjoyed for its accounts of heroism, magic, suspense, suffering and eventual success. It also contains a number of other features which could be discussed with a class. The theme of destiny is continually emphasized. Sundiata is destined to return to Mali, he cannot escape his destiny any more than can an ordinary individual. Another theme is the passing of time and with it the passing of kings, cities and empires. At the close of this epic the bard comments on the mortality of kings and kingdoms: 'How many heaped-up ruins, how many vanished cities! How many wildernesses peopled by the spirits of great kings'. (p.83) The imagery of the epic centres firstly on the emblems of Sundiata's father and mother, that of the lion and the buffalo. Not only is Sundiata frequently referred to as 'Son of the Buffalo' and 'the Lion Prince', he is also associated with majesty and power through the image of the sun. This is used, for example, at the moment when destiny leads him to war with Soumaoro, the sorcerer king (p.40). Other natural images such as light, lightning and floodwaters reinforce the associations of power. A point which is emphasized throughout the epic is the close relationship of the bard or 'griot' and the young prince Sundiata. The loss of his bard – his mentor and praise-singer – Balla Fasseke to Soumaoro makes war between the two inevitable. After his escape from Soumaoro, Balla Fasseke is constantly at Sundiata's side singing his praises and those of his ancestors, exhorting the prince and his allies to victory (see p.63).

Besides recalling the splendour of 'great Mali', this version of the epic underlines the presence of Islam in the region. Soumaoro the enemy king is associated with the fetishes and magic of the old indigenous religion. Sundiata on the other hand is presented as a Muslim leader although he too has strong links with the old religion.

The author

There is no single author of the Sundiata epic, just as there is no single version of it. Although Niane writes in his preface that he took this version from the bard Djeli Mamadou Kouyate it is more likely that he used his own wide knowledge of Sundiata to rework it himself into its present literary form. So, in a sense, he and his Guinean griot are the authors of this version.

The setting

The Kingdom of Mali

Mali first became a force to be reckoned with in the thirteenth century, when, having defeated Soumaoro, Sundiata moved his capital to Niana on the river Niger. He introduced a standing army and extended his territories to the west to include the gold-bearing regions of Wangara and Bambuk. 'By the end of the thirteenth century Mali had become the richest and most powerful of the States of the Sudan, the gold trade was flourishing and Sundiata or Maridjata, as he was sometimes known, had

become a hero to his people.' (Shinnie, *Ancient African Kingdoms*, 1965, p.52)

Mali, like Ghana before it, was famous, well-governed and prosperous, but only for a time. Its most renowned ruler was Mansa Musa, grandson of Sundiata, who made a pilgrimage to Mecca by way of Cairo. So generous was he with his gold that he caused inflation for several years after his visit!

The third and perhaps greatest kingdom of the Western Sudan was Songhai (or Gao). It flourished in the fifteenth and sixteenth centuries and was eventually destroyed in 1587 by the Moroccans, whose use of firearms was a decisive factor in their victory.

The Western Sudan

The term 'Sudan', meaning 'the country of the Black People' was the name given by the Arabs to the savannah region which stretched across Africa from the Atlantic to the Red Sea. The Western Sudan, in which the kingdoms of Ghana, then Mali and finally Songhai flourished is dominated by the river Niger; to the north is the Sahara desert and to the south tropical forest (see T. Hodgkin in Roland Oliver, *The Dawn of African History*, 1961, pp.37–44).

Mali and Islam

The teachings of Islam were brought across the desert from North Africa by merchants as early as the eighth century. From the eleventh century onwards Islam was a vital force in the religious, civic and intellectual life of the Western Sudan. In many instances it existed side by side with traditional religious beliefs and practices.

The bards or griots

The griots are hereditary and full time professional bards. Innes reported that in the Gambia they were formerly attached to the courts of rulers but are now freelance and play for wealthy patrons, praising their families by narrating the history of their ancestors or, if the patron shows himself to be tight-fisted, criticizing both him and his ancestry. The numerous references to song in the text, 'The Hymn to the Bow' (p.21), the 'Hymn to Abundance' and 'Niama', the victory song, give the reader an idea of how in an actual performance the spoken narrative would be interspersed with singing. The harp-like Kora and the xylophone (*balafon* as it is called here) form a musical accompaniment even to the spoken parts of the epic. These days – in the Gambia at any rate – Mandinka griots have access to the radio and use this, where possible, as a means of making a living and establishing a reputation. It also helps them hold their own in the face of stiff competition from contemporary pop music (see Innes, 1974, pp.2–11).

Classroom use

Level of use

With third to fourth years. **Age 13–15.**
The scenes of battle or sections highlighting magic and the supernatural could be taken separately and set beside extracts from the tales of King Arthur, the Odyssey and war poetry such as Drayton's 'The Ballad of Agincourt' or battle scenes from *Henry V*. The epic as a whole could be read as part of a unit on 'Heroes', 'Kingdoms and rulers' or 'The Supernatural'. Epic as a genre with its wide, teeming canvas, its emphasis on heroism, challenges and (frequently) a journey could also be discussed. It would also be a good literature text to use if parallel work on West Africa was planned with Geography and History departments.

   Possible initial difficulties: (a) strange place names; (b) characters often have several names, some of which are praise names and highlight some striking characteristic of their owner, such as good looks or courage; (c) misconceptions about oral literature – 'Is it all learnt parrot fashion?' No. Griots often learn from a number of bards and put together their own versions. Reminders that *The Iliad* and *The Odyssey* were once oral poems might be helpful. The oral origins of *Beowulf* and the Anglo-Saxon tradition of the *scop* could be introduced as parallel examples of oral poetry and oral poets. There is also the Scottish literary tradition of 'flyting'. Medieval Irish and Welsh bardic poetry could also be mentioned as well as Caribbean performance poetry. The merits of spoken or sung poetry as opposed to poetry on the page could be discussed. Ballads, old and new would also fit in well in a general discussion of spoken and sung poetry (see Unit 12 on African Oral Poetry).

Teaching resources are listed at the end of this unit.

Points for focus and emphasis

1 *Sundiata's early childhood*:
   the backward child
   he loses his inheritance and is scorned (p.18)
   'I am going to walk today' (p.19)
   his kindness to the Nine Witches of Mali

2 *Sundiata's early friends*:
   the young hunters: Fran Kamara (pp.23, 31) ⎫
   Kamandjan from Sibi (p.25) ⎬ see Sundiata's
   Manding Bory (pp.23, 27, 29, 49) ⎭ campaigns
   his sympathetic half-sister Nana Triban (p.25 and see 4)

3 *Magic in the epic*:
   Sogolon the buffalo woman (pp.6–11)
   Soumaoro's magic chamber (pp.39–40)
   Soumaoro's magic powers (pp.52, 69, 76)
   the owl challenges (pp.60–1)
   Soumaoro loses his magic (p.65)
   Sundiata's journey to the magic pool (p.71)

4 *Sundiata's enemies*:
   Sassouma Berete's jealousy; the Nine Witches of Mali (pp.24–6)
   Soumaoro: (a) he keeps Sundiata's griot (pp.38–46)
             (b) he steals his nephew's wife and makes an enemy (p.42)
             (c) the battle of Tabon (pp.48–50)
             (d) his magic makes him invulnerable (p.52)

(e) Sundiata consults the sooth-
sayers (pp.56–7)

(f) Nana Triban (see 2) helps
Sundiata

5 *Sundiata's mother, Sogolon:*
the buffalo of Do (pp.7–8)
the ugly hunchbacked girl (pp.6–9)
her powers and her 'defeat' (pp.10–12)
her trials as a wife (pp.15–19)
'I have known exile' (p.33)
her death at Mema (pp.43–6)
Sundiata visits her memorial in Do (p.72)

6 *Sundiata's travels in exile:*
'I will return' (p.28)
the first stop: at Djedeba with Mansa
Kankan the great sorcerer (pp.29–31)
the second stop: at Tabon with Fran Kamara
– their promises (pp. 31–2)
the third stop: the court of the King of
Ghana in Wagadou (pp.32–4)
the fourth stop: with Moussa Tounkara at
Mema; Sundiata is made his viceroy
(pp.35–8)
the 'Merchants' from Mali and their
message (p.45)

7 *Sundiata and his griot:*
Balla Fasseke as teacher (p.23)
Sundiata loses his griot (p. 27)
Balla Fasseke returns (p.57)
he praises the heroes of Mali (p.58)
he praises Sundiata (p.62)
Sundiata rewards Balla Fasseke (p.78)
The Songs: 'The Hymn to the Bow' (pp.21,
56, 71, 80)
'Niama', the victory song (p.79)
'The Hymn to Abundance'
(p.79)

8 *Sundiata's campaigns:*
Stage 1: The Battle of Tabon: Sosso Balla is
defeated (pp.48–50)
the Battle of Negueboria: rival
tactics and Sundiata's gloom
(pp.51–3)
a night attack (pp.53–4)
the gathering at Sibi (pp.54–9)
Stage 2: Sundiata gains an ally, Fakoli
Koroma (p.61 and see p.46)

The battle of Krina (p.64)
The chase (p.65–7)
Stage 3: Celebrations and homage to
Sundiata (pp. 75–9)
Sundiata returns to Niani and re-
builds it (pp. 80–2)

Teaching suggestions

(a) Interpretation and appreciation

1 What claims does the griot Djeli Mamadou
Kouyate make as the epic begins? (pp.1–2)

2 How can you tell that the epic is meant to
be spoken? (pp.1–3)

3 'He saw a man dressed like a hunter
coming towards him.' (p.4) What is his
prophecy? Can you think of any other
examples of prophecy in an epic or legend?
What is the effect of the prophecy on the
reader or listener?

4 'Sogolon's time came'. (p.13) Give the
story of Sogolon up to this point. How is
she 'an extraordinary woman'? (p.11)

5 How does Sundiata's 'slow and difficult
childhood' affect: (a) his mother? (b) public opinion about him? (c) his chances of
becoming king?

6 '"When the seed germinates growth is not
always easy; great trees grow slowly but
they plunge their roots deep into the
ground."' (p.17) Who is this blacksmith
seer talking about? If you were speaking in
a straightforward way to Nare Maghan
what would you say?

7 '"but nothing can be done against a heart
full of kindness ... Forgive us, son of
Sogolon."' (p.26) Explain how Sassouma
Berete's plan misfires.

8 What is the secret message in Sundiata's
song:
'But the gold came only yesterday?' (p.30)
Where is Sundiata at this point? Where
does he go after this?

9 In what ways do you think the two caravan
journeys (to Ghana and to Mema) benefit
Sundiata? (pp.32–3 and 35)

10 'You are at home. Stay here as long as you wish.' (p.36) What does Sundiata achieve during his stay in Mema? (pp.36–8)

11 (a) How does the griot Balla Fasseke come to be at the court of 'The Untouchable King'? (p.38 and see p.27)
(b) What does the song on p.40 tell you about Balla Fasseke and about Soumaoro?
(c) Why is the song a turning point in the epic?

12 "' Maghan Sundiata, I salute you; King of Mali, the throne of your fathers awaits you.'" (p.45) Do you think Sundiata is ready to be King, or not?

13 'and Sogolon received her funeral honours.' (p.47)
(a) What sort of a woman was Sogolon?
(b) How important was she to Sundiata?
(c) How important is she in the epic as a whole?

14 'his sword made heads fall as when someone shakes a tree of ripe fruit.' (p.50) What other similes are there in this paragraph? What do they suggest about the battle?

15 "'Father he is worse than a lion; nothing can withstand him.'" (p.50) Explain who is speaking and what he is talking about.

16 Why is Sundiata 'in a gloomy mood' (p.52) after the battle of Negueboria?

17 Does the description of the meeting on the plain of Sibi add anything to the epic? Could it be left out? (pp.54–6)

18 What difference does the return of Nana Triban and Balla Fasseke make to Sundiata's campaign? (pp.56–8)

19 (a) Would you say the Battle of Krina was an easy victory for Sundiata?
(b) What do you think 'the great black bird' signifies? (p.65)

20 What part do Sundiata's boyhood companions Fran Kamara (later Tabon Wana) and Kamandjan play in his campaign successes?

21 (a) Describe three incidents involving magical powers.

(b) How important is magic and the supernatural in the epic?
(c) Would Sundiata be a more interesting hero if he had no magical powers?

22 'Sundiata ought to have gone straight back to Niana without delaying at Kaba.' (pp.72–8) Give your opinion.

23 List the advantages a citizen of Mali at the time of Sundiata might have experienced. (pp.81–2)

24 What qualities do you associate with Sundiata by the end of the epic?

(b) Creative

1 "'You won't dance in the square any more and have yourself admired by the boys." [p.10] "They never have admired me anyway . . ."' Write your version of Sogolon's story of her life up to this point.

2 What picture of women does the epic provide (Sogolon, Sassouma Berete, Nana Triban, Massiran, poetesses, dancers)?

3 Take one of the following incidents, and consider how you could act it out. (You might need to consider the contrasts in moods, the way people reveal what they feel by the way they walk.) It might be possible to act out all three episodes, with a narrator providing a link from one to the next. **D**

(a) Sundiata's walks (the mocking remarks of people *before* the event, Sogolon's despair, Sassouma Berete's gloating – the changed crowd reactions afterwards).
(b) Sogolon, her children and Manding Bory arrive in Wagadou at the court of the King of Ghana (fatigue, apprehension, crowd curiosity, appearance of city, reception by King . . .).
(c) Koloukan, Sundiata's sister goes to the market at Mema and finds a strange woman selling spices from Mali (market stalls, Koloukan worried about Sogolon's health, discovery – surprise, the news . . .). **D**

4 Imagine that you are with the caravan travelling:
(a) from Tabon to Ghana
(b) from Ghana to Mema (see the map opposite p.vii and pp.32–3 and 35).
You could note the scenery, companions, food, dress, travellers' tales, merchandise and so on.
What are the qualities that are usually attributed to heroes?

5 Compare Sundiata with any other legendary hero you know of, for example, King Arthur, Prince Rama, Odysseus, Gilgamesh. In what ways are they conventional heroes and in what ways are they different? What do you think are the qualities of a real hero?

6 Read in two parts 'the dialogue of the sorceror Kings.' (pp.60–1) What kind of voice would be best – dramatic, challenging, eerie, mysterious?

7 Read aloud any part which you particularly like.

8 Look again at the song with a hidden message on p.30. The message here is, 'I know you've been bribed to kill me'. Try composing a verse or song which contains a hidden message (for example, a challenge, warning, complaint, threat, declaration of love). When do you think people might use songs or poems with a hidden message?

9 'From the top of the hill Djata looked on Niani which looked like a dead city.' (p.80) Describe in prose or verse, Sundiata's return seen from the point of view of someone in the crowd awaiting him.

10 There are many sayings in the epic, for example, 'God has mysteries which none can fathom' (p.15) or 'Man is in a hurry but time is tardy and everything has its season'. (p.6) Collect a number of these (see pp.26, 27, 28, 40, 42, 47, 48). What view of life do they present?

(c) Curriculum-linked

1 (a) Find out what you can about the vegetation, terrain and ways of life along the upper reaches of the river Niger.
(b) List the countries through which it flows.
(c) Name two other major rivers in Africa and the countries through which they flow.

2 This is what the Arab writer El Bekri had to say about the King and court of Ghana in 1067: 'he sits in a pavilion around which stand his horses dressed in cloth of gold; behind him stand ten pages holding shields and gold-mounted swords; and on his right hand are the sons of the princes of his empire, splendidly clad and with gold plaited into their hair' (quoted in Shinnie, 1965, p.47). Make a short study of the Kingdom of Ghana – its methods of government, links with Islam, trade, decline.

3 Find out more about El Bekri and what he said. Compare what you have found out about the Kingdom of Ghana in 1067 with what you know of Britain in the same year.

4 Find out what you can about Sundiata's grandson (Mansa Musa), the most famous of the Kings of Mali.

5 Investigate which, if any, caravan routes operate between North and West Africa today. Are camels still used? Can vehicles cross the Sahara? The routes? Goods? Starting points and destinations? Difficulties?

Topics

The passage of time
Exile
Leaders and heroes
War and glory
The supernatural

Passages for reading

The destroyed city (pp.69–70)
Sundiata's transformation (pp.19–21)
Two leaders (pp.36–7)
The battle of Krina (pp.64–5)
The magic chamber (pp.39–40, 69)

Teaching aids

See items listed under Unit 1, *The African Child*, in particular, *Gambia: River of the Ancestors.*

Audio-visual

Film

The Ancient Africans
Time: 27 mins   Colour   Distributor: Edward Patterson   Hire: £11.50
Includes kingdoms of Western Sudan; uses variety of cinematic techniques; stills, live, maps, animation.

Music

Kora Melodies from the Republic of the Gambia, West Africa Rounder 5001, 1973.
African Journey: a search for the roots of the Blues Vol.1 SONET SONET SNTF 660, London 1974, Side 'A', band 1.
African Music Folkways FW 8852, New York, 1957, especially Side 1, band 3.
Kora Music and songs from the Gambia featuring Alhaji Bai Konte, Dembo Konte, Malamini Jobarteh. Virgin Records, 1982. (Available at Collet's Record Shop, 180 Shaftesbury Ave, London WC2.)
For listening purposes and some copying facilities: The National Sound Archive, 29 Exhibition Road, London SW7 has a large collection of Mandinka poetry and song.

Background reading

History: Relevant sections in **Oliver** (ed.) *The Middle Age of African History,* Oxford University Press, 1967 (p.6), and **Davidson** *Discovering Africa's Past,* Longman, 1978.
Also, for class use the following:
John Addison, *Ancient Africa,* Rupert Hart Davis Educational, 1970.
Both these are informative and well illustrated.
Margaret Shinnie, *Ancient African Kingdoms,* Edward Arnold, 1965.

Africa general

Diana Finley, *The Niger,* Macdonald Educational, 1975.
Very introductory: covers people, environs, trade and history. Maps. A good starting point.
Naomi Mitchison, *African Heroes,* Bodley Head, 1968.
First chapter is on Sundiata and Mali: 'The Kings beyond the Desert'.

African oral literature (teachers)

D. Biebuyck and K.C. Mateene, *The Mwindo Epic,* University of California Press, 1971 (paperback). A Congolese epic; the hero after a series of trials in this world and the underworld comes into his kingdom.
Ruth Finnegan, *Oral literature in Africa,* Oxford University Press, 1970 (available in paperback) Indispensable as a text for general reference, but it makes little mention of epic.
Gordon Innes, *Sunjata: Three Mandinka Versions,* School of Oriental and African Studies, 1974.

Reading links   If the text is being linked with other epics and legends, the following could be considered:

King Arthur
For example, **Antonia Fraser**, *King Arthur and the Knights of the Round Table*, Sidgwick & Jackson, 1970 (hardback).
Also possible excursions into Malory and/or Tennyson.
The Ramayana
For example, **Elizabeth Seeger**, *The Ramayana*, Dent (Children's Classics), 1975.
The Odyssey
For example, **Barbara Leonie Picard**, *The Odyssey of Homer*, Oxford University Press, 1952, repr. 1974.
Beowulf
For example, **Ian Serraillier**, *Beowulf the Warrior*, Oxford University Press, 1954, repr. 1975.
Rosemary Sutcliff, *Dragon Slayer*, Puffin, 1966 (also published as *Beowulf*, Bodley Head, 1961). A beautifully written account which echoes the Anglo-Saxon style of imagery.
Alexander the Great
For example, **Pierre Grimal**, *Stories of Alexander the Great*, Burke (Myths and Legends Series), 1983; and **Plutarch**, *The Age of Alexander*, trans. from the Greek by Scott Kilvert, Penguin Classics, 1973.
Robin Hood
For example, **R. Lancelyn Green**, *The Adventures of Robin Hood*, Puffin, 1956, repr. 1978.
See also: **Camara Laye**, *The African Child* (Unit 1).
Laye's home in Kouroussa in present-day Guinea is in the heart of the Old Mali.
Cheikh Hamidou Kane, *Ambiguous Adventure*, translated from the French by K. Woods, Heinemann (African Writers Series 119), 1972.
A novel contrasting the simple Muslim faith of a community in Senegal with the materialism of French civilization.

Unit 3   *Weep Not, Child*

Ngugi wa Thiong'o

Level of use and scope

Ngugi's *Weep Not, Child* depicts the life of a young boy, Njoroge, who grows up during the years of the Mau Mau emergency in Kenya. The novel creates a strong sense of political turmoil and social unrest. Its atmosphere contrasts sharply with the sad serenity of Laye's *The African Child*. Ngugi's criticism of British appropriation of large tracts of Gikuyu land in the colonial period is forcefully presented in his early description of the land. Such a division, he suggests, can only bring dispossession and poverty to one group and wealth and power to the other. The contrast between the land of the white settlers and the Gikuyu foreshadows the conflict that is to come: 'You could tell the land of the Black People because it was red, rough and sickly, while the land of white settlers was green and not lacerated into small strips'. (p.7) Njoroge's father works for a white farmer, Howlands, who owns what was once the ancestral land of his Gikuyu employee. Both men have a passion for the land, and both die violently during the Mau Mau struggle. As the crisis in the country deepens, Njoroge's brother Boro returns from Nairobi to join the freedom fighters in the forest and he taunts their father Ngotho for not being man enough to take 'The Oath'. The young schoolboy Njoroge, a 'lonely thoughtful boy', sees the gradual disintegration of his family, and clings to education and a belief in God to sustain him.

In the bleak second section of the novel, 'Darkness Falls', Njoroge is forcibly removed from the prestigious boarding school, Siriana, to which he has won a scholarship. The full brutality and viciousness of the war is revealed. He is interrogated and beaten. He returns

Weep Not, Child, Ngugi wa Thiong'o, Heinemann (African Writers Series 7) 1964, reset 1976.

home to find that his father has been accused of the murder of black landowner Jacobo. Ngotho is taken to his family to die, and Njoroge faces the harsh reality of a life seemingly empty of hope or salvation: 'And suddenly Njoroge saw himself as an old man – an old man of twenty.' (p.129).

Another strand in the novel is Njoroge's relationship with Mwihaki, daughter of the wealthy Jacobo. They are friends at school, although the social distance between them is emphasized (pp.15, 18). Their relationship survives even the murder of her father (for which Njoroge's family is blamed) and finally it is she who has the courage to face life in Kenya, terrible though it is. His plea is 'Let's go. Kenya is no place for us'. Her response is different: 'She sat there, a lone tree defying the darkness, trying to instil new life into him. But he did not want to live. Not this kind of life. He felt betrayed.' (p.133) Mwihaki's courage is matched by the endurance and fortitude of Njoroge's mother Njeri. It is she who goes in search of Njoroge and saves him from taking his own life. The 'glowing piece of wood which she carried to light the way' is the lonely symbol of hope with which the novel ends.

Besides dealing sensitively with the issues of war, violence and personal commitment to a cause, the novel shows what it is like to grow up in an unstable society where in the end nothing seems secure and there is only personal courage to fall back on. It could be studied at fourth and fifth-year levels (age 14–16) and would be an excellent component in a CSE or 'O' level course. The descriptions of Njoroge at school learning the alphabet and learning English would also be enjoyed by first and second years, and would compare well with the school sections in *The African Child*.

In general, this early novel of Ngugi's shows his (still unshaken) belief in political art, his determination to articulate his beliefs concerning social, economic and political justice within the framework of literature and in particular, the novel. This early work, covering as it does the period of Mau Mau, is particularly challenging to many readers in this country as it questions assumptions of past colonial and imperial glory and often presents Britain and White British settlers in a highly critical light. Perhaps more than that of any other African writer, Ngugi's work shows the way in which literature can be a powerful instrument for change in its ability to topple prejudices and disturb ideas. Because of their very power to change, and, in some cases, hurt, his novels need to be handled carefully by the teacher.

The author

Ngugi wa Thiong'o is the foremost East African writer and is considered by some to be the leading African novelist writing in English. *The River Between* was his first novel, followed by *Weep Not, Child, A Grain of Wheat* and, in 1977, the widely acclaimed *Petals of Blood*. Like Achebe, Ngugi believes that a writer should be more than an impartial observer of the social and political developments of his time. 'We want,' he writes in 'The African Writer and his Past' (in C. Heywood (ed.), *Perspectives in African Literature*, Heinemann, 1971) 'to create a new society which is reflected in our educational, political and economic structure.' For Ngugi, like writers in other parts of Africa, art and politics are not separate issues. He was imprisoned without trial for twelve months in 1977–78 partly because of government disapproval of his satirical and hugely popular Gikuyu play *Ngaahika Ndeenda* (published in an English translation as *I'll Marry When I Want* by Heinemann (African Writers Series 246), 1982). His latest novel, *Devil on the Cross*, was written during his year in prison, first in Gikuyu and subsequently translated into English. Interestingly, the Gikuyu edition was hugely popular and sold out very quickly. The English version is published by Heinemann (African Writers Series 200) 1982.

The setting [1]

Like Ngugi's other novels and short stories, *Weep Not, Child* is set in Kenya's Central Province which includes the hilly and fertile 'White Highlands'. The Gikuyu suffered most when, during the early years of the twentieth century, large portions of their land were alienated and made available for European settlement. Bitterness and frustration over the loss of land was one of the main causes of the guerilla war of 1952–56 called by the British 'Mau Mau' and the formation of the Land Freedom Army under such leaders as Dedan Kimathi. The time span of the novel covers the period before the Emergency and the terrible war years. The Gikuyu, whether they were combatants or not, were at the centre of the struggle and suffered accordingly. As the Kenyan politician Oginga Odinga expresses it, 'When the Emergency began, the indiscriminate arrest and beating of every Gikuyu tribesman seemed to augur the elimination of the whole tribe' (*Not Yet Uhuru*, 1968, p.117). The fighting itself, although sporadic, was bitter. Odinga continues: 'At the height of the struggle there were several relatively autonomous zones of resistance and fighting: Nairobi, which was the vital supply centre, the Gikuyu reserves, Mount Kenya, and the Aberdare forests and the settler farms of the Rift Valley. In the forests the fighters set up permanent headquarters, which not only resisted government attack, but also launched offensives . . .' (p.117) The fighters in the forest called themselves The Land Freedom Army.

Returned soldiers

Kenyan troops fought in the First and Second World Wars. In the latter they fought against the Italians in Ethiopia and also served in Madagascar and Burma. 'They were told that this was a war against oppression and dictatorship, to secure freedom and independence for all. It was hardly surprising, therefore, that they should carry these ideas back with them and apply them to their own situation . . . Their

[1]For a further note on the setting, see Unit 5 *The River Between*.

return to East Africa after the war gave fresh impetus and force to African political movements.' (from Odhiambo, Ouso and Williams, *A History of East Africa*, p.163). Ngugi makes dramatic use of these events in the figures of Boro, Njoroge's silent and sullen half-brother who becomes a freedom fighter, and the barber.

The detainees

The actual figure of how many people were kept in detention camps during the Emergency varies from estimates of 30 000 to 90 000. Ngugi's account of the torture of Njoroge's father Ngotho, and the treatment of Njoroge himself during interrogation are true to life. Oginga, a Luo and a non-combatant records: 'No detainee was released until he had been passed along a security clearance channel known as the "Pipe Line"; among the Emergency casualties not recorded are the victims of the Pipe Line who were injured and permanently disabled by torture to exact confessions.'

Oathing

In the novel Boro tries to persuade his father to take 'The Oath' and Njoroge is asked during interrogation if he has taken 'The Oath'. The taking of an oath to seal an agreement or to set the seal on one's loyalty to an organization is a normal practice among Gikuyu people. The taking of an oath was an indispensable part of becoming a freedom fighter during Mau Mau. Friedmann in *Jomo Kenyatta* gives an example of 'a typical Mau Mau Oath'. Part of it runs as follows:

I speak the truth and vow before God
And before this movement. The Movement of
  Unity,
The Unity which is put to the test
The Unity which is mocked by the name of
  'Mau Mau',
That I shall go forward and fight for the land,
The lands of Kiringyaga that we cultivated,
The lands which were taken by the Europeans.
And if I fail to do this

May this oath kill me,
May this seven kill me,
May this meat kill me . . .

Friedmann continues: 'The person administering the oath would hold some goat meat in his hand, and those taking the oath would do the same. As the oath was said the person administering it would circle the heads of the others with the meat seven times (seven being the Gikuyu magic number)' (J. Friedman, *Jomo Kenyatta* p.45). The solemn, ritualistic nature of the language and the action is unmistakable.

The Home Guard

These were loyalists, many of whom were Gikuyu who had supported the Church in its stand against female circumcision (see the Background notes to Unit 4). They tended to be well-to-do landowners, tribal police, shopkeepers and government employees. Odinga remarks that great pressure was put on men to join the Home Guard. Those who did not volunteer became suspect to the security forces and in some instances men joined in order to protect their immediate family 'and found themselves helping to betray and kill their own people'. Naturally, to the men of the Land Freedom Army fighting in the forests and to their supporters, the Home Guard were despised collaborators.

Jomo Kenyatta

Kenyatta was President of the Kenya African Union from 1946. He was arrested with other leaders of the KAU when the State of Emergency was declared in 1952 and a month after his arrest he was charged with managing the illegal movement 'Mau Mau'. After a four-month trial at Kipenguria, Kenyatta and his associates were sentenced to seven years' hard labour and were taken to the remote village of Lokitaung in North West Kenya. He was finally released in August 1961 and the country gained its Independence in 1963. In the novel Kenyatta is a distant but charismatic leader, a Black Moses, uniting the people in their longing for the promised land of Independence and freedom from British rule.

Classroom use

Level of use

Fourth and fifth years. **Age: 14–16.** School passages first or second years. **Age 11–13.**

Teaching resources are listed at the end of the unit.

Points for focus and emphasis

1 *The experience of school*:
Beginning (Chapter 2, pp.13–15)
the reading lesson (Chapter 3, pp. 33–8)
an English lesson (Chapter 5, pp.44–8)
Siriana (Chapter 14 and 15, pp.114–16)

2 *The land*:
land divided (Chapter 1, p.7)
the ancestral land (Chapter 2, pp.23 ff. and Chapter 3)
the Bible and the sword (Chapter 7, pp.57–8)
the lost land (Chapter 12, pp.102–3)

3 *The fighting*:
first signs – the strike (Chapter 6 and Chapter 7, pp. 56–61)
involvement (Chapter 8)
the trial of Jomo (Chapter 9)
combatants (Chapter 10 and Chapter 12)
the casualties (Chapter 11, pp. 84–6, Chapter 12)
torture (Chapter 15)

4 *Families*:
the brothers and the land (Chapter 5, pp. 40–4)
families in conflict – Ngotho and Jacobo (Chapter 7)
father and son divided – Ngotho and Boro (Chapter 8)
Kamau provides (Chapter 11)
'about to break' (Chapter 15)
reconciliation – Ngotho and Boro (Chapter 16)
revenge (Chapter 17, pp.127–9)

the settler and his family (Chapter 3, pp.29–32; Chapter 10, pp.76–8)
the two mothers (Chapter 18)

5 *Njoroge and Mwihaki*:
early days (Chapter 2, pp.13–15; Chapter 4, pp.36–8)
exams and after (Chapter 7, pp. 55–6)
after a long time (Chapter 11, pp. 88–96)
farewells (Chapter 13, pp. 105–7)
a changed relationship (Chapter 18)

6 *Dreams and disillusion*:
'He clung to books' (Chapter 5, pp.48–9)
his optimism (Chapter 11, pp.94–7)
his hopes (Chapter 13)
fear and guilt (Chapter 15)
'You're fired' (Chapter 17)
lost (Chapter 18)

Teaching suggestions

(a) Interpretation and appreciation

1 (a) Why is Njoroge so eager to go to school? Read the description of Njoroge's first two years at school (Chapters 2 and 3).
  (b) Talk or write about your first school. Say whether it was in any way similar to Njoroge's school.

2 (a) What are the differences between Njoroge's and Mwihaki's families?
  (b) How does their friendship develop in spite of these differences?

3 (a) Describe the barber and Nganga (pp. 9–20).
  (b) What is their importance later in the novel?

4 Compare Howlands' and Ngotho's attitudes to the land (see Chapter 3).

5 'And he could tell a good story. This was considered a good thing for a man.' (p.20) What part does 'story-telling' play in the novel?

6 Read (aloud if possible) the creation story told by Ngotho (Chapter 2, pp.23–4). Then read the account of creation in the book of Genesis in the *Old Testament*. In what ways do the two accounts differ?

Have they any points in common? What other creation stories do you know? Are there points in common to most of them? What are they? G

7 Why do you think Ngugi puts the Gikuyu creation story into the novel at this particular point?

8 'He clung to books and whatever the school had to offer.' (p.48) Explain Njoroge's feelings about school and education up to this point.

9 *The strike* 'The men also talked of the strike. All men who worked for white men and Serikali (the Government) would come out on strike . . .' (p.50)

(a) The strike issue divided Njoroge's parents for the first time: '"But he's paying you money. What if the strike fails?" "Don't woman me!" He shouted hysterically . . . She sensed this note of uncertainty and fear and seized upon it . . .' (p.53) Why is there a call for such a strike?

(b) How does Ngotho behave at the strike meeting?

(c) Is his behaviour there out of character? Understandable?

(d) What are the consequences of his actions?

10 *Jomo* Why is Jomo such an important figure in the novel, although he never actually appears? Can you think of other leaders (contemporary or historical) who have exerted a similarly powerful influence on people's minds?

11 Enter Rumour, painted full of tongues.

Rumour: Open your ears; for which of you will stop
The vent of hearing when loud Rumour speaks?
I, from the orient to the drooping west,
Making the wind my post-horse, still unfold
The acts commenced on this ball of earth:
Upon my tongues continual slanders ride,
The which in every language I pronounce,
Stuffing the ears of men with false reports.
I speak of peace, while covert enmity,
Under the smile of safety, wounds the world;
And who but Rumour, who but only I,
Make fearful musters and prepar'd defence;
Whilst the big year, swoln with some other grief,
Is thought with child by the stern tyrant war,
And no such matter? Rumour is a pipe
Blown by surmises, jealousies, conjectures;
And of so easy and so plain a stop
That the blunt monster with uncounted heads,
The still-discordant wavering multitude,
Can play upon it . . .

(from the opening to Shakespeare's *Henry IV* pt.2)

In what way is the technique Shakespeare uses here similar to that employed by Ngugi in the section 'Interlude', between Part One, 'The Warning Light', and Part Two, 'Darkness Falls'? How useful is the 'Interlude' to the reader?

12 'Boro would soon be executed while Kamau would be in prison for life. Njoroge did not know what would happen to Kori in detention.' (p.134) Trace what has happened to any one of Njoroge's brothers from the start of the Emergency up to this point.

13 Outline Kamau's contribution to the family as a son and as a brother.

14 'Mwihaki, dear, I love you. Save me if you want. Without you I am lost.'
      She wanted to sink in his arms and feel a man's strength around her weak body. She wanted to travel the road back to her childhood and grow up with him again. But she was no longer a child. (p.133)

(a) How do these lines show you Mwihaki's strength as well as her weakness?

(b) Show how relations between Njoroge and Mwihaki have altered since their childhood.

15 Mwihaki comes from a 'family of the rich', Njoroge from a poor family.

   (a) How does this affect their friendship?

   (b) Can you think of any other figures in the books you have read who are placed in a similar position? Possible comparisons could be made with Lorna Doone and John Ridd in *Lorna Doone*; Catherine and Heathcliffe in *Wuthering Heights*; Pip and Estella in *Great Expectations*, or the young boy and girl in Alex La Guma's short story 'A Glass of Wine'; also with Joe Lampton and Susan Brown in John Braine's *Room at the Top*; Shell and Rosalie in Michael Anthony's *Green Days by the River*. Compare the way in which Ngugi and any one of the above writers explore the problem of love across class or social or racial barriers.

16 'He saw the light she was carrying and falteringly went towards it.' (p.135) The book begins and ends with Njoroge and his mother. Discuss the relations between Njoroge and his mother: a) when he first goes to school; b) at the time of his father's death; c) after he has been rejected by Mwihaki.

17 Compare Ngotho's relationship with Boro and with Njoroge. Discuss whether or not he is a failure as a father. (Compare Ngotho as a father with Camara Laye's father in *The African Child*.)

18 Compare the three families in the novel: Jacobo and his family; the Howlands family; Ngotho and his two wives and their sons. Points of comparison could be: standards of living; relationships within the family; duties of individual members; general happiness of each family; their position in the community; their roles in the novel.

(b) Creative

1 (a) Compare Isaka's and Lucia's techniques as teachers. Say which of the two seems to you the better teacher, and why.

   (b) Describe your first memories of learning to read or of learning a second language. G

2 What impression of life in Kipanga do you gain from the description of the land and the shops? (pp.7–10) Describe an urban or rural landscape which you have seen (or seen pictures of) and which shows up differences in people's standard of living. G

3 'because to me the whole world is the true home of all the creatures that were placed there at the beginning of time. No tribe can claim any portion of the globe as its own to the exclusion of others, because we all have to give way to posterity …' (from Mtutuzeli Matshoba, *Call Me Not a Man*, p.46). What do you think the speaker of these words would have to say about the Gikuyu creation story?

4 (a) Make a list of the civilian casualties of the Emergency mentioned in Chapters 11, 12 and 15.

   (b) List the ways in which members of Njoroge's family are affected by the Emergency.

5 Have you seen any programme or news item on television describing the flight of civilians in a war situation? In what way were the conditions similar to those described in *Weep Not, Child* (disruption of home, physical brutality at hands of armed forces, lack of food and so on . . .)?

6 Discuss the problems people might encounter when they love someone outside their own class, religion, social or ethnic group. G

7 'Children came to the shop. They were coming from school. Njoroge saw their hopeful faces. He too had once been like this when he had seen the world as a place where a man with learning would rise to power and glory.' (p.129)

   (a) How useful do you think Njoroge's education has been to him?

   (b) Suggest and argue the case for one change which you would like to see in the organization/teaching/subjects offered at your own school.

8 Compare *Weep Not, Child* with another novel or autobiographical account of growing up in wartime. (For instance Eva Figes, *Little Eden: A Child at War*, Faber 1978; *The Diary of Anne Frank*, Pan, 1954; David Rees, *The Missing German*, Dennis Dobson, 1976; Johanna Reiss, *The Upstairs Room*, Oxford University Press, 1973; Puffin, 1979 or Robert Westall, *The Machine Gunners*, Macmillan, 1975.

9 After the strike, Juliana rebukes Jacobo: '"I have always said that such *Ahoi* were dangerous. But a man will never heed the voice of a woman until it is too late. I told him not to go but he would not listen!"' (p.56) Work out (in writing or orally) a suitable dialogue for Juliana and Jacobo at this point. G

10 *Dramatize* a scene in which you focus on a member of a family returning home for a secret visit during wartime. Re-read Boro's visit to the family, pp.124–5, but the dramatization could be based on any war and set in any historical period. (W.H. Auden's ballad 'O What is that sound?' might help to bring in to focus the tensions and dangers of such a situation.)

(c) Curriculum-linked

1 *Prepare a talk* on the life of Jomo Kenyatta, concentrating on his early political career.
2 *Debate* the question of compensation to settlers for land they have to leave after a country becomes independent. (Countries to refer to, besides Kenya, could be Algeria, Zimbabwe or Northern Ireland.) Should they be forced to leave? Where should compensation come from if they do go – from the colonial government or from the new post-independence government?
3 *Interview* (use a tape recorder if possible *and* take notes) a relation, friend or neighbour about their wartime experiences as combatants or civilians and report back to the class.

4 (Could link with Geography or Development Studies.) Prepare a report on farming at the present time in the Central Province of Kenya. Include topics such as land allocation: co-operatives, small-holdings or large farms; crops grown; livestock.
5 Write a short piece (or make a tape recording) about your home for someone living in a different continent.
6 Dedan Kimathi, chief commander of the Land Freedom Army was captured by colonial government forces in October 1956, tried, and executed by hanging in February 1957.
   (a) Write the report of his capture which might have appeared in a contemporary British newspaper.
   (b) Write (or record on tape) the report of his capture as it might have been told by a fellow guerilla fighter to his companions.
   (c) What is propaganda? How do two sides in a war or conflict make propaganda out of an event? What are the advantages and disadvantages of propaganda, particularly in a war situation? Is propaganda moral? Immoral? Necessary? Avoidable?

Topics

War
Dispossession
Schools and education
Parents and children
Love and class
Inequality

Passages for reading

The strike (Chapter 7, pp.56–9)
The reading lesson (Chapter 4, pp.33–8)
An English lesson (Chapter 5, pp.44–8)
The casualties of war (Chapter 12, pp.99–102)
Why are we fighting? (Chapter 12, pp.102–3)

Teaching aids

Audio-visual

Films

Black Man's Land: Images of Colonialism and Independence in Kenya
A series of three films:
1 *White Man's Country*
2 *Mau Mau*
3 *Kenyatta*
Time: 3 × 50 mins   Colour   1973   Distributor: The Other Cinema
Hire: £24 each or £50 for three
Controversial. Would provide a heightened awareness of the social and political forces at work in the period in which the novel is set.

African Odyssey: The Two Worlds of Musembe
Time: 15 mins   Distributor: Rank Aldis   Hire: £9.95
Musembe lives in Nairobi but returns with his father to their family's village. He wants to stay but cannot. Illustrated urban/rural contrast in ways of living. Difficulties of reconciling two cultures. Relates in a general way to *Weep Not, Child*.

Slide sets

A School in Kenya
CWDE 1979. £5.50 + VAT
20 colour slides with notes. Looks at a few individual children, their school and its facilities. Might help in giving the atmosphere of schools in *Weep Not, Child* and *The River Between*; shows difficulties faced by schools in rural areas.
See also: *Freedom Railway*
            A Fair Share of What Little We Have
            films from Kenya High Commission (see Section 3, Resources p.136).

Background reading

E.S. Atieno Odhiambo, T.I. Ouso and J.F.M. Williams, *A History of East Africa*, Longman, 1977.
Julian Friedman, *Jomo Kenyatta*, Wayland 1975.
Provides an excellent pictorial and written account of Kenyan political and social history with particular emphasis on the Gikuyu and Kenyatta. Makes use of key material from contemporary sources. Useful in class.
Mugo Gatheru, *Child of Two Worlds*, Heinemann (African Writers Series 20) 1966.
The autobiography of a young Gikuyu.
G.M. Hickman, W.H.G. Dickins with E. Woods, *The Lands and Peoples of East Africa*, Longman, 1977.
Godfrey Muriuki, *People Round Mount Kenya – Kikuyu, Embu and Meru*, Evans, 1979.
Provides useful background on Kenya's peoples, history and traditions. Illustrated with line drawings. Would be useful in class.

Oginga Odinga, *Not Yet Uhuru*, Heinemann (African Writers Series 38) 1968, repr. 1977.
See the chapters 'Peasants in Revolt' and 'From Battalions to Polling Booths'. Contains photographs from Emergency period-detention camps, arrests, searches, gallows and a photograph of the leader of the Land Freedom Army, Dedan Kimathi.
M.P.K. Sorrenson, *The Origins of European Settlement in Kenya*, OUP, 1962.

Criticism

G.D. Killam, *An Introduction to the Writings of Ngugi*, Heinemann, 1980.
Ngugi Wa Thiong'o in *African Writers Talking*, D. Duerden and C. Pieterse (eds), pp.124–31.
A discussion of *Weep Not, Child* and *The River Between*.
Eustace Palmer, *An Introduction to The African Novel*, Heinemann, 1972.
Essays on Ngugi's first three novels.
C.B. Robson, *Ngugi wa Thiong'o*, Macmillan, 1979.
Adrian Roscoe, *Uhuru's Fire: African Literature East to South*, CUP, 1977.
See pp.170–90.
Michael Simmons, 'Chronicler of the Winds of Change', *The Guardian*, 7 January 1981.
An interview with Ngugi in London.

Reading links

Maina wa Kinyatti (ed.), *Thunder from the Mountains: Mau Mau Patriotic Songs*, Zed Press, 1980.
A collection of oral songs sung by the guerillas during the war.
Ngugi wa Thiong'o, *Secret Lives*, Heinemann (African Writers Series 150), 1975. Could refer to in teaching *Weep Not, Child* or *The River Between*.
A Grain of Wheat, Heinemann (African Writers Series 36), 1967 reset 1975. Suitable for sixth form. Age 16–18.
Petals of Blood, Heinemann (African Writers Series 188), 1977. Suitable for sixth form. Age 16–18.

Other books by Kenyan writers

Leonard Kibera and Samuel Kahiga, *Potent Ash* (Short stories), East African Publishing House, 1968.
Deals with experiences of Mau Mau, city and rural life, Quite racy. Should be enjoyed up to fifth year. Age 14–16.
Leonard Kibera, *Voices in the Dark*, East African Publishing House, 1970, repr. 1974.
An irreverent study of life in post-independence Kenya. Should be popular up to fifth year. Age 14–16.
Charles Mangua, *Son of Woman*, East African Publishing House, 1971, repr. 1978.
Fast-moving, racy, might be a starting point for those who don't usually read much. Depicts with gusto the seamy side of city life.
A Tail in the Mouth, East African Publishing House, 1972, repr. 1974.
Samson Moira fights back when luck turns against him. Amusing and eventful. Could be tried on reluctant readers.

Books on the theme of struggling for independence or emancipation

Pepetela, *Ngunga's Adventure: A story of Angola*, Young World Books, 1980.
About the active involvement of a young boy in the Angolan war of independence. Deals in a realistic way with war and politics.
V.S. Reid, *The Young Warriors*, Longman Caribbean (Horizons), 1979.
Sixty Five, Longman Caribbean (Horizons), 1980.
Both tell the stories of young people caught up in the struggle for independence in Jamaica. For lower secondary. Age 11–13.
New Day, Heinemann (Caribbean Writers Series 4), 1973.
Suitable for sixth formers. Age 16–18. About the events leading up to the 1865 Morant Bay rebellion in Jamaica and the struggle for independence from British rule and a measure of self-government.
Morna Stuart, *Marassa and Midnight*, Heinemann (New Windmill), 1969.
The story of twin slaves born in Haiti, separated, and involved in Toussaint L'Ouverture's revolution and the 1789 French revolution.

For follow-up reading on African myths and legends

J. Knappert, *Myths and Legends of the Swahili*, Heinemann (African Writers Series 75), 1970.
Myths and Legends of the Congo, Heinemann (African Writers Series 83), 1971.

Schoolchildren in Kenya

Unit 4 *Tell Freedom*

Peter Abrahams

Level of use and scope

This is the autobiography of one of the first Black South African writers to place on record the experience of growing up in a segregated society where race is linked with status and opportunity. Abrahams depicts with vividness and intensity the relationships within his own immediate family. He provides us with careful portraits of his frail but strong-minded mother, his domineering yet finally defeated and pathetic Aunt Mattie, his brother Harry, a victim of the system, and his 'laughter loving' sister Maggie. The opening pages of the book also provide a brief glimpse of his Ethiopian father who died in Abrahams' early years. Social and economic circumstances make it impossible for the family ever to live under the same roof after his father's death but even the poverty and enforced separations of his early years are not enough to destroy the strong family bonds.

The book also charts Abrahams' development from an underfed boy to a (still underfed) poet, writer and spokesman for Coloured and Black people in South Africa in the late 1930s. Abrahams seems to have wanted to become a writer from an early age. Even before the idea of writing or even of attending school has occurred to him, he recalls 'dreaming long dreams on the soft grass' (p.50), perhaps nurturing the imaginative power that was later to produce the poetry, the novels and the autobiography itself. The novelist's ability to observe and to present the complexity of things is constantly evident in *Tell Freedom*. See for instance, the account of the sacking of the man who in his anger has blinded the boy Nondi in one eye (pp.101–2), the descriptions of the

Tell Freedom, Peter Abrahams, Allen and Unwin (schools ed.), 1963.

Afrikaans Headmaster of the Coloured Vrededorp school, 'The old devil! And they thought him too mad for a white school . . .' (p.126), and the account of the black railway worker cursed by angry women as he tries to catch the small boy who has stolen coal from the railways (p.52).

Most of the people featured in the autobiography do not understand why their life is as it is. They merely suffer or endure and survive as best they can: the young Lee (Peter Abrahams) and his friends in the gang supplement their diet by stealing from the Indian traders, the Reverend Rogerson sings in his 'rich, deep voice', prays to the Lord and expects succour from his ragged flock, Aunt Mattie sells illegal liquor, his mother works for a white family in Upper Vrededorp. Many inhabitants of Vrededorp never find work and only the gaiety and brilliance of the annual carnival relieves their year of 'drabness and want' (p.100). Only in the latter section of the book, when Abrahams has gone beyond the confines of his immediate community, does he meet others, such as his school friend Jonathan, and later the trade unionist Max Gordon, who question the nature of their society.

Abrahams' consciousness of a world outside Vrededorp, his understanding of social and political injustice come to him through education. His introduction to Keats and Shakespeare radically changes his attitude to himself and to his environment: 'I lived in two worlds, the world of Vrededorp and the world of those books. And, somehow, both were equally real . . . My heart and mind were in turmoil.' (p.127) Education becomes a weapon which enables Abrahams to articulate the grievances of the oppressed. His poetry is published in the black Johannesburg newspaper *The Bantu World*. Its contents are controversial and touch on political topics that 'should not be mentioned' (p. 178). The young Abrahams is, however, an artist, not a propagandist: 'You look at too many sides of a question. And it'll get worse as you develop . . . You may, as a writer, exert an influence on events from afar *if* you succeed. You can do damn all from here.' (p.191) The autobiography ends with Abrahams turning his face to Europe in the hope that there he will find the personal freedom he needs if he is to become a writer and 'tell freedom'.

There are a number of points which could be explored with classes: Abrahams' account of how he published his first poems, his editing of the college magazine at Grace Dieu, his newspaper articles and his editing of the Liberal Study Group's bulletin in Durban, could provide the basis for a discussion of how one becomes a writer; how many writers write full time; the payment one gets for newspaper articles; magazine articles; radio and television scripts; writing a book. Discussion could even extend to matters such as printing processes, copyright, contracts and so on. The question of protest literature could also be followed up: the white sergeant in Durban asks Abraham '"Who's behind this? . . . These meetings and this Bulletin of yours?"' (p.219) Questions such as what dangers do people face in producing protest pamphlets, bulletins and leaflets in authoritarian societies could be followed with wider discussion on the relationship between literature and politics, art and propaganda. Can art be more effective than propaganda in exposing particular injustices?

The theme of racial discrimination is a central one in the autobiography. Abrahams provides a number of instances which focus on his own humiliation, for example when the Elsburg farmer forces his Uncle Sam to beat him for being cheeky. These and his later attempts to oppose legalized racism could form a useful framework for class discussion on race prejudice and race discrimination.

Perhaps most valuable of all, however, are Abrahams' accounts of his childhood and adolescent relationships, his school years, his experiences of the world of work, looking for work and his struggle to achieve a sense of identity in a society that was often alien and hostile.

The author

Abrahams was born in Johannesburg in 1919. His father was Ethiopian and his mother a 'Cape Coloured'. He left South Africa at the age of 20 and after a period as a sailor he settled in London and later moved to Jamaica where he now lives. Abrahams' novels are for the most part set in South Africa; as a writer his themes are varied, and include a study of the conflict for land between Boer and Ndebele in *Wild Conquest*, relationships across the Colour Bar in *Path of Thunder*, urban segregation and migrant workers in *Mine Boy* and a portrait of an imaginary African leader in *A Wreath for Udomo*.

The setting

Vrededorp

This area of Johannesburg, close to the centre of the city, was laid out in 1892 and was originally set aside for Afrikaner transport riders who had lost their occupation when the railway was extended to Johannesburg. Destitute white farmers soon followed. By the 1920s its crowded streets housed only the poorest of Afrikaners and a far larger number of people of mixed race, known in South Africa as 'Coloureds'.

Segregation and the Coloured people

During the 1920s and 1930s the Coloureds' position was favourable compared with that held by Africans, but they too were at the receiving end of racialist legislation and white prejudice. In the Cape Province and in Natal Coloured men had the franchise, but in the Transvaal and the Orange Free State they could only elect one European to Parliament as their representative. Coloureds were not debarred from skilled work in the mines as were Africans and Indians, and generally their employment prospects were better. They were also admitted to white trade unions but these unions made no effort to bargain for better wages for their Coloured members: Coloured miners and teachers, for instance, received only 60–80 per cent of the salaries of their white counterparts. The historian Eric Walker notes that the mass of Coloured people were (in 1936–37) what they had always been, low grade urban or rural labourers or indifferent domestic servants. 'The majority who lived in towns lived at below subsistence level; those on farms led a squalid existence . . .' (*A History of Southern Africa*, 1957, 3rd ed. p.650). Educational facilities were segregated and were poor, they were best in the Cape and worst in the Orange Free State. It was possible for Coloureds to attend university in the Cape or at the University of the Witwatersrand, but here too, they would be isolated.

The pass laws

Although these laws have never been applied to Coloured South Africans they are referred to in *Tell Freedom* (pp.101–2; 143–4) and serve as a reminder of the racialist legislation that affects the lives of a large section of the population. Pass laws laid severe restrictions on the free movement of Africans. From 1923 onwards all African men had to carry evidence of being registered in urban areas where influx control was applied. Contracts of employment had to be registered and men who had not found work within a certain time could be forced to leave the town. Certain people such as landowners and some teachers did not have to carry passes but after 1952 all African men and women had to carry a 'reference book', i.e. a pass at all times. (See Unit 11: *Sizwe Bansi is Dead*.)

Black writing and Black journalism in the 1930s

Abrahams' feeling of isolation as a writer is very evident in the third section of his autobiography. What literary tradition was there he could look to for guidance? He looked back to the English Romantic poets and was also fired

with enthusiasm by the 'New Negro writers' whose books he came across in the library of the Bantu Men's Social Centre (p.154). The writer and critic Ezekiel Mphahlele, who was at school with Abrahams in Johannesburg in 1935, remembers him as 'a dreamy boy who wrote a good deal of verse inspired by Marcus Garvey's call to the American Negro to come back to Africa and most probably by Langston Hughes' verse' (*The African Image*, 1962, p.177).

The Bantu World, to which Abrahams sent his youthful poems of protest was the only English language paper catering for Black writers and readers. Writers using Zulu could turn to the Johannesburg *Umteteli weBantu* or the Durban *Ilanga laseNatal* and these papers did also quite frequently print poetry and articles in English. H.I.E. Dhlomo, whom Abrahams mentions as being editor for a time of *The Bantu World*, wrote poems and plays in English. His best known poem is the romantic epic *Valley of a Thousand Hills* which recalls the former glories of the Zulu people. Other writers such as the novelist R.R.R. Dhlomo and the poet B.W. Vilakazi chose to use Zulu as their literary language. Thomas Mofolo, author of the historical novel *Chaka* (1931) had written in Sotho. The only novel of the period which might have influenced Abrahams was Sol Plaatje's *Mhudi* (1930). There was also William Plomer's novel *Turbott Wolfe* (1925) which provided a sharply critical view of accepted black-white relationships and the earlier *Story of an African Farm* by Olive Schreiner. Yet these on their own could not provide Abrahams with a sense that there was a South African literary tradition with which he could identify.

Classroom use

Level of use

As a whole: fourth and fifth year. GCSE. **Age 14–16.** In parts: the sections on his early life in Vrededorp, his friendships, his first school and life in Elsburg could be used for third year work (age 13–14).

Teaching resources are listed at the end of the unit.

Points for focus and emphasis

1 *His family*:
the lost father (Book 1, Chapter 1)
at Elsburg with Aunt Liza and Uncle Sam (Book 1, Chapter 1)
reunion, sickness and poverty (Book 1, Chapter 2)
life with Aunt Mattie (Book 1, Chapters 3, 4 and 5)
Harry's troubles (Book 1, Chapters 4 and 5)
Maggie's and his mother's devotion (constant references)

2 *The environment*:
the harshness of Elsburg (Book 1, Chapter 1)
Vrededorp; colourful and poverty-stricken (Book 1, Chapter 2)
the carnival (Book 1, Chapter 4)
the white suburbs (Book 2, Chapter 1)
the city centre (Book 1, Chapter 5)
the rural peace of Grace Dieu (Book 2, Chapter 3)
the terrible Cape Flats (Book 3, Chapter 2)

3 *Work*:
selling firewood (Book 1, Chapter 3)
the smithy (Book 1, Chapter 4)
basket-carrying at the market (Book 2, Chapter 2)
a hotel boy (Book 2, Chapter 2)
an office boy (Book 2, Chapter 2)
teaching on the Cape Flats (Book 3, Chapter 2)
writing (p.174, p.219)
'the best trimmer I ever shipped with' (p.221)

4 *Friends*:
Dinny and the gang (Book 1, Chapters 3 and 4)
'mad' Nondi (Book 1, Chapters 4 and 5)
Ellen (Book 1, Chapter 5)
Anne (Book 2, Chapters 2 and 3)
Jonathan, the country boy (Book 2, Chapter 3)

Max Gordon, the trade unionist (Book 3, Chapter 1)

5 *Portraits*:
Oupa Ruiter, the drover (Book 1, Chapter 3)
Rev. Rogerson, the singing evangelist (Book 1, Chapter 3)
Visser, 'the Mad Boer Poet' (Book 1, Chapter 5)
Teka (Book 2, Chapter 3)
Fatty, the café owner (Book 2, Chapter 3)
Roderigues, a religious fanatic? (Book 3, Chapter 2)

6 *Episodes*:
begging in the city centre (Book 1, Chapter 5)
saved by a red-head (Book 2, Chapter 2)
the 'Burning Meat' encounter (Book 2, Chapter 2)

7 *Schools and teachers*:
'the story of Othello jumped at me and invaded my heart' (p.115)
Visser's school (Book 1, Chapter 5)
self-education (Book 2, Chapter 2)
a worker-scholar at Grace Dieu (Book 3, Chapter 1)
a changing outlook (Book 3, Chapter 1)

8 *Becoming a writer*:
'my greatest wealth' (p.127)
'What do you want to learn?' (p.150)
the poems and *The Bantu World* (Book 2, Chapter 3)
influences: the English Romantic poets
Black American writing (Book 1, Chapter 5)
'Best thing you've done. Better than your poetry' (p.214)

9 *'Reserved for Europeans Only'*:
an insult and its consequences (Book 1, Chapter 1)
'And remember to say "baas" or "missus"' (p.81)
the laughing girls (Book 2, Chapter 2)
passes (Book 2, Chapter 2, pp.140–4, 161–2)
trade unions, Christianity and Marxism (Book 2, Chapter 3; Book 3, Chapters 1 and 2)
protest (Book 3, Chapters 2 and 3)

Teaching suggestions

(a) Interpretation and appreciation

1 (a) Why does Lee (Peter Abrahams) go to
       live in Elsburg?
   (b) What sort of treatment does he receive
       from Aunt Liza and Uncle Sam?
   (c) What qualities of character do you
       think he shows during his Elsburg stay?

2 'One morning Maggie, Aunt Betty and I
   saw my mother off to Krugersdorp.' (p.75)
   Describe Lee's home life in Vrededorp up
   to this point.

3 (a) 'I went out and walked aimlessly about
       the bleak, cold world.' (p.110) What
       do you consider are Aunt Mattie's
       strong and weak points as head of the
       family? (pp.75–110)
   (b) 'Quite often, Aunt Mattie would sit in
       a corner listening while tears ran down
       her cheeks.' (p.128) Describe the
       changes that have taken place in the
       family by this time. How has Aunt
       Mattie changed?

4 'He and his wife fought interminably . . .'
   (p.128) How sympathetic a portrait of his
   brother Harry does Abrahams give?

5 Compare Lee's stay in Elsburg with his life
   in Vrededorp. In what ways are the two
   places different? Would you say one is
   better than the other?

6 Which experiences make the young
   Abrahams aware of the differences in
   living standards between the white people
   and most of the inhabitants of Vrededorp?

7 What do you consider to be a) the pleasant
   and b) the unpleasant aspects of Abrahams'
   childhood?

8 Which of Abrahams' jobs do you think was
   the worst? Which was the best? Why?

9 Abrahams talks of 'a dear warmth of pure
   motiveless friendship.' (p.187) Describe
   his friendship with Dinny or Ellen or
   Jonathan.

10 How big a part does luck, or coincidence
   play in Abrahams' life?

11 What characteristics do you think
   Abrahams shows in his childhood and
   youth?

12 '"You've changed," she said slowly,
   frowning.' (p.175) How has he changed
   and what do you think has brought about
   the change?

13 (a) How does Abrahams build up a repu-
       tation as a writer? What difficulties
       does he encounter?
   (b) '"The Bible says 'And Jesus wept'. I
       suppose that would be too simple for
       you. Read the Bible if you want to see
       how good English should be written."'
       (p.171) Discuss Abrahams' style.

14 Why does Abrahams find that both Christianity and Marxism leave him unsatisfied?
   What elements in each appeal to him?

15 'Really, my mother had performed a
   miracle in giving us a sense of family without the support of a husband.' (p.206)
   How has his mother managed to do this?
   What difficulties has she had to face?

16 What details does Abrahams concentrate
   on in his description of the carnival,
   Nondi's accident, his work as a hotel boy?

17 '"You look at too many sides of a question."' (p.191) Is this a weakness in
   Abraham's writing? Select an incident
   where you think he does present more than
   one side of a question and comment on his
   presentation.

18 Discuss Abrahams' use of dialogue in his
   presentation of people.

(b) Creative

1 How are the Coloureds in the novel affected
   by unemployment? What effects do you
   think unemployment has on an individual,
   the family, the community as a whole?

2 'My aunt was as loud and assertive as my
   mother was quiet and retiring.' Compare
   two people you know (or invent two) who
   are related but who are different in many
   ways.

3 Dramatize any of the following incidents:
'Life with Aunt Mattie' (pp.77–85)
stealing the coal
the insults and the whipping that followed (pp.30–5)
the police asking for passes in the cafe (pp.160–2)
the market and the red-head
looking for work as a docker in Cape Town and Durban (pp. 2–3, 220–2)
Granny Pietersen and the visiting preacher (pp. 94–7) **D**
4 Read again Abrahams' description of the coon carnival (pp.97–100). Write about a carnival or a fair which you have been to. In what ways was it similar to the Vrededorp carnival?
5 'His clothes hung drably on him. His shoulders slouched. An oily cap sat far back on his head, showing the dust in his hair. His eyes were sullen.' (p.78) How far do you think Harry's environment has brought about the change in him? How important is environment in forming a person's character and general attitudes to life? Does where we come from help us to make us what we are (suburb, inner city, village and so on)?
6 '"Me, I'm going brother!"
"Where?"
He pointed at the setting sun.
"There! I'm going to see what it's like where the sun sets."' (p.103)
Write 'Nondi's story'.
7 What does the book tell you about the effects of race discrimination on people?
8 Imagine you are a reporter for *The Bantu World* and write a report on one of the following: Nondi's accident (pp.101–3); Mr Rathebe's visit to Harlem (p.153); Market boys and police harassment (pp.133–7).

(c) Curriculum-linked

1 Links with *History* or *Economics*: make a study of the effects of the world depression of 1930 on South Africa.
3 Links with *History*: make a study of African Nationalism and opposition groups in South Africa in the period 1920–40 or from 1950–80.
3 Links with *Geography*: plot a route for Abrahams' journey from Cape Town to Durban (include rail, road and walking).
4 Many books by African writers are written in their own country but often published overseas in London, or in the USA. How do you think this affects what writers write about? What are the problems and advantages of indigenous publishing houses? What are the disadvantages? Examples of indigenous publishers are: South Africa: Ravan, Ad Donker; Nigeria: Fourth Dimension; Kenya: Transafrica, East African Publishing House.

Topics

Families
Childhood
Friendship
Discrimination
Rich and poor
The city
Politics

Passages for reading

City lights (p.157)
Confrontations (pp.161–2)
Parting (pp.165–7)
The writer and repression (p.178)
Growing up, growing away (pp.175–8)

Teaching aids

Audio-visual

Film

Cry the Beloved Country, based on the novel by Alan Paton.
Time: 103 mins   Colour   Distributor: Connoisseur Films   Hire: £20
A black priest from Zululand goes to Johannesburg to look for his son and daughter – an exposé of Johannesburg slum life and slum violence generated by apartheid.

Photographic sets

Children Under Apartheid
Available for hire at £4.50 from IDAF, Canon Collins House, 64 Essex Street, London N1.

Background reading

David Killingray, *A Plague of Europeans*, Penguin Educational, 1973.
There have been westerners in Africa since the fifteenth century. This contains an excellent brief account on South Africa. After charting early European–African contact and European expansion in South Africa, Killingray concentrates on discriminatory legislation introduced since the National Party came to power in 1948 and charts African responses to discrimination. The illustrations and diagrams are a valuable source of information.
Peter Walshe, *Black Nationalism in South Africa, A Short History*, Sprocas/Ravan (Johannesburg), 1973.
A short but comprehensive account of black politics in South Africa from the early part of the twentieth century through to the 1970s.
Apartheid in Practice, United Nations Publication, 1976.
This sets out the legal restrictions imposed by apartheid laws. It is useful as a reference document on racism in South Africa and as an example of how race domination can be institutionalized.
John Addison, *Apartheid*, Batsford (Today's World Series), 1981.
Discusses how apartheid operates today and examines its development and existence under other names before it became institutionalized in 1948.

Criticism

Christopher Heywood, 'The Novels of Peter Abrahams' in C. Heywood (ed.), *Perspectives in African Literature*, Heinemann, 1971.
K. Ogungbesan, *The Writing of Peter Abrahams*, Hodder and Stoughton, 1979.
Russell Daniels, *Tell Freedom, Peter Abrahams*, Longman Guides to Literature, 1981.

Reading links

Charles Dickens, *Great Expectations* and *David Copperfield* (relevant parts).
Alex La Guma, *A Walk in the Night*, and other stories, Heinemann (African Writers Series 35), 1968.
Experience of Coloured society in Cape Town. Title story very useful for fourth and fifth years. Age 14–16. Michael Adonis is pushed ever nearer to the sleazy underworld of Cape Town's District Six. Crisp prose. Vivid images of decay.
Mtutuzeli Matshoba, *Call Me Not a Man*, and other stories, Ravan Press, 1979; Longman (Drumbeat 42), 1981.
Life in Soweto and South Africa as a young urban Black. First published collection, satiric, covers rural and urban experience.
Mbulelo Mzamane, *My Cousin Comes to Jo'burg and Other Stories*, Longman (Drumbeat 41), 1981.
Life in Soweto by 'one who knows'. Fourth years and above. Age 14+.
Alan Paton, *Debbie Go Home, and Other Stories*, Penguin, 1965. Enjoyed by third and fourth years. Age 13–15.
Samuel Selvon, *A Brighter Sun*, Longman (Drumbeat 4), 1979; *Turn Again Tiger*, Heinemann (Caribbean Writers Series 19), 1979.
Alan Sillitoe, *Mountains and Caverns: Selected Essays*, W.H. Allen, 1975.

Other novels by Peter Abrahams

Mine Boy, Heinemann (African Writers Series 6), 1963.
A country youth learns of the harshness of life in Johannesburg. Fourth and Fifth years. Age 14–16.
Path of Thunder, Faber, 1952.
Traces the difficulties of love across the Colour Bar in South Africa. Fifth years. Age 15–16.
Wild Conquest, Faber, 1951; Nelson (Panafrica Library), 1981.
A historical novel of the journey of the Matabele across the interior. Eventful. Fourth and fifth years. Age 15–16.
A Wreath for Udomo, Faber, 1965.
Explores the difficulties of nationalism and independence in an imaginary West African state, closely resembling Nkrumah's Ghana. Sixth form. Age 16–18.
See the books recommended for Unit 1: *The African Child*.

Poetry

M. Chapman and Achmat Dangor (eds), *Voices from Within, Black Poetry from Southern Africa*, Ad Donker, 1982.
B. Feinberg (ed.), *Poets to the People*, Heinemann (African Writers Series 230), 1980.
Political poetry, some very good poems, some impassioned but flat.
Mafika Gwala, *No More Lullabies*, Raven (Staffrider Series 15), (Johannesburg), 1982.
A pioneer poet of the Black Consciousness movement of the 1970s, but Gwala is based in Natal, not Soweto. See particularly 'Words to a Mother' and 'To My Daughter on Her 16th Birthday'.
Claude McKay, *Selected Poems*, Harcourt Brace Jovanovich (New York), 1953.

Could be used to show the kind of Black American poetry which influenced Peter Abrahams: issues of oppression, efforts to define identity, blackness, roots, idealism, the romantic. McKay is one of the best known of the writers of the 'Negro literary renaissance of the 1920s'. He died in 1948.

Robert Royston (ed.), *Black Poets in South Africa*, Heinemann (African Writers Series 164), 1974.

Poems from this collection could be used to illustrate the themes of racism, urban poverty and alienation, all of which Abrahams explores in *Tell Freedom*.

Swazi women and baby, Swaziland (David Rycroft)

Unit 5 *The River Between*

Ngugi wa Thiong'o

Level of use and scope

The River Between, originally called *The Black Messiah*, is Ngugi's first novel. The story centres upon the figure of Waiyaki who from his earliest years seems marked out as a leader. When his father Mugo tells him in the solemn secrecy of 'the sacred grove' that he is the last in a 'long line of seers' and that he is destined to be a saviour of his people, the boy is frightened, not exhilarated. He tries to forget his father's words, partly because he does not understand them. Although he is a traditionalist, Mugo sends his son to the mission school, Siriana, in order to understand the white man's ways. It is after Waiyaki leaves Siriana that he begins to emerge as a leader and organizer of his people. He becomes known as 'the Teacher', 'the pride of the hills' and 'the champion of the tribe's ways and life' (p.70).

Waiyaki, however, is destroyed, partly by his own blindness and partly by his own people. At first he believes single-mindedly in education as a means of salvation; he longs for unity and reconciliation between the devout but inflexible Christians of Makuya ridge and the passionate traditionalists of his own Kameno ridge. He realizes too late that there is a need too for political action to defend his people's rights against the encroaching colonial administration and the seizure of Gikuyu land. The tension between Waiyaki's growing consciousness of what should be done and the build-up of forces hostile to him continues to the book's final pages. Finally he is forced to choose between his love for the 'impure' Christian Nyambura and a rigidly defined loyalty to his own group. He is accused of

breaking the oath of loyalty and in a final dramatic scene he presents his defence to the people, all those who had praised him as 'their teacher, their saviour' (p.149) and who then betrayed him: 'they did not want to read their guilt in one another's faces. Neither did they want to speak to one another, for they knew full well what they had done to Waiyaki and yet they did not want to know'. (p.152)

Apart from the strong storyline which holds the reader's interest, Ngugi instils from early on a sense of impending doom and tragedy. He does this through the use of omens such as Waiyaki's uncontrollable crying during the first simple ceremony of being 'born again' (pp.11–12), dreams and presentiments of disaster. Thus as Waiyaki watches Nyambura pray, on the very spot where as a young boy he was circumcised, he experiences 'a frightening sensation, as if she and he were together standing on an altar ready for sacrifice' (p.104). Ngugi forces the reader to share the consciousness of his characters. It is because of his sensitive portrayal of Waiyaki that the book is not merely about issues but is also an exploration of an individual struggling to reconcile opposing factions and trying to understand what it means to be both leader and lover.

Although the book is at present (1981–83) set as an 'A' level text for the London University Examinations Board, it could equally well be studied at 'O' level and included in CSE work on 'Leaders', 'Heroes' or 'Parents and children'. It is suitable for the 14+ age group. It could also be used with senior forms for work on misunderstanding and conflict between older and younger generations (Waiyaki's implacable enemy is the elder Kabonyi); and for work on the subject of prejudice or sectarian rivalry. In its emphasis on conflict between parental (or senior)

The River Between, Ngugi wa Thiong'o, Heinemann (African Writers Series 17), 1965, repr. 1978.

authority in the figure of Nyambura's father Joshua and the aspirations of youth, it has links with Achebe's *No Longer at Ease*. The book is also about the problem of asserting and affirming one's own culture in a way that is neither narrow nor sectarian. It reflects changing cultural patterns, making the point – which, in the novel itself, Kabonyi and the stubborn, conservative elders of the tribe resist – that culture is never static but always, in some form or another, innovative.

The author

See Unit 3 *Weep Not, Child*.

The setting

The novel is set in Kenya's Central Province, the traditional territory of the Gikuyu. This fertile, heavily populated and intensely cultivated area with its parallel ridges and intersecting valleys was the focus of land expropriation in the time of expatriate settlement. The period is the late 1920s and early 1930s when settlers were increasingly encroaching on what the Gikuyu regarded as their land (see below). The profound division in Gikuyu society over the issue of female circumcision came to a head in the late 1920s (see below) and resulted in the setting up of independent, non-missionary Gikuyu schools. These latter events are central to the plot of the novel.

Discussion before reading the novel could focus firstly on prejudice and how it operates between two groups divided on ethnic, political, religious or economic grounds; how such groups often do not want to understand each other or communicate; how particular slogans, symbolic dress, code words and so on become associated with a particular group. Another topic for discussion could be rebelling against authority or the assertion of independence in the teeth of opposition. The example of a son or daughter who chooses a career or life-style disapproved of by the family could be used; or the class could talk about cases where children have opposed the political or religious views of their parents. An example could be the school-children of Soweto, South Africa, who in 1976 took independent action against the White authorities. Initiation could also be discussed, first of all in a general sense, as a way of making an individual a fully fledged member of a group. School and in some cases college initiations, baptism and confirmation could be mentioned. The question of how does one prove one is 'a man' could be explored; how do girls express changed status and identity? Initiation as a 'rite of passage' could then be introduced (see below).

The 'Kiama'

The term is used to mean a council of Gikuyu elders who were responsible for judging cases in the community over which they had jurisdiction. Normally each ridge ('*mbari*') would have its own Kiama and only older men would be eligible for a place on it.

Oathing

Oath-taking as a means of binding a group together and reinforcing loyalty amongst the members of a group is common in a traditional context among the Gikuyu and their neighbours the Kamba. In the Emergency in Kenya, all persons involved in the Independence struggle took an oath. Oathing still takes place and in the 1969 elections it had to be banned as some politicians were using oath-taking as a means of ensuring that people voted for them (see also Unit 3, Setting).

Circumcision

In traditional Gikuyu society circumcision for both males and females is an important rite of passage signifying entry into adulthood, and the responsibilities of adulthood. It is an essential preliminary to marriage. The circumcision of women, which involves cutting off a piece of the clitoris, is not seen as an act of cruelty or degradation. At one point in *The River Between* Waiyaki tries to assess its significance: 'Circumcision of women was not important as a physical operation. It was what it did inside a person. It could not be stopped overnight . . .' (p.142) Earlier in the novel Ngugi speaks more directly to the reader: 'Circumcision was an important ritual to the tribe. It kept people together, bound the tribe. It was at the core of the social structure, and a something that gave meaning to a man's life. End the custom and the spiritual basis of the tribe's cohesion and integration would be no more'. (p.68) Female circumcision has, however, in recent years become an increasingly controversial topic. Although it is still practised in large regions of East Africa and elsewhere in Africa, the physical, psychological and sexual hazards it involves make it a very questionable practice in the eyes of many Africans and non-Africans. Some people though (often African men) take the line of argument represented in *The River Between*, that where female circumcision is an integral part of a traditional culture it should be upheld. For a careful discussion of the subject see *Minority Rights Group Pamphlet No.47: Female Circumcision, Excision and Infibulation: the facts and proposals for change*, M.R.G., London, 1980, £1.20. For a Gikuyu account and point of view, see Jomo Kenyatta, *Facing Mount Kenya*, Heinemann Educational Books, (Nairobi), 1971, Chapter 6, 'Initiation of Boys and Girls'.

The independent schools

So incensed did the members of the Scottish Mission become over the issue of female circumcision that they banned all 'heathen' Gikuyu from their schools. The independent Gikuyu schools which sprang up in 1931 and in the years following were a response by some Gikuyu to what they saw as an attempt to suppress and denigrate their customs and to prevent them from obtaining western education.

Land

During the period of European settlement in the early years of this century it was largely Gikuyu land which was alienated and put aside for private farms. Land was divided along racial and tribal lines with Crown-owned African Reserves on the one hand and privately owned 'White' Highlands for the Europeans. As overpopulation, land hunger and poor terms of employment on White-owned farms intensified, Gikuyu bitterness increased.

The legend of origin

History recalls that the Gikuyu entered what is today northern Kenya in the sixteenth century and made their way to their present lands in the eighteenth and nineteenth centuries. Legend speaks of the origin of the Gikuyu people in the story of Mumbi and Gikuyu. Legends of origin often serve as a source of unity and inspiration to a particular people; in the case of the Gikuyu the focus of the legend is not on power given to a particular lineage but on territory. Mugo Gatheru refers to the legend as follows:

In 1953, during the trial of those who were accused of organizing Mau Mau among my people, frequent references were made to certain alleged secret rituals in which they referred to themselves as the 'Children of Mumbi and Kikuyu'. But I, who was born long before Mau Mau, learned of Mumbi and Kikuyu — the story which was handed down from father to son about the origin of our people . . . According to our legends, Ngai took Kikuyu to the top of Mt Kenya, among the shining snow-covered peaks, where no man's foot had ever left a print, and showed him the beautiful country for miles around. There were great forests of cedars, bamboos and olive trees, and between them were vast open spaces where herds of antelopes and gazelles were peacefully grazing. Many rivers of clear, cool water flowed through the land. Far, far away to the south could be seen the snow-capped peaks of what is now called Mt Kilimanjaro. To the west was the mountain 'Myandarua' or Aberdare and to the south, the big hill called Kirima-Mbogo — the hill of the buffaloes.

Ngai said to Kikuyu: 'This is yours . . .' (from Mugo Gatheru, *Child of Two Worlds*, Routledge and Kegan Paul, 1964, p.3).

For another version which again stresses the sacred right of the Gikuyu to their land, see Ngugi's *Weep Not, Child*, Chapter 2, pp.23–4.

Classroom use

Level of use

As a whole: fourth and fifth year in GCSE; also sixth form, 'A' level or CEE. **Age 14–18.**

Teaching resources are listed at the end of the unit.

Points for focus and emphasis

1 *Waiyaki's early life*:
His 'second birth' (Chapter 3)
the importance of the past: heroes and leaders (Chapters 4 and 5)
the prophecy of 'a saviour' (Chapter 5)
initiation and circumcision (Chapters 9 and 10)
2 *Muthoni's rebellion*:
her reasons (Chapter 6)
womanhood (Chapter 9)
her death (Chapters 10–12)
the consequences (Chapter 12)
3 *The antagonists*:
Joshua and Kabonyi as friends (Chapter 12)
Christian anger, traditionalist outrage (Chapters 11 and 12)
Kabonyi and the Kiama (Chapters 13, 18, 19 and 20)
Joshua's fervour (Chapter 17)
conflict between Church and Kiama (Chapters 20, 22 and 24)
4 *Waiyaki as leader*:
his belief in education (Chapters 13, 14 and 20)
a speech, an omission (Chapter 18)
the teacher (Chapter 18)
conflict with Kabonyi and the Kiama (Chapters 16, 18, 20, 23 and 24)
'traitor' or 'Saviour'? (Chapters 23 and 24)
5 *Nyambura and Waiyaki*:
the moonlight encounter (Chapter 15)
a meeting (Chapter 17)

proposal and rejection (Chapter 19)
Kamau's jealousy (Chapter 19, pp. 107–8)
victims of prejudice (Chapter 21)
their courage (Chapter 24)

Teaching suggestions

(a) *Interpretation and appreciation*

1 An exercise for a first sampling of the book: Read the paragraph on p.20 containing the words, 'And keep on remembering, salvation shall come from the hills. A man must rise and save the people in their hour of need. He shall show them the way; he shall lead them'. Then turn to p.135, read the paragraph containing the words 'Outside he heard a faint noise. At first it had seemed distant but now he could hear some words – Teacher . . . traitor . . . A heavy dejection came over Waiyaki. He knew now that he was not wanted by them in spite of all he had done for the hills'. Speak or write about what you think has happened in the story between those two points.
2 (a) Why do you think Waiyaki finds the visit to the sacred grove such an uncomfortable experience?
(b) What are Waiyaki's feelings towards his father?
3 Muthoni's act of defiance and her death mean different things to different people:
(a) 'There was something in Muthoni that somehow called forth all his sympathy and admiration. Was he himself capable of such a rebellion?' (Waiyaki, p.49)
(b) 'To him Muthoni had ceased to exist on the very day that she had sold herself to the devil.' (Joshua, pp.53–4)
(c) 'This was a punishment to Joshua.' (Chege, p.54)
(i) Why did Muthoni act as she did? What is your opinion of her action? (ii) Plan and act a dialogue between Muthoni and Joshua over the issue of her circumcision. (iii) Think of a situation where you might find yourself in a position similar to Muthoni's. Improvise a scene around that situation.

4 What are the real differences between the Church group and the traditionalists? (Consider terms used by the Church group: 'a pagan rite' (p.23); 'children of darkness' (p.67); 'this wicked generation' (p.32). What have the groups in common with each other? How irreconcilable are their positions in reality? Can you think of other societies which are similarly divided over religious, political or social issues? **G**

5 Compare the descriptions of the boys' circumcision ceremonies in *The River Between* and *The African Child* (pp.100–8 Fontana edition). What is the importance of the ceremony to the individual and to the community? How different are the techniques of the two writers (Ngugi and Camara) in their accounts of circumcision?

6 'Waiyaki was becoming the pride of the hills and the pride of Kameno. Already they had started calling him the champion of the tribe's ways and life.' (p.70) But is he such a champion? Compare his outlook with that of Kinuthia (see for instance p.64).

7 'Nyambura was not circumcised. But this was not a crime. Something passed between them as two human beings untainted with religion, social conventions or any tradition.' (p.76) Compare the situation of Waiyaki and Nyambura with that of Romeo and Juliet as shown in the following extract from the play, Act 2, Scene 2:

JULIET: O Romeo, Romeo! Wherefore art
　　　thou Romeo?
　　　Deny thy father and refuse thy
　　　　name;
　　　Or, if thou wilt not, be but sworn
　　　　my love,
　　　And I'll no longer be a Capulet.

ROMEO (Aside): Shall I hear more, or shall
　　　I speak at this?

JULIET: 'Tis but thy name that is my
　　　　enemy;—
　　　Thou art thyself though, not a
　　　　Montague.

What's Montague? It is nor hand,
　　　nor foot,
Nor arm, nor face, nor any other
　　　part
Belonging to a man. O, be some
　　　other name!
What's in a name? that which we
　　　call a rose,
By any other name would smell as
　　　sweet;
So Romeo would, were he not
　　　Romeo call'd,
Retain that dear perfection which
　　　he owes
Without that title:—Romeo, doff
　　　thy name;
And for that name, which is no
　　　part of thee,
Take all myself.

ROMEO : I take thee at thy word:
　　　Call me but love, and I'll be new
　　　baptiz'd;
　　　Henceforth I never will be Romeo.

8 Chapter 18 describes the first Parents' Day at Marioshoni school.
　　(a) What impression does Wiayaki make on the gathering?
　　(b) What danger signs are there? If you had to send a 20-word telegram to Waiyaki *warning* him of … what would you say?

9 'Nyambura was not happy.' (p.102) What are the difficulties of her position? What would you say if you had to give her advice *before* Waiyaki's proposal (p.107) and again shortly afterwards? Send Waiyaki another telegram!

10 'The old rivalry went on … Waiyaki did not like to be identified with either side; he was now committed to reconciliation.' (p.110) Compare this attitude with Kinuthia's warning on p.112 '"they are taking the new oath in your name"'. How realistic are Waiyaki's aims?

11 Kabonyi feels himself to be 'the saviour for whom the people waited' (p.144). What has he to offer the tribe compared with Waiyaki?

12 'And he said loudly, "I shall go there to-morrow."
"Where?" Kinuthia asked . . .
"To the hill south of Kameno. To the sacred grove."
"To the sacred grove?"
"Yes, it is a long story."' (p.138)
Discuss whether or not Kinuthia is right to revisit the sacred grove? Is it for instance, a waste of valuable time? A move which plays into his enemies' hands? A valuable source of inspiration to him? G

13 Turn to the account of Waiyaki's and Joshua's speeches in their final confrontation (Chapter 26). 'He began to speak. At first he made a small speech; thanked the people for coming . . .' (Waiyaki, p.146); 'He was once a Joshua follower. Now he was the leader of the Kiama . . .' (Kabonyi, p.147) Turn both these into *direct speech*. Deliver the speeches. Try to dramatize the whole scene, bringing in Waiyaki, Nyambura, the elders, Kinuthia, the observers from across the river, the crowd. G

14 Why does Waiyaki win the people's support the first time he speaks against Kabonyi (Chapter 19, pp.91–6) but lose on the second occasion? Compare the final scene with *Julius Caesar*, Act III Scene 2, where Brutus and Mark Anthony address the Roman crowd after Caesar's murder. G

15 'Had Kinuthia betrayed him? Had Kinuthia been in league with Kabonyi?' (p.151) Compare Kinuthia's treatment of Waiyaki with Peter's denial of Christ (see St Matthew 26; St Mark 14).

16 Ngugi begins and ends the novel with a reference to the river Honia, which meant 'cure or bring-back-to-life' (p.1). Why do you think he does so?

17 Discuss the use of omens and dreams in the novel.

18 Muthoni, Nyambura and Waiyaki are all rebels but what is the cause they are each fighting for?

19 Do you think *The Black Messiah* would have been a better title for the novel?

(b) Creative

1 Using Chapter 24 as your basis for information, write an account in your diary of the day's events from the point of view of Waiyaki, Nyambura or Joshua. (Use whatever style of entry you like in your diary: telegraphic, impressionistic, descriptive and so on.)

2 Read the description of Waiyaki's being 'born again' (Chapter 3, pp.11–12). Note particularly the sentences, 'People became frightened. This was not what usually happened.' Think of occasions in real life when things have gone wrong at a special event, for example, prolonged crying of a baby at baptism, sudden inexplicable weeping of one of the partners during a wedding ceremony, and so on. Consider the effects on those present: possible concern for the future, alarm, the feeling that the person is special in some way. How could such an event be a useful device in a story or a play?

3 Discuss the same piece from the point of view of Waiyaki: 'He felt the pain of fear inside himself'. Write or speak about a time when you have been the centre of attention, for example when you were singing or playing an instrument solo or in a group, at a birthday party, a celebration for you, a punishment. What were your feelings at the time. Do you think Waiyaki's reactions are unusual in any way?

4 The following poem by the Australian poet, Justina Williams, raises the question of women's right to choose for themselves on a number of issues (including circumcision) rather than accept the demands of custom and authority:

v
Women Carrying Banners
We are carrying banners sacred as
    childbirth,
Words for women who demand liberation
    as women,
slogans that slip like new skin over
    wounds.
O masters, we take back control of our
    bodies,

of minds no longer truncated, of feet no
longer bound,
the fingers of our left hand no longer cut off
to placate ghosts, of our genitals mutilated
to deprive us of joy, of our virginity sold
in the market. We take back the right to
conceive
or not to conceive, to resume our lost
creativity.
We will sustain one another with friendship and bread
not seeking revenge nor the turning of
tables,
and go proudly as women, as comrades
and lovers,
as workers tending the furnace of change.

from 'Song Cycle of Venus',
Justina Williams.

(a) What specific practices does the writer
object to? Do you consider her points to
be fair ones? Is she persuasive? What are
your own feelings about the kind of
equality for women which the writer
advocates?

(b) 'Equality, Sweet Equality': Write a prose
piece (or act a short sketch) with this title
about a morning in the life of two people
(or a family) who have very different
views on the subject of women's rights. **D**

(c) Curriculum-linked

1 (Could link with History) Compile a list of
men and women who have had a great contribution to make to their society but who
failed in some way or were destroyed. You
could divide this into historical and contemporary sections, for example:

Joan of Arc	Malcolm X
Vercingetorix	J.F. Kennedy
Deacon Book of Jamaica	Steve Biko
L'Ouverture of Haiti	Tom Mboya
Parnell	Kwame Nkrumah

Can you make any generalizations about
such figures?

2 (Could link with Religious Knowledge)
What has 'the sacred grove' in common with
holy places in any of the world's religions?

3 (Link with Religious Knowledge) What are
the parallels between Waiyaki's story and
the life of Christ?

4 Make a short study of two groups in your
own community who are deeply divided
over a religious, political or social issue.

Topics

Leaders: heroes and martyrs
Sacrifice
Rebels
Parents and children
Factionalism
Prejudice

Passages for reading

Muthoni's rebellion (Chapter 8, pp.33–86)
Moonlight encounter (Chapter 14, pp.73–84)
The seasons of the long rains (Chapter 16,
pp.79–80)

Teaching aids

See items listed for Unit 3: *Weep Not, Child.*

Recorded sound	The BBC Radio 4 1981 Schools Broadcast tape on *The River Between* is now held by the National Sound Archive, see Section 3, Resources p. 133.
Reading links	**Chinua Achebe**, *No Longer at Ease*. See Unit 7. **Michael Anthony**, *Green Days by the River*, Heinemann (Caribbean Writers

Series 9), 1973.

An account of how a young boy comes to terms with marriage and commitment.

James Baldwin, *The Fire Next Time,* Penguin, 1964.

Earl Lovelace, *The Schoolmaster,* Heinemann (Caribbean Writers Series 20), 1979.

The story of the building of a road and a school in a village, and of the changes these bring.

Ngugi wa Thiong'o, *Secret Lives,* Heinemann (African Writers Series 150), 1975. Short stories.

See particularly 'The Village Priest' and 'A Meeting in the Dark' which deal with the conflict between Christian and traditional values.

William Shakespeare, *Romeo and Juliet.* The theme of sectionalism versus romantic love could be compared in the play and the novel, see also *West Side Story* for a modern version of the Romeo and Juliet story.

Julius Caesar. The political themes in the two works could be an area for comparison.

Criticism   **Diana Bailey,** *The River Between,* Nexus Books, British Council/Rex Collings, 1982.

Young girls taking the sacrifice of the new yam to the chief, Nigeria (John Picton)

Unit 6 *Things Fall Apart*

Chinua Achebe

Level of use and scope

Things Fall Apart is Achebe's earliest novel and perhaps the best known of all African novels written in English. Achebe is a didactic writer. He states that his aim as a writer is 'to help my society regain its belief in itself' (quoted in Roscoe, *Mother is Gold*, p.121). Elsewhere he remarks, 'I would be quite satisfied if my novels (especially the ones I set in the past) did no more than teach my readers that their past — with all its imperfections — was not one long night of savagery from which the first Europeans acting on God's behalf delivered them' (Achebe, 'The novelist as teacher' quoted in Zell, Bundy and Coulon, 1983, p.345).

In *Things Fall Apart* the central character, Okonkwo, is himself a tragic figure. Through him Achebe portrays his Igbo society, analyses and interprets it. The novel is in three parts and is carefully structured. The first section is not idyllic but it portrays a confident, regulated society. People live in harmony with the cycle of the seasons (p.21); the wrestling matches portray an aspect of their cohesive social life (pp.33–5); political and religious affairs are conducted by those who represent the ancestral spirits of the clan. Achebe, though, also integrates the harsher side of their life. The captive Ikemefuna who has become as a son to Okonkwo has to die because the oracle ordains it; twins are cast out to die in the forest.

Together with the portrait of the small Igbo community are constant references to Okonkwo's character. His central flaw is the fear of being thought weak (pp.9 and 20). He fears that he will die poor and a failure like his flute playing, indolent father. He is impatient with his wives, but worst of all, his fear of appearing weak leads to his taking part in the killing of Ikemefuna. There are hints of a retribution to come as his friend Obierika remarks, 'it is the kind of action for which the goddess wipes out whole families' (p.46). Okonkwo's status and success is in fact destroyed at a stroke of fate. He accidentally kills the son of the very man who advised him earlier: 'That boy calls you father, bear no hand in his death' (p.84). At this point the sense of change to come is introduced. Okonkwo's son Nwoye becomes a Christian, thus destroying his father's sense of his family's unity. The third and final section depicts the breakdown of the old order and the self-destruction of Okonkwo.

Although the novel is currently (1981–83) set as an 'A' level text by London University Examinations Board it could be studied at lower levels (from age 16+) and it could be linked with other novels under the topic Social Change.

The author

Achebe's youth was spent in a large village, Ogidi, in Eastern Nigeria where Christians and traditionalists co-existed, each group keeping its distance from the other. He later studied at University College, Ibadan, and worked for some years for the Nigerian Broadcasting Corporation. He was Director of External Broadcasting when he left the Corporation in 1966. During the Nigerian Civil War he campaigned actively for the Biafran cause. He now devotes all his time to writing and lives in Nsukka, in the eastern state of Anambra.

Things Fall Apart, Chinua Achebe, Heinemann (African Writers Series 1), 1958, repr. 1978.

The setting

The novel is set in south-east Nigeria at the end of the nineteenth century and in the early years of this century. This period saw the penetration of missionaries into Igboland and in 1900 the imposition of direct administration by the British. Between 1891 and 1906 there were government stations at Asada, Onitsha (the town 'on the bank of the Great River' mentioned on p.123), and Awka. The turmoil and instability which followed Direct Administration is brilliantly portrayed in the third and final section of *Things Fall Apart*.

The incidents in the novel are in some cases based on actual events. The murder of the man on the bicycle (p.97) is based on an actual incident in which Dr Stewart, a missionary, was travelling by bicycle and was murdered at the village of Mbaise in 1905. (See *A History of the Igbo People*, Elizabeth Isichei, Macmillan, 1976). Achebe's description of the attraction of Christianity for some sections of the Igbo community (for example pp.103–4 and p.124) is also authenticated by historians:

> The bulk of the first Christian converts were drawn from the poor, the needy and the rejected: the mothers of twins, women accused of witchcraft, those suffering from diseases such as leprosy which were seen as abominable. Finding little satisfaction in the world around them they turned to Christianity with a single-minded devotion which astonished all who beheld it.
>
> (Isichei, p.162)

Masks and masquerading

Masked figures generally represent ancestors or some other kind of spirit, and because of this the masquerader becomes the mediator of power normally beyond human control; the power to cure the sick, make the barren fertile, punish and sometimes execute offenders and so forth. In a small-scale community where everybody is likely to know everybody else, the mask and its costume serves as a device which temporarily re-defines the social person, diverting attention from his everyday role in the community to the one expected of the masked spirit. The dramatic and theatrical possibilities of masquerading are obvious and in some places the aesthetic content of masquerading, including poetry, song and dance, is developed to a high degree far beyond the necessities of religion and politics.

Classroom use

Level of use

Fourth to sixth form. **Age 16–18.** Parts such as folk tales could be used with second years, from the age of 12 upwards.

Teaching resources are listed at the end of unit.

Points for focus and emphasis

1 *Family life*:
(i) *the stories*:
Vulture and Sky (pp.37–8)
Mosquito and Ear (p.53)
The Snake-lizard and his Mother (p.59)
Tortoise at the Feast (pp.67–9)
(ii) *Okonkwo's children*:
Ezinma's illness (Chapter 9)
the priestess Chielo carries off Ezinma (Chapter 11)
Nwoye and Ikemefuna (pp. 20 and 23 and Chapter 7)
Nwoye's grief (p.43) and his rebellion (pp.106–8)
(iii) *Okonkwo's wives*:
Ezinma's illness
preparations for the Feast of the New Yam (pp.27–30)
Ekwefi's love of the wrestling contests (p.28)
her lost children (pp.54–6)
her daughter Ezinma (pp.56–61)
(iv) *Okonkwo's kinsmen*:
help from Uchendu, his mother's brother (Chapter 14)
the farewell feast (pp.117–18)

2 *The Land*:
  how Okonkwo earned his first seed yams
    (pp.14–18)
  yam-planting and the Feast of the New Yam
    (pp.23–8)
  Ekwefi and Ezinma harvesting cassava
    (p.116)
3 *Ceremonies and celebrations*:
  Obierika's family has a marriage party
    (Chaper 12)
  the wrestling contest (Chapter 6)
  the Feast of the New Yam (p.23–8)
  Okonkwo's farewell feast for his mother's
    family (pp.117–18)
4 *Religious belief: the oracles, the deities and
    the ancestral spirits*:
  the Evil Forest (pp. 13 and 105)
  the oracle of Agbala (pp.12–13 and 75–6)
  The Week of Peace and the Feast of the New
    Yam (pp.21–3)
  Ani the earth goddess (pp.26 and 147)
  the ancestral spirits dispense justice
    (Chapter 10)
  Ezeudu's funeral (Chapter 13)
  desecration (pp. 131–2) and vengeance
    (pp.132–5)
5 *Change: the destruction of the old order*
  Church and Government (p.123)
  the destruction of the 'egwugwu' (p.131)
  imprisonment (p.136)

Teaching suggestions

(a) *Interpretation and appreciation*

1 Read the stories listed under *Family Life*.
  Do you think these are most important for
  their entertainment value or because they
  teach a lesson? Look for examples where a
  speaker uses a story in conversation or
  when addressing a gathering. How are
  stories used in Britain?
2 Why is Ezinma so precious to her mother?
  What is an *ogbanje*? Can you think of any
  reason why such a belief came into existence? How does Okonkwo help during her
  illness? What emotions do you think
  Ezinma experienced during her journey

with Chielo? Draw a map (use the text as a
basic guide) of the route taken by Chielo
(see pp. 70–8) the nine villages, the forest,
the oracle etc.
3 What do you think are Okonkwo's good
  points as a father? What goes wrong in his
  handling of Nwoye? Could he have
  avoided the split with him? If so, how?
4 Where is Ikemefuna from and how does he
  come to be in Okonkwo's household?
  What advice does Okonkwo ignore with
  regard to Ikemefuna? What link is
  there between Ikemefuna's death and
  Okonkwo's seven-year banishment
  (pp.86–7)?
5 How do Okonkwo's wives help each other
  (e.g. pp.27–30)? What do you think might
  be the benefits of being a wife or child in a
  polygynous household?
6 What relation is Uchendu to Okonkwo?
  What sort of assistance does he give
  Okonkwo during his exile? (e.g. advice,
  material help, moral support etc.)
7 Outline how Okonkwo overcomes the disadvantages of his early life. Work out how
  many yams Okonkwo should have had for
  himself in his first year of share-cropping
  (p.16). What characteristics of Okonkwo
  (good and bad) are brought to the fore by
  his early experience?
8 'Yam, the king of crops, was a man's crop.'
  (p.16) How does the book bring out the
  importance of yam in people's lives? G
9 What makes the drumming such an important part of the wrestling contest? 'There
  were seven drums and they were arranged
  according to their sizes in a long wooden
  basket. Three men beat them with sticks
  working feverishly from one drum to
  another. They were possessed by the spirit
  of the drums.' (p.33) Draw a picture to
  illustrate this.
10 'Okonkwo never did things by halves.'
  (p.117) How is that proved true in the
  farewell feast he gives for his mother's
  people?
11 Why is it necessary to have the Week of
  Peace before the Feast of the New Yam (pp.
  21–8)? What deity is being thanked? Can

you think of any similar religious observances in other religious beliefs?

12 By what means do the *egwugwu* project their awesomeness? (pp.63–6 and 84–6) What is their role?

13 'The egwugwu with the springy walk was one of the dead fathers of the clan.' What is the point of this change of role on Okonkwo's part?

14 'It was clear from the way the crowd stood and sat that the ceremony was for men.' (p.62) What important part in the proceedings do the men have?

15 'And how is my daughter Ezinma?' (p.34) Read pp.34–5 and then pp.70–6. How is Chielo's behaviour different on the two occasions? What causes the difference?

16 'The land of the living was not far removed from the domain of the ancestors.' (p.85) Does the book succeed in showing the truth of this remark?

17 'It was the poetry of the new religion, something felt in the marrow.' (p.104) Explain as carefully as you can what attracts Nwoye to the new religion.

18 'Suppose when he died all his male children decided to follow Nwoye's steps and abandon their ancestors?' (p.108) What does Okonkwo fear and despise about 'the new religion?'

19 What effect does his exile have on Okonkwo? (Chapter 14)

20 How could Okonkwo derive comfort from the song
   'For whom is it well, for whom is it well? There is no-one for whom it is well'?
   (p.95)

21 Explain how Obierika helped Okonkwo during his years of exile.

22 What changes await Okonkwo when he returns to Umuofia?

23 Compare the policies of Mr Brown and Mr Smith. Why was the former more successful than the latter? **G**

24 'He has put a knife on the things that held us together and we have fallen apart.' (p.125) Is this an accurate assessment of what has happened? **G**

25 'That man was one of the greatest men in Umuofia. You drove him to kill himself and now he will be buried like a dog.' (p.147) Discuss.

26 'Okonkwo never did things by halves.' (p.117) To what extent is this shown to be true in the novel?

27 What reasons does Okonkwo have to remember his father's words 'It is more difficult and bitter when a man fails alone'?

28 'Men who made a great art of conversation'. Does the speech (the dialogue and the public addresses) in *Things Fall Apart* show this to be true?

29 'One of the most infuriating habits of these people was their love of superfluous words.' (p.146) Would you agree with the Commissioner's judgement?

(b) Creative

1 Read again the part describing Ekwefi's illness (pp.53 and 60–1). Write an account of or talk about a time when you or someone you know were seriously ill.

2 Read again the description of Ezinma's night journey on the priestess Chielo's back. Try and put yourself in Ezinma's place and write about or describe to an audience what happened to you that night; what you saw, felt like, feared might happen and so on.

3 'Nwoye remembered this period very vividly until the end of his life.' (p.25) Write about a time in your life when you have been very happy.

4 'but it was a dream.' Imagine that Nwoye (or Isaac as he later calls himself) dreamt of Ikemefuna many years after his death. What was the dream?

(c) Curriculum-linked

1 How would you define exile? What effect do you think exile has on people? How do they remember their motherland? Do they change because of exile? What happens if they return? Work out a short questionnaire on exile, interview someone known to you

who is in some sense an exile. Report back to the class on your findings.

OR Think of famous political or historical figures who have been in exile or banished. Compare them.

2 *Home Economics* Egusi, bitter leaf, foo-foo, are dishes mentioned in the book. Find out about how these are prepared, the ingredients, recipes.

3 *Geography* Markets are mentioned frequently in the novel (e.g. p.79). Find out as much as you can about markets in Eastern Nigeria – who runs them, what commodities are sold, how prices are controlled and goods transported.

4 *Religious Education/History* Work on missionary activities in Eastern Nigeria during the late nineteenth and early twentieth centuries. The Church Missionary Society (CMS) was the most active at that time.

5 *History* Work with the history department on British penetration and conquest of Eastern Nigeria and Igbo struggles against British domination.

6 *Religious Education* Discuss the sacred places and deities mentioned in the novel, the attitudes to the power of the gods and the ties with the ancestors, the idea of the Evil Forest.

7 *Art/Religious Education/Social Studies* Masks and masquerading are still an important and colourful element in Nigerian life. Find out more about how masks are used – by what societies – religious, political – when they appear in public, their appearance, how they are made.

Teaching aids

Audio-visual

Slide sets

Nigeria in Change, 2 slide sets: 1 Modern Nigeria. 2 Traditional Nigeria – Oyo. CWDE (order no. S1 and S2) £5.50 + VAT each. *See also* Resources, p.138.

Recorded sound

The BBC Radio 4 1981 Schools Broadcast tape on *Things Fall Apart* is now held at the National Sound Archive. See Resources p.141.

Reading links

Chinua Achebe, *Arrow of God*, Heinemann (African Writers Series 16), second ed., 1974.
Depicts the tragic clash of traditional religious belief and the forces of change.
No Longer at Ease, Heinemann (African Writers Series 13), 1960.
Can be seen as a sequel to *Things Fall Apart*. See Unit 7.
Girls at War, Heinemann (African Writers Series 100), 1972. Short stories.
Kathleen Arnott, *Auta the Giant Killer and Other Nigerian Folk Stories*, Oxford Univeristy Press, 1971. Illustrated by Uzo Egonu.
For other novels of Igbo life see Section 3, p.149, entries under *Emecheta*.
M. Crowder and H. Nzekwu, *Eze Goes to School*, African Universities Press, (Lagos), 2nd ed., 1971. Available in the UK from Edward Arnold., 41 Bedford Square, London WC1.
Short paperback for top primary but useful as supplementary background reading.

Romanus Egudu and Donatus Nwoga (eds and translators), *Igbo Traditional Verse*, Heinemann (African Writers Series 129), 1973.
Contains a scholarly and readable introduction to Igbo culture and a collection of poems that are often rich in poetic techniques, entertaining and cover a variety of subjects.
William Golding, *The Inheritors*, Faber, 1955.
Thomas Hardy, *The Mayor of Casterbridge*, (for comparisons of Okonkwo and Henchard and social change).

Background reading

General

M. Crowder and G. Abdullahi, *Nigeria, An Introduction to its History*, Longman, 1975.
Dennis Duerden, *African Art: An Introduction*, Hamlyn, 1974.
A good introduction with some material on masks and masquerading.
Colin Latcham, *Looking at Nigeria*, A & C Black, 1976, has excellent illustrations, a useful introductory text on economic and social life (he says nothing about religious life, though, except a curious reference to *juju*) and a good map.
Rems Nna Umeasiegbu, *The Way We Lived*, Heinemann (African Writers Series 61), 1969.
The first section on 'Customs' contains short, very readable entries on 'A first child in the family', 'Breaking a kola nut' and so on; the second section, 'Folklore', contains mainly stories but also a few songs, for example 'An Unmarried Mother's song'.
Victor C. Uchendu, *The Igbo of Southeast Nigeria*, Holt, Rinehart and Winston, 1965.
Not too long and excellent.
Laurens van der Post, *African Cooking*, Time/Life Books, 1970.
Large and glossy, in two parts, one general text and one recipe book.
Richard White, *Africa: Geographical Studies*, Heinemann, 1978.
Up-to-date and useful on Nigeria.
R.O. Williams, *Miss Williams' Cookery Book*, Longman, Nigeria, 1957, repr. 1975.

Criticism

C.L. Innes and B. Lindfors (eds), *Critical Perspectives on Chinua Achebe*, Heinemann Educational, 1979.
G.D. Killam, *The Writings of Chinua Achebe*, Heinemann Educational, 1977.
Eustace Palmer, *An Introduction to the African Novel*, Heinemann Educational, 1972.

Unit 7 *No Longer at Ease*

Chinua Achebe

Level of use and scope

The novel is a sequel to the celebrated *Things Fall Apart* and the issues it explores relate to the earlier work. The central character, Obi, is the grandson of Okonkwo. On his return to Lagos after taking an English honours degree in London, Obi Okonkwo has to come to terms with the conflicting demands of custom and kinship on the one hand and personal affection on the other. Soon after his return he discovers that Clara, the girl he loves, is an *osu* – an outcast. Marriage to an *osu* would be unthinkable for most of his fellow Igbo, Obi is told. As the reality of his situation becomes clear Obi begins to feel 'a stranger in his own country' (p.65). His alienation from his fellow Umuofians in Lagos shows itself in his inability to behave as one of them when he attends Lagos meetings of the Umuofia Progressive Union. He realizes his distance from his own parents when on a visit to Umuofia village the subject of marriage to Clara is broached. His father warns him solemnly against such a union; his sick mother promises to commit suicide if he should marry an *osu* in her lifetime. His isolation increases when Clara too refuses to see him and their engagement is broken off. Besides his personal difficulties over Clara, Obi runs into financial trouble. Because of his position in the Civil Service he is expected to live in an expensive Europeanized suburb, Ikoyi, where the cost of living is high. He finds that he cannot pay his bills, let alone repay money owing to the Umuofia Progressive Union who helped support him while he was overseas. Obi's isolation and sense of stress is intensified by the news of his mother's death. The Umuofia Progressive Union who come to help him mourn, are by this time too disapproving of his lifestyle to offer him any real comfort. It is at this point when Obi feels most disillusioned with 'our noble fatherland' (p.36), and without support or understanding that he begins to accept the bribes which have always been within his reach. The ending of the book contains the ironic question: 'everybody wondered why' (p.154).

Achebe's study is a sympathetic one. He puts before the reader the dilemma facing members of the new elite who have to reconcile attitudes inculcated through western education with the demands of custom and kin. He is critical of the high standards of living the elite take for themselves yet he also points an accusing finger at aspects of Igbo custom such as the prejudice against anyone who is an *osu*. Achebe's presentation of Obi compares interestingly with Armah's treatment of the elite in *The Beautyful Ones are Not Yet Born*, with Aidoo's characters and with Ngugi's degenerate creations in *Petals of Blood*.

The book would fit well with work on the subjects of 'Conflict' (culture conflict and parental conflict), and 'City life'. Obi's loneliness and the way in which his overseas education and elevated social status have isolated him from most of his fellow-countrymen would make the book a useful inclusion on the topic of 'Outsiders'.

The book would be a good CEE text (age 16–18) but would also be enjoyed by fifth years (age 15–16).

The author

See Unit 6 *Things Fall Apart*

No Longer at Ease, Chinua Achebe, Heinemann (African Writers Series 3), 1963.

The setting

Umuofia and Lagos

The eastern, Igbo, region of Nigeria is very densely populated and because of the shortage of land and the traditional individualism of the Igbo there has been much migration of Igbo people to other parts of the country. Far-flung rural and urban links are nevertheless maintained through organizations such as the 'Umuofia Progressive Union' of the novel; such organizations provide scholarships for illustrious sons and offer support to members in times of need. In this way many people escape loneliness and find some protection against the hardships of the city.

Umuofia, near Onitsha in south-eastern Nigeria is approximately 300 miles from Lagos. The novel is set in the 1950s in the years preceding Nigerian Independence (1960).

An 'osu'

Such a person would in the last century have been a captive consigned to serve a particular duty in a village and totally cut off from communication with all but other *osu*.

Classroom use

Level of use

The novel would be enjoyed at sixth form level; the difference in aspirations and values of parents and son would also make good teaching material for fifth years. **Age 15–18.**

Teaching resources are listed at the end of the unit.

Points for focus and emphasis

1 *Custom and solidarity*:
   Obi's departure (Chapter 1)
   The Umuofia Progressive Union welcome Obi in Lagos (Chapter 4)
   Umuofia welcomes Obi (Chapter 5)

Conflict with the Umuofia Progressive Union (Chapter 8)
   The Umuofia Progressive Union pay a sympathy call (Chapter 18)
2 *Obi's family*:
   Obi sees his family again (Chapter 6)
   Obi's parents' refusal (Chapters 13 and 14)
   his mother's death (Chapter 18, pp.144–16)
3 *City life*:
   Village links: the Umuofia Progressive Union in Lagos (see Chapters noted above)
   Lagos slums (Chapter 2)
   high-life (Chapter 11, pp.99–104)
   Obi's office and the first bribe offer (Chapter 9)
   Miss Tomlinson and Mr Green (Chapter 11, pp.95–7)
   Mr Green's views (Chapter 11, pp.105–6 and Chapter 17, pp.139–40)
4 *Love*:
   The ship home (Chapter 3)
   Clara is an *osu* (Chapter 7)
   uncertainty (Chapter 13)
   the break with Clara (Chapter 15)
   the abortion (Chapter 15)
5 *Contradictions and pressures*:
   ideals and reality (Chapter 4, p.27, Chapter 5, pp.35–6 and 38–40)
   bribery refused (Chapter 9)
   financial worries (Chapters, 10, 13 and 17)
   capitulation (Chapter 19)

Teaching suggestions

(a)   Interpretation and appreciation

Numbers 1 and 2 should precede the first reading of the book.

1 Read p.94 which has on it a poem 'God bless our noble fatherland' and then read p.136 where Obi destroys the poem. Write a short account of what you think has happened to make him do this.
2 Read Chapter 2, p.25, 'They heard Macmillan bang his cabin door . . .
   "Leave me," she whispered.
   "I love you."

She was silent for a while seeming to melt in his arms.'

Then turn to Chapter 17, p.142 '"I can understand your not wanting to set eyes on me again. I have wronged you terribly. But I cannot believe that it is all over. If you give me another chance, I shall never fail you again."' What do you think has happened in between these two points in the story?

3 What are the advantages of beginning with the court case where Obi is tried for accepting bribes and only then turning to the events leading up to this?

4 'He rose, cleared his throat and began to intone from an enormous sheet of paper' (p.28) ... 'Obi's English, on the other hand, was most unimpressive. He spoke "is" and "was".' (p.29) Why do the elders not like Obi's speech? Write, and read out, a new speech for Obi which you think would be more to their taste. G

5 What is the attitude of members of the Umuofia Progressive Union towards bribery? (Chapters 4 and 8)

6 '"He is a son of Iguedo," said old Odogwu.' (p.48) Why is his speech at the welcome ceremony at Obi's home so impressive?

7 Do you think Obi could have handled his second meeting with the Umuofia Progressive Union better? (Chapter 8) Give some practical suggestions as to what he could or ought to have done.

8 'Henceforth he wore her sadness round his neck like a necklace of stone.' (Chapter 6, p.5) What is the link between his mother's illness and Obi's later break with Clara?

9 '"You cannot marry the girl," he said quite simply.' (p.120) Do you have any sympathy with Obi's father's point of view? Can you think of any similar cases where something like this might happen in our society? G

10 What are Clara's strong points as far as character is concerned? Does Achebe suggest any faults in her personality? (Chapters 3, 10, 11 and 15)

11 What are the difficulties which Obi is up against on his return from London? List the people who do not understand his problems.

12 What are the various bills and financial obligations which Obi cannot eventually meet? List as many of these as you can.

13 Is it true to say that Obi is a man 'paralysed by his own thoughts'? (p.134)

14 Obi says he feels 'a stranger in his own country' and he is called 'Beast of no nation!' (p.138). How does Achebe bring out the gap between Obi and many of his fellow countrymen? (Market place, lorry drivers, kinsfolk, talk at hospital.)

15 Look at the songs on pp.42, 101–2 and 117. How do they underline the themes of the book?

(b) Creative

1 Debate whether or not what happens to Clara is justified.

2 Conduct a mock trial of: Obi or of Mr Green, for misunderstanding Nigeria and its people; or of the President of the Umuofia Progressive Union for failing to give necessary support to Obi Okonkwo. Discuss the issue before appointing speakers for the defence, speakers for the prosecution, judge and jury. D

3 What do you think you would like about Lagos? What would you find strange?

4 Compare the advantages and disadvantages of arranged marriages and 'love matches'.

5 Pick out three examples of conflict between western and traditional values in the novel. Are you aware of any conflict of values between your own and your parents' generation? Talk about these in groups. In what ways can it be said that culture is constantly changing?

(c) Curriculum-linked

1 Find out as much as you can about the pattern of housing, transport and communications, commerce and local amenities of a

West African city, for example Lagos, Ibadan, Accra, Abidjan, Freetown or Dakar.

2 Prepare a talk on the first ten years of Nigerian Independence, i.e. 1960–70.

3 Prepare a short talk or a series of talks on women in Africa. Choose such headings as work opportunities, marriage, women's organizations, links with family, difficulties.

Topics

Love
Custom and conflict

Prejudice
City life
The village
Parents and children

Passages for reading

Reunion and mistakes (pp.28–30)
Bribery on the road (pp.38–42)
'I am an *osu*' (pp.64–9)
Money troubles (pp.89–93)
Mother's room, Father's room (pp.114–17)
Marriage with an *osu*? (pp.120–4)

Teaching aids

Audio-visual

Films   See also films listed in Unit 10.
Xala
Time: 123 mins   Colour   Distributor: Contemporary   Hire: £30
Director: Sembène Ousmane (Also available as a novel, see below.)
A film about the elite of Dakar, Senegal. Obi's comparative innocence could be compared with the extravagance and lack of morality shown by El Hadji Abdou Kadar Beye.
The Money Order
Time: 90 mins   Colour   Distributor: The Other Cinema   Hire: £30
Director: Sembène Ousmane (Also available as a novelette, see below.)
Shows a simple townsman who becomes embroiled in a tangle of officialdom, corruption and false friends when his nephew in Paris sends him a money order. Satirical and could be useful for drawing comparisons between his position and Obi's.

Slide sets   *Nigeria in Change* (1) Modern Nigeria.
CWDE, 1979 (order no. S.1) £5.50 + VAT. 20 slides, with notes.

Photographic   *Nigeria in Change* (1) Women and Children in Nigeria.
CWDE, 1979 (order no. P.2) £1.60 + VAT. 16 b/w photos, with notes.

Background reading   B.W. Hodder, *Africa Today*, Methuen, 1978.
Chapter 3. 'Ethnicity and elitism in Africa'.
Colin Legum, *Africa Handbook*, Penguin, 1970.
Useful section on Nigeria although now a little dated.
S. Leith-Ross, *African Women: a study of the Ibo in Nigeria*, Routledge and Kegan Paul, 1965

K. Little, *West African Urbanization: a study of voluntary organizations in Social Change*, Cambridge University Press, 1965.
African Women in Towns: an aspect of Africa's Social Revolution, Cambridge University Press, 1973.
A.M. O'Connor, *The Geography of Tropical African Development*, Pergamon, 1978.
Has chapters on 'The Role of Transport' and 'Urbanization'.
D. Okafor-Omali, *A Nigerian Villager in Two Worlds*, Faber, 1965.
Easy to read and extremely helpful as background for the novel.

Criticism

Emmanuel Obiechina, *Culture, Tradition and Society in the West African Novel*, Cambridge University Press, 1975.
G.D. Killam, *The Writings of Chinua Achebe*, Macmillan (Commonwealth Writers Series), 1979.
See also Unit 6.

Reading links

Buchi Emecheta, *The Bride Price*, Allison & Busby, 1976; Collins (Fontana), 1978.
A young Igbo girl chooses her own lover with tragic consequences.
The Slave Girl, Allison & Busby, 1977; Collins (Fontana), 1979.
The story of an Igbo girl fighting for dignity in the face of rigid and repressive custom.
Chukwuemeka Ike, *Toads For Supper*, Fontana, 1965.
A similar conflict between customs and affection.
Festus Iyayi, *Violence*, Longman (Drumbeat 1), 1979.
A study in morality: Two families, one wealthy and the other poor. Long but powerful.
Sembene Ousmane, *The Money Order*, with *White Genesis*, Heinemann (African Writers Series 92), 1974, translated from the French by Clive Wake.
Xala, Heinemann (African Writers Series 175), 1976, translated from the French by Clive Wake.
Wole Soyinka, *The Interpreters*, Heinemann (African Writers Series 76), 1970.
John Braine, *Room at the Top*, Penguin, 1959.
Albert Camus, *The Outsider*, Penguin Modern Classics, 1961.
Iris Murdoch, *Under the Net*, Chatto and Windus, 1954.
John Wain, *Hurry on Down*, Penguin, 1960.

Unit 8 *When Rainclouds Gather*

Bessie Head

Level of use and scope

Bessie Head concentrates on a small village community in rural Botswana, but the issues she explores in this setting have a wide application. The central character, Makhaya Maseko, is an outsider, a refugee from South Africa, and Head analyses his attempts to integrate into the small community and live a new life. The theme of the outsider who seeks acceptance in a new society recurs constantly in Head's novels and short stories (see *Maru* and the short story 'Life', for instance). In this case the village of Golema Midi itself is not a long-established settlement but a new one made up of wanderers, outcasts, those who have nowhere else to go or those who wish to start afresh. Such groups, Head suggests, may accept and even seek change with the greatest readiness. She is interested in the relationship between people and their environment and this leads her in the Botswana context to consider the crops planted, the cattle, drought and rain and the introduction of new methods of agriculture. She creates a sense of place with a skill at times comparable with that of D.H. Lawrence in *Kangaroo* or *The Sea and Sardinia*. Head also explores the role of authority, the traditional authority of the chiefs, the dubious claims to authority of some politicians and the authority of the people themselves.

The book is by no means an idyllic tale of rural life – it presents with great power the harshness and beauty of the land, and the folly and courage of those who live on it. Head is in some ways a polemical writer, and, like such writers as Bernard Shaw and D.H. Lawrence, she tends at times to overstate her case: men, politicians, chiefs and Christianity are all sub-

When Rainclouds Gather, Bessie Head, Victor Gollancz, 1969, Heinemann (African Writers Series) 1987.

ject to scathing attack at various points in the book. Nevertheless, her interest in people and human relationships and her skill as a literary artist prevent the polemics from dominating the novel.

The book would be very useful for fifth formers of mixed ability (age 15–16). In addition the sections describing Paulina Sebeso's children, the Botswana landscape and land and the drought would be useful for topic work with lower secondary forms. The polemical pieces themselves might be useful as points of debate!

The author

Bessie Head is a Black South African who now lives in Botswana, and her novels and short stories are set for the most part in the country of her adoption. She is thus in a sense outside the mainstream of South African political and protest writing and concentrates instead on personal and social relationships in rural Botswana. She is not in any sense escapist, though, and the South African situation is often a bleak and sombre element of her writing, intruding into the lives of the characters she creates. Her works include *Maru*, *A Question of Power*, *Serowe*, *Village of the Rain-Wind* and *The Collector of Treasures*.

The setting

The focus of the book is the village of Golema Midi in southern Botswana. The events take place immediately before Independence (1966) when the country became known as Botswana and was no longer the Bechuanaland Protectorate. The drought mentioned is based on the actual drought of 1965–66 in which 200 000 cattle out of 1.4 million are thought to have died. The long, desolate border with the Transvaal and Cape Provinces of South Africa means that political refugees often slip across in order to escape from their pursuers or would-be pursuers. The distance between centres of habitation and the vastness of the landscape are stressed in the novel. In size Botswana is larger than France, but it has only 600 000 inhabitants as opposed to France's population of more than 50 000 000.

The climate

As so much of the novel is about rain or the absence of rain it would be worth discussing the topic before beginning the novel with a class. Life in Botswana revolves around rain – it is the lifeblood of the country. The annual rainfall is sporadic and haphazard. In a good year it is 30 inches, but it fluctuates with devastating results in bad years. May to October are the dry months, with light showers sometimes falling in June and July. The rainy season itself is November to April. So important is rain that the Setswana word *pula* (rain) is used to conclude large meetings and to express acceptance or pleasure (from G. Winchester-Gould, *The Guide to Botswana*, Gaborone, 1968). It is also the name of the national currency.

Life at the cattle posts

This aspect of Botswana life might also be a useful point for discussion before the novel is read. The cattle posts are often many miles from people's villages. Men, and often young boys, spend a great deal of the year there and for this reason many boys start school later than girls. The easiest time of the year is February to April when there is plenty of grass and water for cattle. This is the time of year described in the following passage from Naomi Mitchison's *The Family at Ditlabeng*. Sello has been away with the cattle whereas Kabi has been at home in the village:

Sello was away at the cattle post most of the time now; when he came back he talked about the food there. Some of the grown men were good shots; there was often a buck roasting on the fire or a big turkey bustard. Above all there was milk, fresh or sour, not as much milk as in a good year but still more than they had at Ditlabeng. And one could ride the oxen. There was a big boy, Molotsi, who always rode an ox. When he beat the ox it plunged about but he always stuck on. Even when it fought with another ox! One day he too would do that.

Somehow Sello always looked well when he came back. His skin was shining. There was fat on his bones. Kabi did not look so well. You could count his ribs and his knees seemed to stick out of his legs. (pp.42–3)

April to August is the dry season, when cattle stay longer outside their enclosure and so the boys (and men if they are there) have to watch them carefully. They may move the cattle to a river or borehole if water becomes very scarce. August to October is the end of the dry season and is a very hard time for herdboys and cattle. They have few visitors from home and little time to play. There is little or no milk from the cows now so they eat porridge without milk. The rains usually come in late October and after a month or so the oxen will be ready to plough the lands for planting maize, sorghum or millet. (Source: The Botswana Oxfam Education Department Wallet.)

Classroom use

Level of use

Fifth form. **Age 15–16**. Selected passages describing Paulina's children could be used with third and fourth forms. **Age 13–15**.

Teaching resources are listed at the end of the unit.

Points for focus and emphasis

1 *A sense of place*:
   First impressions (Chapter 1, pp.16–17)
   Golema Midi (Chapter 2, pp.22–3)

Grass (Chapter 3, pp.36–7)
Makhaya and the setting sun (Chapter 6, pp.77–8)
July (Chapter 9, p.122)
The sun (Chapter 9, p.140)
Drought (Chapter 10, pp.145–8 and Chapter 11, pp.159–64)

2 *Farming*:
Gilbert's methods (Chapter 2 and Chapter 3, pp.36–42)
Tobacco and the women (Chapter 7, pp.99 and Chapter 8)
Makhaya as instructor (Chapter 3, p.36 and Chapter 8)
The model village (Chapter 8, pp.107 and 113–18)
Cattle – cattleposts or fenced fields? (Chapter 2, p.35, Chapter 9, pp.141–2 and 154–5)

3 *Authority and leaders*:
Paramount Chief Sekoto (Chapter 4, pp.49–58)
Chief Matenge (Chapter 3, pp.43–8, Chapter 5, pp.64–6 and Chapter 12, pp.178–82)
George Appleby-Smith (Chapter 4, pp.55–61, Chapter 11, pp.166–7 and Chapter 12, pp.178–82)
Gilbert as innovator (Chapter 3) as adviser (Chapter 10, p. 149)
Paulina (Chapter 7, pp.94 and 100 and Chapter 8)
Makhaya (Chapter 12, pp.177–8)

4 *Friends and enemies*:
Dinorego and Makhaya (Chapter 1, pp.20–1)
Gilbert and Makhaya (Chapter 2, pp.29–35, Chapter 6, pp.82–8 and Chapter 7, pp.99–107)
Mma Millipede befriends Makhaya (Chapter 5, pp. 67–71 and Chapter 9, pp.126–32)
Maria and Gilbert's wedding party (Chapters 6 and 7, pp.83–104)
Matenge (Chapter 3, pp.43–8 and Chapter 12, pp.174–82)

5 *Makhaya the outsider*:
The fugitive (Chapter 1)
Political refugee (Chapter 4, pp.54–61)

His despair (Chapter 9, pp.124–34)
Acceptance by the women (Chapter 8, pp.104–8)

6 *Makhaya and Paulina*:
The widow and her children (Chapter 6, pp.75–8, Chapter 8, pp.120–1 and Chapter 9, pp.141–2)
Working together (Chapter 8)
Makhaya comes to tea (Chapter 9, pp.137–44)
Isaac's death (Chapter 10, pp.148–64 and 170)
Makhaya the comforter (Chapters 10–11, pp.152–70)

Teaching suggestions

(a) *Interpretation and appreciation and* (b) *Creative*

1 An exercise for a pre-reading of the book: Read pp.119–21 from 'The small girl looked at her startled . . .' to 'He had tuberculosis'. Discuss or write an outline of what you think happens to Isaac.

2 Give your own version of the following, based on a reading of Chapters 1 and 2: a) Makhaya's reasons for leaving South Africa; b) How he reaches Golema Midi; c) The landscape and the land; d) The people he meets on the way to Golema Midi; e) Your impressions of Makhaya; f) Farming methods in Golemi Midi. **G**

3 *Improvisations* Give an improvised account of Gilbert interviewing Makhaya (see pp.30–4). Improvise the scene where a deputation of old men come to ask Gilbert why he has fenced the land (see pp.37–40). Work out a short dramatized version of Makhaya's first day with the women who are to work on the tobacco growing project (see pp.104–12). **GD**

4 (a) Prepare two progress reports from Gilbert to the voluntary organization funding his work (e.g. Oxfam, Christian Aid, War on Want). They should cover items such as progress with methods of cattle farming; crops being

grown; level of community participation; any particular difficulties; successes; hopes for the coming year; interesting events; new developments. (See Chapters 2, 3, 9 and 10.) **G**

(b) Prepare a police report on Chief Matenge's death (see pp.177–82).

(c) Draft the advertisement which might appear in a national or regional newspaper advertising Gilbert's post in Golema Midi.

5 Read from 'She sat for a moment . . .' (bottom of page 89) to the end of the chapter, p.90. Write out your version of the conversation which takes place after '"I have a surprise," Mma Millipede said.'

6 'happiness, anyway, was dirt cheap in Botswana. It was standing still, almost in the middle of nowhere, and having your face coloured up gold by the setting sun.' (p.141) Give your own short definition of. 'happiness'.

7 Give your opinions on how well or how badly the following use their positions of authority: a) Paramount Chief Sekoto; b) Chief Matenge; c) Police Constable George Appleby-Smith.

8 It was to amaze Makhaya after all this that an old woman . . . named Mma Millipede was to relieve his heart of so much of its ashes, frustration and grief.' (p.126) In what way does Mma Millipede influence Makhaya?

9 Gilbert thinks of Makhaya as 'someone he now leaned on heavily for courage to push ahead with his ideas' (p.100). Discuss the friendship between Makhaya and Gilbert. What factors do you think are important in a friendship? Write or talk about one of your own close friends.

10 Consider the ways in which the women of the village organize themselves. Discuss their importance in the life of the village (the wedding, the tobacco farming, comforting Paulina, their solidarity). **G**

11 Compare the attitudes of Maria and Paulina towards marriage and towards men. Say whether you agree with either of them (see pp. 88–9; p.77 and p.119).

12 '"Most men want to achieve great victories," he said. "But I am only looking for a woman."
The old man nodded his head profoundly, but at the same time he sensed snags in that simple statement.' (p.97) Trace the events in Makhaya's life from that point until, '"So much has happened so quickly," he said. "I forgot to ask you if you'd like to marry me."' (p.188)

14 'Without turning round he asked, "Where's the boy?"
'"He's at the cattle post looking after the cattle," Paulina said.' (p.141) What are the different points of view on education, cattle and money, put forward by Makhaya and Paulina in the argument that follows? Can you think of any other examples where parents might say they *cannot* send their children to school? What do you think is the best course of action in such cases? **G**

15 (a) Read the passages describing Isaac's carvings (p.163–4 and p.170). Discuss what it would be like to be in Isaac's position. Write or tape-record what his thoughts might have been as he was at work on one of the carvings. **G**

(b) 'But the handwork on the little crocodile was different from the small boy's rough strokes. It had the smooth, polished finish of an old professional hunter.' (p.170) Write your own version of Isaac's meeting with the hunter.

16 How well do you think Bessie Head writes about Isaac's death?

17 Read from 'At first not a thing stirred around him . . .' (p.16) to 'and that somehow he had come to the end of a journey.' (p.17) Use it as a model for your own writing on first impressions of a place.

18 Try to find as many examples as possible of references to the sun (for example, pp.16, 65, 71, 77 and 140). Discuss Head's use of the sun as a symbol.

19 'One might go so far as to say that it is strong, dominating personalities who play a decisive role when things are changing . . .' Read what Head has to say about

leaders on p.75. Say which figures in the novel you regard as leaders and give your reasons.

(c) Curriculum-linked

1 What would you find strange, novel or hard to get used to if you were to visit Botswana? What do you think you would like about the place and the people?
2 (This and question 3 could link with Geography and Development Studies.) Compare Golema Midi (or a small town such as Serowe) with a village or small town in Britain. You could use headings such as: postal services; transport; occupations of inhabitants; educational facilities; recreation of inhabitants; land tenure; prominent individuals.
3 There is only one store in Golema Midi. Draw up a list of what you think it should stock to serve the needs of the villagers, and make some profit. Write about an average day in the life of the storekeeper. This is what a Kenyan leader has to say about his shop-keeping experience in Kenya in the 1940s:

Ours was the only shop in Maseno and I must admit we often let our customers down badly. We learnt about stocking through our losses. There was depreciation to be taken into account; and the people's needs and tastes in the locality. I learned to buy tea and sugar, dishes and cutlery, exercise books and socks. I bought the goods from the wholesaler, loaded them into the truck, drove the truck, stacked the goods on the shelf, counted the cash, did the account books, and trained and supervised the staff.

(from Oginga Odinga, *Not Yet Uhuru*, Heinemann (African Writers Series 38), 1967, p.83)

Topics

Authority
Childhood
Escape
The land
New beginnings

Passages for reading

Marriage (pp.88–90)
A child's death (pp.161–3)
Vultures (p.165)
Dictatorship or democracy? (pp.82–3)
Work (pp.136–8)
Brother and sister (pp.119–21)

Teaching aids

Audio-visual

Film   Bitter Melons
          Time: 30 mins   Colour   Distributor: Royal Anthropological Institute Film Library   Hire: £9
          From the San (Bushman) series by John Marshall. A carefully shot and memorable film showing the daily life of a small band of Gwi San of the Kalahari in Botswana. (See Reading links, p.61: Elizabeth Marshall-Thomas.)

Photographic   Botswana; Country and People, Oxfam Education Department Wallet, Oxfam, 1977. Available CWDE (order no. PA-1) £1.90 + VAT.

An excellent source of information on many aspects of life in Botswana. It has large black and white photographs as visual back-up material.

Botswana
A collection of illustrated and carefully written pupil and teacher materials mainly for 15–16 year-olds. CWDE (order no. B-114) £2.50 + VAT.
See also Resources, p.136.

Background reading

Anthony J. Dachs, *Khama of Botswana*, Heinemann Educational, 1971.
This is of general background and historical interest. It is concise, informative and has interesting photographs from the period covered.
Isaac Schapera, *Praise-Poems of Tswana Chiefs*, Oxford University Press, 1965.
This has background material on Tswana society, language and oral art. The praise-poetry itself contains much vivid imagery and often a sense of action, excitement and adventure. Extracts from the praise-poems would be of use in dealing with topics such as war, heroism and authority.

Reading links

Bertolt Brecht, *The Caucasian Chalk Circle*, ed. M. Marland, Blackie, 1968.
This has links in its emphasis on corrupt leaders and the essential goodness of the human spirit.
Albert Camus, *The Outsider*, Penguin Modern Classics, 1961.
Nadine Gordimer, *Some Monday for Sure*, (short stories) Heinemann (African Writers Series 177), 1976.
The title story is about political activists and exile.
Thomas Hardy, *The Woodlanders*, Macmillan Educational, 1975.
Bessie Head, *The Collector of Treasures and Other Botswana Village Tales*, Heinemann (African Writers Series 182), 1977.
Stories such as 'Life', 'The Wind and a Boy' and 'Snapshots of a Wedding' would complement class study of *When Rainclouds Gather*.
Elizabeth Marshall-Thomas, *The Harmless People*, Penguin, 1969.
Also an account of life with the San in two parts of the Kalahari. It has excellent passages which could be used on topics such as accidents, disasters, encounters, survival. It also contains useful photographs.
Edgar Mittelholzer, *Corentyne Thunder*, Heinemann (Caribbean Writers Series 2), 1970.
A novel about farming on the coast of Guyana and the pressures on one family.
Ezekiel Mphahlele, *The Wanderers*, Macmillan, 1972.
This is about a South African political exile and his family in West and East Africa. It would be useful as further reading for interested pupils.
Samuel Selvon, *Turn Again Tiger*, Heinemann (Caribbean Writers Series 19), 1979.
Also about adapting to new social conditions and new people. In the sequel to *A Brighter Sun*, Tiger goes to work on a Trinidadian sugar cane estate and the process of his creolization is continued.
Laurens van der Post, *Lost World of the Kalahari*, Penguin, 1964.
This is used as a CSE text (Age 14–16) and is liked by classes. It is an account of the author's sojourn among the San people (Bushmen) of the Kalahari.

*Books set in
Botswana and
suitable for
middle and
junior
secondary
levels*
Age 11–14

Susheela Curtis, *Mainane: Tswana tales*, Botswana Book Centre, Gaberone, 1965.
The tales are often allegorical and sometimes didactic. They are full of magic, fantasy and common sense.

Naomi Mitchison, *The Family of Ditlabeng*
Collins, 1969 (hardback).
This would be useful in a class library and would also be good as background preparation for *When Rainclouds Gather*.

Sunrise Tommorrow, Collins, 1973 (hardback).
About school, work and ways of being 'modern' and yet true to one's own culture.

Note also the following books by Naomi Mitchison written for primary school readers but useful at any level for conveying the flavour of life in Botswana:

Snake, Collins, 1976 (hardback).

Ketse and the Chief, Nelson, 1965 (hardback; a school edition available).

Unit 9 *Anowa*

Ama Ata Aidoo

Level of use and scope

Aidoo sets her play in the southern Fante region of Ghana in the late nineteenth century. She uses as a story outline the motif of a folktale which is found in Ghana and elsewhere in Africa: a girl marries a handsome man (often a stranger) of her own choice, with terrible consequences. For instance he is often in reality a monster and his limbs fall off one by one shortly after they leave the girl's village! Anowa chooses Kofi Ako in the face of opposition from her mother in particular. She calls Kofi Ako a 'good-for-nothing-cassava-man' and a 'watery male of all watery males' but Anowa refuses to listen to her warnings. Aidoo is interested in Anowa as a girl who is independent and who all her life questions the confines of the role she is expected to play as a married woman. In a number of traditional African societies such women often become diviners or priestesses, but Anowa does not do this. She marries instead.

Aidoo's second concern in the play is to explore the issue of slavery in her own society's past. Anowa's husband Kofi Ako soon wants to buy slaves to share their workload. Anowa resists, but before long 'he is buying men and women as though they were only worth each a handful of the sands on the shore' (p.39). Aidoo links the moral destructiveness of slavery with the barrenness and sterility of the couple's marriage (pp. 40 and 61–2). To Kofi Ako, however, and to the diviners whom he constantly consults, the cause of their childlessness is Anowa's 'restless soul'. In the second of the play's three acts (or 'Phases' as Aidoo names them, referring to the phases of the marriage) Kofi begs his wife to enjoy their

wealth. He asks her, in effect, to bury her conscience: 'Shamelessly, you rake up the dirt of life. You bare our wounds. You are too fond of looking for the common pain and the general wrong.' (p.38) In the third and final 'Phase' of the play Aidoo contrasts Kofi Ako's great wealth with Anowa's isolation and unhappiness. A brilliant scene of gaiety and triumph where a great throng of people greet and praise the richly dressed Kofi Ako is followed by one in which the lonely Anowa (thinking of the Atlantic slave trade) recalls questions she asked herself in childhood and which no-one answered: 'What happens to those who were taken away?/Do people hear from them?/How are they? (p.46) Anowa's refusal to accept affluence or to stop questioning the moral basis of slavery leads to the last bitter confrontation between husband and wife and the final tragedy.

The play could interest fourth or fifth years and even older readers in a number of ways. In the early stages the lack of understanding on the part of Anowa's mother could lead to discussion of conflict and the causes of conflict between parents and young adults. Interestingly, although Anowa's decision brings her great unhappiness she never regrets it; the thought of returning home and asking forgiveness is never introduced. What becomes increasingly clear, though, is that she is not conforming to expectations of what a wife should be. She asks herself ironically at one point, 'O – why didn't someone teach me to grow up to be a woman?' (p.52). Some members of the class might feel that Anowa behaves wrongly in flouting her parents' wishes and that having chosen her husband she should support him however much she disagrees with his actions. Others might see Anowa's position in a different light. This could lead to discussion of roles in marriage and of women's roles in a wider context.

Anowa, Ama Ata Aidoo, Longman, 1970, Longman (Drumbeat 19), 1980.

The issue of morals and money is a major theme in the play. Kofi Ako defends the purchase of slaves at one point by saying, 'Everyone does it . . .' (p.30). For Anowa this is not sufficient justification. Questions such as how one resists popular opinion or an easy, comfortable decision could also be raised. The play's exploration of slavery is closely related to the 'easy decisions' issue. Aidoo involves not only 'the pale strangers' in her presentation of slavery but also those in the community who profited from it. Moreover, Akan society itself made great use of slaves, and Aidoo will not let this pass unnoticed or without comment.

Besides being a useful class text *Anowa* would make an interesting form or even school drama production. It is enjoyable and often funny; even towards the end when Anowa is in many ways a pathetic figure, the young 'Boy' and 'Girl' slaves introduce a note of liveliness and humour – as well as pathos. Anowa's bad-tempered mother is often unintentionally amusing and the elderly observers who so often take the audience into their confidence are a source of comedy as well as critical comment. The large colourful crowd scenes in Phase Three would provide scope for music, dance and group work and would allow for involvement of large numbers of actors.

The author

Ama Ata Aidoo was educated in Ghana and America. She is probably best known for her collection of short stories, *No Sweetness Here*, which marked her as a writer who was determined to fashion her work from the material of everyday life in post-Independence Ghana. Her first play, *Dilemma of a Ghost*, explores the position of a black American in Ghana and looks at the conflict in modern and traditional expectations of marriage. *Anowa*, although a historical play, is built around issues of contemporary concern, namely slavery and the position of women in society. Aidoo writes with a great awareness of the spoken word – she once said, 'I write to make my readers listen' – and as the daughter of a Fante chief she is able to draw on a considerable knowledge of Akan tradition and history. She was teaching at the University of Cape Coast, Ghana, until 1982 when she took up the post of Secretary for Education in the PNDC administration of Flight-lieutenant Jerry Rawlings. Her most recent publication is *Our Sister Killjoy*, Longman, 1977; Longman (Drumbeat 35), 1981.

The setting

Ghana (the Gold Coast) and the Atlantic slave trade in the nineteenth century

In the first half of the nineteenth century, despite the anti-slavery legislation in European countries and the constant patrolling of the British navy, the Atlantic slave trade from the west coast of Africa actually increased in scale. Slavery remained legal in the southern states of America until 1863, and the trade to Brazil continued until the 1880s. As European and American traders dropped out for fear of reprisals their places were taken by Afro-Brazilians (Oliver and Atmore, 1967, p.35). Aidoo turns her attention to the wealthy middlemen who made their money by selling slaves to the foreign traders. Kofi Ako was such a man.

Akan societies: the Ashanti and the Fante

The two major groupings, the Ashanti and the Fante, make up over one half of the total Akan-speaking population in Ghana. Whereas the process of almost continual conquest in the eighteenth century – brought about by the acquisition of guns and the sale of slaves – led to the creation of an Ashanti confederacy under a common ruler the Asantehene, the Fante nearer the coast remained in a number of loosely independent political units. The 'Bond of 1844' (p.8) refers to a treaty between several Fante states and the British. The alliance was made for mutual protection against the Ashanti to the north.

The position of women in Akan societies

Akan societies are matrilineal. This means that inheritance is through one's mother and therefore the mother and her family are of great importance. A mother's brother has great influence, more so than the father, in decision-making as regards the children. Hence in the play Osam tells his wife Badua to consult her brothers about Anowa's unconventional behaviour and bad choice of husband. He himself remains fairly passive, though more sympathetic to Anowa than his wife is.

Slavery in Akan societies

Aidoo makes the point that slavery in however mild a form is still slavery. Note for instance the pathos of the young girl (p.50) who longs to be given her freedom. Slaves in Akan societies were expected to perform heavy manual tasks but could also amass wealth and sometimes carried out political functions. They were also often made members of free lineages and their children could marry into the families of former owners (Foster, *Education and Social Change in Ghana*, 1965, pp.20–5). All this seems a far cry from conditions on the plantations of the American south, Cuba, Brazil and the Caribbean. Yet Aidoo looks critically at slavery in general and looks most closely at abuses within her own society.

Places mentioned in the text

Abura is in the Fante coastal region near Cape Coast, although not actually on the sea. Aidoo refers in the Prologue to the legend of how the Fante came to their present area: they were led by the legendary figures of the Three Elders, Osuno, Odapagyan and Obromankoma.

'*Those forts standing at the door*' (p.6) Forts such as Fort George, Fort William, Elmina and others at Shama, Cape Coast and Christianborg Castle in Accra were reception centres for slaves who were kept there in dungeons before being shipped across the Atlantic. The Portuguese, Dutch, Danes and British were in turn administrators of these castles.

Oguaa is the Fante name for the town of Cape Coast, now capital of the Central Region.

Classroom use

Level of use

Fourth and fifth years, GCSE. **Age 14–16.** The questioning of roles in marriage, the topic of principles and profit, slavery and the subject of the writer's role in society might also make it useful for CEE work. **Age 16–18.**

Teaching resources are listed at the end of the unit.

Points for focus and emphasis

1 *Anowa and her parents*:
   their worries about her
   ought she to have been a priestess?
   why hasn't she married?
   she chooses the 'wrong' man
   the quarrel with her mother.
   the rift
2 *Anowa and her husband, Kofi Ako*:
   their early hardships
   the beginning of dissension; a second wife or slaves?
   they begin to 'trade with white men' (p.33)
   she is childless
   they become very wealthy
3 *Anowa*:
   her beauty
   her unusual and independent nature
   she helps her husband despite misgivings
   wealth and disillusion
   abhorrence of slavery (pp.44–6)
   her isolation
   Anowa the conscience of the play
4 *The chorus of Old Man and Old Woman*:
   importance in setting location and stating themes
   focus on 'a bigger crime' (p.6)
   past connivance in the slave trade

early comment on Kofi Ako
early comment on Anowa
the folly of trading in slaves
the old woman criticizes Anowa
the old man and woman have the last
   word
5 *Structure of the play*:
focus on Anowa
ironic linking of wealth and unhappiness
ironic linking of celebration and isolation
increasing importance of slavery issue
increasing tension within Anowa
resolution

Teaching suggestions

(a) *Interpretation and appreciation*

1 Improvisations based on themes in the
   play. Act out a short sketch based on one of
   the following situations:
   (a) A confrontation between parents and a
       daughter who wants to marry against
       her wishes. (Brothers, sisters, aunts,
       uncles etc. can also be involved.)
   (b) A difference of opinion between two
       friends or two people in the same
       family over a decision involving a
       moral issue.
   (c) A group discusses someone they know
       who has done well financially but has
       gained his or her money in a dubious
       way – the person they are talking about
       enters . . .
   (d) Two or more women discuss a couple
       they know who have no children. **D**
2 What issues does the Prologue focus on?
3 What is your impression of Anowa from
   the Prologue?
4 'But my only daughter shall not be a
   priestess.' (p.11) Why is Badua so against
   her daughter becoming a priestess? Can
   you think of any similar situations today
   when a mother might have similar views?
5 'Mother, Father, I have met the man I want
   to marry.' (p.14) What is the reaction?

How do you think the actors should convey their emotions here? Try acting this
short piece.
6 Why is Badua so against Kofi Ako as a
   husband for Anowa?
7 'But Father, Mother is driving me away.'
   (p.19) Compare Anowa's relationships
   with her mother and with her father.
8 How do the Old Man and the Old Woman
   differ in their opinions about what has
   happened? (pp.19–21)
9 'Is it the same thing to ask an older person
   about a woman's womb as it is to contract
   medicines in pots and potions which would
   attract good fortune and ward off evil?'
   What does Anowa mean?
   Kofi Ako answers, 'I swear by everything it
   is the same' (p.26). What important differences in outlook are beginning to show
   here?
10 'Anowa, I shall be the new husband and
   you the new wife.' (p.27) How happy and
   successful is their marriage so far?
11 Do you think the storm is symbolic at all?
   Of what?
12 'But your soul is too restless.' (p.28) Is this
   an accurate description of Anowa?
13 'Everyone does it . . . does not everyone do
   it?' (p.30) What serious differences of
   opinion come to light now?
14 'But she is my child' (p.32). Do you feel any
   pity for Badua here?
15 'What is the matter? . . . Be my glorious
   wife, Anowa, and the contented mother of
   my children.' (pp.34–9) What signs of
   strains between husband and wife are there
   in this section?
16 Why do you think the Old Woman is so
   against Anowa? (pp.39–42) Can you think
   of any modern parallels where an elderly
   woman might say similar things?
17 'I remember once . . . I see a woman who is
   me and a bursting as of a ripe tomato on a
   swollen pod.' (p.44–7)
   (a) Describe Anowa's state of mind here.
   (b) Discuss the effectiveness of the change
       to verse and then back to prose on
       pp.45–6.

(c) Compare Kofi Ako's praises 'He is coming!' (p.43) with Anowa's verse (pp.44–6).
What is the connection between his praises and her memories?

18 What does the Boy and Girl interlude (pp.47–51) tell us a) about Anowa; b) about slavery?

19 (a) Why does Kofi Ako want to divorce Anowa (pp.53–61)?
(b) How does she attempt to defend herself?

20 In her production notes Aidoo writes that the play could end with Anowa's exit. Which ending would you prefer, and why?

21 Why does the marriage of Kofi Ako and Anowa fail?

22 In what ways is *Anowa* very much a modern play?

23 'You rake up the dirt of life.' (p.38) Collect other comments people make about Anowa. What kind of person is she? What difficulties does she face?

24 Have you any sympathy for Kofi Ako at any point in the play?

(b) Creative

1 In a group, discuss the way in which the scene where Anowa leaves home (pp.17–19) could be best acted. Think first about why Badua feels that she as a mother knows best. What are Anowa's feelings? How can they best be shown?

2 Improvise a situation where a daughter is leaving home against her parents' wishes. Work out the reasons. Think of the parents' responses (hostile? indifferent? sympathetic?). You could add brothers and sisters – would they be on their sister's side? Critical? Apprehensive? **D**

3 Do you think writers should 'rake up the dirt of life' as Aidoo does in this play? Can you think of any other writers who do so?

4 'Don't laugh. Have you seen how you yourself will end?' (p.49) Write and act out a short scene between the Boy and the Girl, twenty years after this remark. **D**

5 'Oh yes, they're doing very well for themselves – but have you heard … ?' Two people discuss a local couple. Work out their dialogue and then act it. **D**

6 Do you think there is more pressure on girls to conform than there is on boys?

7 Look again at Anowa's remembered nightmare (p.46). Write your own nightmare in which you dream of something that worries you in your waking life.

8 Three suggestions for sections to act or to plan for performance:
(a) The multitude scene at the opening of Phase 3 (grouping? colours of costumes? gestures?). Then move on to Anowa's soliloquy.
(b) The passage on pp.34–9. How successful are they now? Is Kofi Ako happy? Has he a right to be complacent about 'bonded men'? Is Anowa over-anxious? How does the tension build up?
(c) The final confrontation between Anowa and Kofi Ako (pp.53–62). Anowa's state of mind? Has she changed? Kofi's feelings? Why does she call in 'everybody?' Their reaction? She realizes he is impotent. *His* accusation, *her* accusation. Suicide – why? **D**

(c) Curriculum-linked

1 *History* Find out what you can about British connections with the Gold Coast slave trade. How did the British traders and merchants defend their actions? What were the views of the British public on slavery?

2 Find descriptions of the journeys across the Atlantic in the slave vessels. What were the hardships for the captured slaves? What might they have missed and longed for most? Read *Equiano's Travels* (ed. Paul Edwards) under Olaudah Equiano in Section 3, p.154.

3 Find out which West African states prospered through the slave trade. How was other trade affected?

4 *Women* Compare the position of women in two societies, one in Africa and the other in any other society elsewhere in the world. Compare for instance, their positions in

their own families when young; opportunities to earn money; work and marriage; influence in family affairs; in public and political life.

Topics

Family relationships
Convention
Marriage
Money
Roles (of men and women)
Slavery

Passages for reading

An excuse: 'Everyone does it . . .' (p.30)
Too many questions: 'I remember once . . .' (pp.44–6)
Mother and daughter: 'I am in disgrace . . .' (pp.17–19)
Slaves and a quarrel: 'why must you always bring in this . . .' (pp. 37–8)

Teaching aids

Audio-visual

Films

Kentu
Time: 28 mins   Colour   Distributor: Concord   Hire: £14.20
Focuses on a group of Congolese women, who prefer a life of independence with their children to the confines of customary marriage. Useful for discussion of women's roles in African societies and could relate to Anowa's dilemmas. *See also Malawi – The Women*, Resources, p.135.

The Ancient Africans
Useful as general historical background. Includes Ashanti and the Atlantic slave trade. See Resources, General Films p. 139.

The following films, available from the Ghana High Commission:
This is Ghana   35 mins
Panoply of Ghana   20 mins
Wealth in Timber   20 mins
Ghana at a Glance   35 mins
Ghana Dances   20 mins
Deer Hunt Festival   10 mins
Ghana Builds Part 1 and 2   50 mins
Volta River Project   30 mins
Ghana – Gateway to Africa   30 mins
Industrial Development in Ghana   30 mins
Independence Celebration   35 mins

Slide sets

Kwadjo of Ghana, UNICEF 1978. Available CWDE £6.45 + VAT.
Thirty-two colour slides about the life of a teenager, eldest son of a tax-collector. Informative on modern Ghana. Could use to stimulate discussion on links between past and present. Includes notes.
Town and Village in Northern Ghana, CWDE 1973 £3.25 + VAT.

Twelve colour slides on urban and rural life. Not about Fante or Ashante region but could be used for discussion.
Ashanti Gold-weights, M. McLeod £3.25. Order: Audio-visual library services. Powdrake St., Grangemouth, Stirlingshire K3 9UT.
Slide booklet, 12 slides and commentary. Fascinating miniature figures used for weighing gold dust, representing aspects of Ashanti life.

Photographic **Mylene Remy**, *Ghana Today*, Jeune Afrique, Paris, 1977.
Covers different regions and cultures, economic life, industry, agriculture, politics.
Victor Engelbert, *Camera on Ghana: the world of a young fisherman*, Harcourt Brace Jovanovich (NY) 1971.
Seascape, boys watching fishermen, playing, going to school, father in ceremonial dress. Evocative. Set in Ewe East coast region.
Paula Jones and Fay Bourne, *Ghana*
Available CWDE £1.50. Comb-bound collection of class materials about Ghana and Ghanaian life, including maps.
Oxfam topic booket, *Ghana – The Road to Wonoo*
Available CWDE 50p. Designed for middle schools. Informative, aimed at stimulating interest and discussion. Set in Ashanti region around Kumasi. Illustrations.
Commonwealth Institute:
Country fact sheet, *Ghana*, 30p
Topic series, *Life in Ghana*, 30p

Music Aklowa Centre. Specializes in West African and particularly Ghanaian music (see Section 3: Resources, p. 142).
Steel and Skin dance group. Specializes in dancing from Ghana, Dahomey, Nigeria (see Section 3: Resources, p. 144).
Ekomé. An African and Caribbean dance group based in Bristol (see Section 3: Resources, p. 143).
See also the entry under *National Sound Archive*, p.141.

Background reading **Basil Davidson**, *Black Mother: Africa and the Atlantic Slave Trade*, Gollancz 1961.
See part six, especially pp.246–253.
Ruth Finnegan, *Oral literature in Africa*,
Chapter 6 and Chapter 17 especially pp.486–97 on Akan drum poetry.
Kwabena Nketia, *African Music in Ghana: A Survey of Traditional Forms*, North Western University Press, 1963.
R.S. Rattray, *Art and Religion in Ashanti*, Oxford University Press, 1927.
J.B. Webster and A.A. Boahen, *The Growth of African Civilization: The Revolutionary Years. West Africa Since 1800*, Longman 1967, repr. 1970.
Designed for West African schools. Contains maps, photos, line drawings. See Chapters 6, 9 and 14.

Reading links   Drama: *The Dilemma of a Ghost*, Longman 1964; Longman (Drumbeat 27),
                       1980.

Other works   A black American girl marries her Ghanaian boyfriend and returns with him
by   to Ghana. Her romantic ideas about Africa soon crumble and both husband
Ama Ata Aidoo   and wife have much to learn. Fifth year and sixth form. Age 15–18.
                       Prose: *No Sweetness Here* and other stories, Longman (Drumbeat 16), 1979.
                       Stories of urban and rural – and particularly women's – experience in
                       post-independence Ghana. Humourous, perceptive, often critical. Would be
                       enjoyed by fourth and fifth years, also sixth form (age 15–18). Good for
                       reading aloud. See Section 2 p.117.
                       See also Aidoo, Section 3: Bibliographies, p.150.

Akosua Abbs, *Ashanti Boy*, Collins, 1959.
A young boy's struggle for education in pre-Nkrumah Ghana. Lots of detail
of family and school life. Age 14–15.

Ayi Kwei Armah, *The Healers*, Heinemann (African Writers Series 194),
1979. EAPH, 1978.
Exciting historical novel set in nineteenth-century Ashanti. Like Aidoo he
looks critically at the past including the slavery issue. Parts could be read with
fifth years, otherwise sixth form. Age 15–18.
See also Armah, Awoonor and Adali-Mortty and Sutherland in Section 3:
Bibliographies, pp.148, 150.

Francis Bebey, *Ashanti Doll*, Heinemann (African Writers Series 205), 1978.
A love story which also introduces readers to the powerful market women of
Accra. Fourth and fifth years. Age 14–16.

Buchi Emecheta, *The Bride Price*, Allison & Busby, 1976; Collins (Fontana),
1978.
A moving story of a young Igbo girl who flouts custom in her marriage with
tragic results.
The Joys of Motherhood, Allison & Busby, 1979; Heinemann (African
Writers Series 227), 1980.
Emecheta's best novel, set in rural and urban Nigeria. The central character
struggles for stability, happiness, fulfilment and respect. She achieves almost
nothing.

Edward Kamau Brathwaite, *Rights of Passage*, Oxford University Press,
1967.
Parts could be read aloud. See 'Tom', pp.11–15; 'The Journeys', pp.34–5;
these touch on West Coast–Caribbean links.

Asare Konadu, *A Woman in her Prime*, Heinemann (African Writers Series
40), 1967.
A happy marriage which lacks only one thing: children. Short, set in pre-
colonial Akan society. Strong position of women emphasized. Fourth year.
Age 14–15.

Thomas Hardy, *Far from the Madding Crowd*, Macmillan Educational,
1975.
Tess of the D'Urbervilles, Macmillan Educational, 1975.
Also more suitable for sixth form (age 16–18) but both novels focus on
women searching for independence and happiness.

Henrik Ibsen, *The Doll's House*, Everyman, 1961 (drama).
Too difficult for fourth and fifth years, but theme similar to *Anowa*. Here too, a central character questions her prescribed role.

Julius Lester, *Long Journey Home*, Stories from Black History, Puffin, 1979.
Meant for young readers (age 11–13). An excellent collection of stories relating to slavery.
To Be A Slave, Puffin.
An excellent collection of first-hand accounts of the experience of slavery. Age 16–18.

Nigerian market scene

Unit 10   *The Lion and the Jewel*

Wole Soyinka

Level of use and scope

In this early play Soyinka holds up to ridicule the hapless schoolteacher Lakunle who enthusiastically embraces western styles and modernity without any real understanding of what he is doing. Balancing the verbose yet likeable Lakunle is Baroka, the village chief or *Bale*, a wily conservative who regards modernity as a threat both to his authority and to his comforts. Sidi, the village beauty, is both lively and level-headed, as we see from her spirited exchanges with Lakunle early in the play. Yet she, like Lakunle, is no match finally for the cunning and confident Baroka.

Although the play places tradition and modernity in opposition, it is not simply about 'a clash of cultures'. The *Bale* may be able to gain yet another wife; he may succeed for a time in buying off prospective surveyors. Yet it is implied that he will eventually have to come to terms with Lakunle's school and with the progress represented not by his fake stamp machine, but by the real stamp with its image of a bridge. This, like a road, provides a passage not only for traffic and goods but for ideas. Another theme of the play is the opposition of youth and age, depicted in the tensions between Lakunle and Baroka. Lakunle's bumptious arrogance is set against the *Bale*'s age and his experience of life. In the words of a Yoruba proverb, 'A young man can have a cloth like an elderly person, but he cannot have rags like an elder' (Gbadamosi and Beier, 1959, p.6).

A further theme focuses on the figure of the *Bale*'s senior wife, the unpredictable Sadiku. She appears at first the model of wifely obedience yet as Eldred Jones points out, 'under her

The Lion and the Jewel, Wole Soyinka, Oxford University Press (Three Crowns), 1963.

basic conformity seethes a basic resentment against her prescribed role' (1973, p.30). Sadiku in her victory dance at the *Bale*'s 'impotence' hints at a hidden animosity between the sexes and briefly celebrates the temporary overthrow of male dominance.

The play is also about the choices one sometimes makes in marriage: Sidi chooses the *Bale* partly because his rich experience as a lover renders him irresistible, but also because he shares her conventions about marriage. Lakunle in his half-baked way stands for a new set of conventions and attitudes and Sidi cannot commit herself to them.

Besides exploring the presentation of tradition and modernity, youth and age, female rebellion and marriage, classes could discuss — and act out — the kinds of comedy which Soyinka exploits. The comedy comes to some extent from the use and misuse of language by characters, particularly Lakunle. It also stems from the interaction and repartee between Lakunle and Sidi and also later in the play the exchanges between Lakunle and Sadiku — one the anxious 'lover' and the other the hoodwinked wife. The dramatic techniques of flashback through mime and the use of song and dance provide for comparison with modern dramatists such as Brecht and Arden. They enable the teacher to point as well to the rich tradition of performed art in Yoruba culture.

Whether the play is used with a class at fourth, fifth or sixth form level (ages 14–18) it needs to be seen not merely as a literary text but as drama, where the total effects arise from the interaction of language gesture and movement, and from communication betwen actors. Even if there is no intention to perform the play or any part of it, it is important to include acting of parts of the text, mime and improvisation in classroom work.

The author

Soyinka was born in Abeokuta in 1934. After two years at University College, Ibadan, he went to Leeds University where he took an English honours degree in 1957. His involvement in theatre while at university was followed in 1958 by work for the Royal Court Theatre. His first two plays, *The Swamp Dwellers* and *The Lion and the Jewel* were ready for production in 1958 and received their first performance at the Ibadan Arts Theatre in 1959. Soyinka's active promotion of drama in Nigeria came to an abrupt halt during the Civil War of 1967–70 when he was imprisoned and accused of spying for Biafra. Besides a number of plays he has written two novels, poetry, an account of his imprisonment and a collection of critical and philosophical essays. He is at present Professor of Drama at the University of Ife. Many consider him to be one of the greatest writers of our time.

The setting

The Yoruba deities

Two of the deities in the Yoruba pantheon are invoked or referred to, Sango (S pronounced *Sh*) and Ogun. Sango is invoked several times, usually by Baroka or Sadiku. A Yoruba deity is usually an ancestor, 'a hero-king, or the founder of a city who personifies some aspect of the divine power' (Gbadamosi and Beier 1959, p.12). Sango, the god of thunder, is said to have been third King of the town of Oyo. The deity Ogun, the god of iron, is worshipped by iron-users, particularly warriors, hunters and blacksmiths. He is associated with physical strength, courage and death and is linked in stories with the conquest and settlement of present-day Yorubaland. Other deities are Obatala, the god of creation; Oshun, the mother goddess, healer and protector of the town of Oshogbo; Erinle, hunter god of the river of the same name; Eshu, the deity of fate, unpredictable and potentially dangerous. Eshu's symbolic colour is black, those of Sango, red and white.

Yoruba masquerades

Masquerades occur mainly in the southern forest areas of West Africa (which includes Yorubaland). They involve costumes – in particular masks – music and dancing. The masquerades, performed by members of men's secret societies are often referred to as 'plays' and involve enactment and representation by the masked figures. The Gelede society of the Yoruba combines carnival-like entertainment as well as ritual in its performances. The Egungun society (concerned with the worship and appeasement of the dead) make use of stories and mimes in their performances, but they do not introduce anything like a complicated plot. Although no specific masquerades are used in *The Lion and the Jewel*, the drummers, dancers, mime and the masked figure are familiar elements from Yoruba culture which Soyinka has integrated into the play.

Yoruba popular theatre

This developed first from various breakaway churches' dramatizations of biblical stories for the benefit of their congregation. Then in 1945 Herbert Ogunde's Theatre Party was formed (and is still in existence). It used biblical themes, farce and topical themes often on political issues. Ogunde's songs were written and the dialogues improvised. He solved the difficult problem of keeping his actresses by marrying them all, after which, apparently, stability and harmony in the company were assured. E.K. Ogunmola's Yoruba 'opera' was rather more serious but Beier regards the plays as less interesting. He cites *Love of Money* in which a man follows a woman and loses all, as Ogunmola's best play. Duro Ladipo, the third major figure of Yoruba popular theatre, has made the most use of music for dramatic effect and has incorporated into the plays the difficult singing techniques and dancing steps of Yoruba hunters, worshippers of Sango and masqueraders. The language of his plays draws heavily on Yoruba traditional poetry (Beier, 1971, pp.243–54). Although Soyinka's plays are not part of this *genre*, the exponents of popular theatre, like Soyinka, have experimented in combining Yoruba performed art with new dramatic forms.

The brideprice

'I've told you, and I say again
I shall marry you today, next week
Or any day you name.
But my brideprice must first be paid.' (p.7)

In the play Soyinka uses the issues of the brideprice to illustrate Sidi's respect for custom and Lakunle's overhasty rejection of outmoded 'ignoble' ways; much of the comedy of their relationship turns on their opposed attitudes to the custom. The practice of bridewealth involves goods, kind (or nowadays frequently money), passing from the prospective bridegroom and his family to the father of the wife-to-be. Defenders of the custom which is found in societies in Southern, East and West Africa point out that it does not mean women are bought. It is part of the marriage contract, signifying the obligations of the husband and sealing the wife's rights in marriage. Young men though, sometimes regard it as a means by which avaricious fathers use their daughters to make as much money as possible. Feminists argue that bridewealth is one of the most fundamental ways in which men maintain their control over women in a particular society.

Classroom use

Level of use

The play could be studied from fourth to sixth form level. **Age 14–18.**
The comedy of situation could be stressed at fourth form level (age 14) and the themes explored; fifth and sixth forms (age 16–18) could also work on the range of language usage, the kinds of comedy, satire and the imagery drawn from English and Yoruba experience.

Teaching resources are listed at the end of the unit.

Points for focus and emphasis

1 *Lakunle* (1):
Lakunle tries his luck
where does he belong?
his aspirations
his talent for mimicry

2 *Lakunle* (2):
Lakunle and Sadiku
the unwilling bridegroom
he accepts defeat – regretfully?

3 *The use of flashback, mime, song and dance*:
the arrival of the photographer
the surveyor changes his mind
the victory dance
the marriage procession
the dramatic effects and purpose of the above

4 The *Bale* (1):
his attitude to Lakunle
his praise names
his lack of scruples (second mime)
his disappointment and the plan

5 The *Bale* (2):
his reception of Sidi
the seduction and his techniques
his attitude to progress

6 *Sidi*:
has Lakunle anything to teach her?
the effect of the magazine photos
her mockery of the *Bale*
the final outcome

7 *Sadiku*:
the loyal wife
she mocks Lakunle
the victory dance
return to normality
her comic role

8 *Tradition and modernity*:
Lakunle's position
the *Bale*'s attitude
Sidi's position – ambivalent?
how does the play define progress?

9 *The language used*:
Lakunle's inflated style
the *Bale*'s rich verse
prose for Sadiku
how effective is the loose blank verse?

Teaching suggestions

(a) Interpretation and appreciation

1 'Oh you with your fine airs and little sense.' (p.3) What prompts Sidi to say this to Lakunle? What is your impression of Lakunle so far?

2 'Not till you swear to marry me.' (p.6) In what ways are Sidi's and Lakunle's ideas about marriage different?

3 'A savage custom . . .' (p.7) What is unusual about Lakunle's language in this speech? Can you think of any other characters in literature who use language in a similar way? (Mrs Malaprop? Uriah Heep?)

4 'Ignorant girl . . .' (p.8) Do you find Lakunle convincing here? Does Sidi find him convincing?

5 Do you think the first flashback works dramatically? Is it too abrupt? Does it forward the dramatic interest of the play at all?

6 How do the magazine photos introduce a comic element?

7 'Hurray! I'm beautiful!
Hurray for the wandering stranger.' (p.13) How do the magazine photos influence Sidi a) at this moment? b) in the play as a whole?

8 How much sense, if any, is there in Lakunle's speech, 'Within a year or two I swear . . .'? (pp.36–8)

9 Are there any signs of stage-managing on Baroka's part at the beginning of Sidi's visit?

10 'But the other matter! Did not the Bale send . . . did Baroka not send . . . ?' (p.40) What success does Sidi score in her duel of wits with Baroka?

11 How essential is the wrestler? (A stage prop? Indispensable?) Act the scene with Baroka, Sidi and the wrestler. Can you think of any other plays where a *silent* character is in fact quite important? **D**

12 'Take warning my masters
We'll scotch you in the end.' (p.33) Do you find Sidi and Sadiku's behaviour

here surprising? Understandable? Can you think of any other situation where this temporary revolt could happen?

13 How important in the seduction plan is 'the strange machine'? (p.50)

14 Point to ways in which Baroka a) flatters Sidi b) impresses her c) puts her off her guard. Does he use any other techniques?

15 'He told me . . . afterwards, crowing,
It was a trick.' (p.59)
(a) Act out Sidi's speech and the responses of Lakunle and Sadiku.
(b) Work out a script for or improvise the exchange that took place when Baroka told her 'It was a trick.' **D**

16 Compare the techniques used by Baroka and Lakunle in attempting to win Sidi.

17 'Sadiku: I invoke the fertile gods . . .' (p.64) What is Sadiku's role here? How do you reconcile it with her earlier mocking dance?

18 What picture of old age does the play present (played out; wisdom of age; ripeness of age)?

19 In what ways is the play about marriage (monogamy or polygyny; new style or old style; old husband or young husband)?

20 Is the play critical of western values or only of Lakunle's idea of them?

21 How far, if at all, do you think Baroka comes to terms with modernity?

22 Point out what Lakunle and Sadiku contribute to the comedy of the play.

23 'A court jester would have been the life for you.' (p.17) Is that a fair assessment of Lakunle?

24 What would the play lose if the mime, song and dance sequences were cut?

(b) Creative

The first mime scene

1 What are the villagers' reactions to the traveller? How typical are their reactions to this outsider? Try miming the surveyor's arrival in the village – follow Soyinka's directions for the mime. **D**

2 What difficulties might arise when people with very different ideas about marriage

(or from different cultures or racial groups) decide to marry?

3 What effects do you think publicity (newspaper, magazine, television) has on a person's self-image (vain; confident; deluded; good for the morale; addictive)?

4 *The second flashback*
Try miming this. How is it different in mood from the earlier mime scene? How does it influence your opinion of both Lakunle and Baroka? **D**

5 Improvise a situation where (like Sidi) the visitor is persuaded by the other party to change his or her mind on an important point (for example, an angry parent confronting a headteacher, a neighbour complaining about noise). **D**

6 Improvise a scene were Baroka plans how he is going to use 'the strange machine' (p.50). This could be followed by another improvisation where he tells the village blacksmiths what he wants them to make. (Would he say – or hint at – why he really wanted it?) **D**

7 Improvise a scene where you (singly or in a group) give Lakunle advice about the best way to go about winning Sidi, *or* write him a letter giving him useful tips, *or* work out a short improvisation/write a short story with the title 'Failure in love!' **D**

8 After careful planning perform the mocking 'dance of impotence'. Consider first of all such points as why does Sadiku enjoy it so much? Why is there emphasis on 'tolerant respect' and 'taunts and tantalizing motions'? How would Baroka enact 'his decline and final downfall'? Note also Lakunle's enjoyment of the scene. **D**

9 Write up or act out a scene where the wrestler tells his wife (or men friends) what happened whilst he was with Baroka (his attitude could be admiring, scornful, puzzled; how much did he know about the plan? What will his wife's/friends' reaction be?). **D**

10 Lakunle and Sidi meet, five years after the end of the play. Give a *written or dramatized* account of their meeting. **D**

(c) Curriculum-linked

1 What are the effects of a new road through a small village, a) in Britain b) in, for example, Kenya or Nigeria? Ngugi's *Petals of Blood* charts the gloomy history of a small Kenyan village where just this happens. Could there be advantages and disadvantages? Consider the effects on community life, size and variety of population, amenities.

2 Refer again to Lakunle's speech on progress (pp.33–7). How would you define 'progress'?

3 Outline a range of the possible kinds of marriage relationship (for example, obedience; equality; separate friends; in each other's company constantly; separate social life). What factors do you think are most important for harmony?

Topics

Marriage
Progress and development
Authority
Education

Passages for reading

marriage and 'a life of bliss' (p.20)
development 'within a year or two' (p.36)
'I do not hate progress' (p.52)
'ignorant girl' (pp.8–9)

Teaching aids

Audio-visual

Film

My Brother's Children
Time: 47 mins   Distributor: Concord   Hire: £9.80
Film made in the style of Yoruba folk opera for a Nigerian audience. It features one of the most famous actor/managers Kola Ogunmola, performing in traditional style and is partly improvised.
The Yoruba of Nigeria.
Time: 24 mins   Open University TV. A 100/02F P01   Cost: £40
The Lion and the Jewel. Video-recording of an excerpt from the play. Available on application to the Director, Audio-Visual Services, University of Leeds, Leeds LS2 9JT.

Slide sets

Nigeria in Change, 2 slide sets: 1 Modern Nigeria. 2 Traditional Nigeria – Oyo. CWDE (order no. S1 and S2) £5.50 + VAT.
Provides excellent introduction to theme of two cultures in the play.

Music

Yoruba Music: See Aklowa Centre under Resources, p. 142.
For popular Yoruba music, records by any of the following:
Sunny Ade; Dele Abiodun; Sonny Okosun; Femi Akineymi's Stars.

Recorded sound

The BBC Radio 4 1981 Schools Broadcast tape on *The Lion and the Jewel* is now held by the NSA. See Resources, p.141.

Exhibition

Permanent exhibition at the Museum of Mankind, Burlington Gardens, Piccadilly, London: 'Yoruba Religious Cults'.

Background reading

M.A. Abidekun and E. Ariaze, *The Yoruba Family in Nigeria*, Commonwealth Institute pamphlets.
W. Bascom, *The Yoruba of Southwest Nigeria*, Holt, Rinehart and Winston, 1969.
A comprehensive introduction to Yoruba life and culture.
Saburi Biobaku (ed.), *The Living Culture of Nigeria*, Thomas Nelson (Nigeria), 1976.
Colourful, evocative and informative.

Critical works

M. Banham, *The Lion and the Jewel*, British Council/Rex Collings, 1981.
E.D. Jones, *The Writing of Wole Soyinka*, second ed., Heinemann, 1983.
G. Moore, *Wole Soyinka*, Evans 1971, second ed. 1978.
O. Ogunba, *The movement of transition: a study of the plays of Wole Soyinka*, Ibadan University Press, 1975.

Yoruba poetry	**B. Gbadamosi and U. Beier**, *Yoruba poetry*, Ministry of Education, Nigeria, 1959.

A special publication of the influential journal *Black Orpheus*. Out of print but with fuller comment than the 1970 publication.

U. Beier, *Yoruba Poetry*, Cambridge University Press, 1970.

Reading links

The play could be linked with other books or plays, which emphasize having to choose betwen two very different marriage partners. See:

Chukwuemeka Ike, *Toads for Supper*, Collins (Fontana), 1965.

An Igbo university student has to choose between the girl selected for him by his parents, and a fellow student who is Yoruba. Sixth form (age 16–18).

Michael Anthony, *Green Days by the River*, Heinemann (Caribbean Writers Series 9), 1973.

One of the strands of the novel deals with having to choose between two girls.

Earl Lovelace, *The Schoolmaster*, Heinemann (Caribbean Writers Series 20), 1979.

A novel about the coming of progress to a village, the building of a road and a school, and the destruction of traditional values.

Other plays by Soyinka

Kongi's Harvest

A trial of wits and character between a ruthless upstart and an effete ruler representing the old order. Thematic links with Shakespeare's *Henry IV* Parts 1 and 2 and *Richard II*.

The Trials of Brother Jero

A talented charlatan makes a living as priest of his own independent church, but events threaten to catch up with him. Has been successfully performed in schools in Britain and the Caribbean.

Jero's Metamorphosis

A bleak comedy, bitterly attacking unscrupulous property developers and corrupt justice. Jero must become part of it all to survive.

Madmen and Specialists

An exposé of the destructive effect of war on individuals and the social fabric. Possible comparisons with Brecht's *Mother Courage*.

All above in W. Soyinka, *Collected Plays*, Volume 2, Oxford University Press, 1974.

Unit 11 *Sizwe Bansi is Dead*

Athol Fugard, John Kani and Winston Ntshona

Level of use and scope

Athol Fugard is widely acclaimed as one of the most powerful and original of contemporary South African writers. *Sizwe Bansi is Dead* is the result of Fugard the writer working closely with two actors, John Kani and Winston Ntshona. In his introduction to *Statements*, Fugard describes how the idea for *Sizwe Bansi* and another play, *The Island*, grew from a complex structure of images which he had. These were then given shape and body by the two actors, working creatively and in collaboration with Fugard rather than merely being interpreters of the idea. Fugard notes that the starting point for *Sizwe Bansi* was 'my fascination with a studio photograph I had once seen of a man with a cigarette in one hand and a pipe in the other' (Introduction, *Statements*). This satiric and compassionate play centres on the efforts of one man to remain in the city in order to obtain work and so support his family who live 150 miles away in the dry, dusty and poverty-stricken Black homeland of the Ciskei. He eventually finds a way to do this by taking over the identity and the passbook of a dead man. Sizwe Bansi 'becomes' Robert Zwelinzima, thereby acquiring a new Native Identity number, an address and most important of all, a 'work-seeker's permit'. The basic theme of the play deals with identity and the way in which the oppressive and bureaucratic laws in South Africa depersonalize individuals, reducing them to an 'identity number'. Thus in one of the most moving moments of the play, Sizwe Bansi, called at this point simply 'Man' rehearses the various scenes (work, shops, church, police encounters) where he must produce not merely his new name but also his Native Identity number – N-I-3-8-1-1-8-6-3 (pp.39–42).

Fugard's earlier plays such as *The Blood Knot* and *Boesman and Lena* have used two actors and a sparse set. In *Sizwe Bansi* the part of the photographer Styles and of the generous friend Buntu is played by the same actor, while that of Sizwe Bansi or the representative 'Man' is played by a second actor. A great deal of the play's success depends on the versatility of whoever takes the Styles/Buntu role. As Styles he has to recreate a number of scenes himself and act out the parts of the characters in each incident. As Buntu, the same actor has to persuade the fearful Sizwe Bansi of the need to lose his *name* (ironically his first name means 'Wide-Country' and his second name 'The-Difficult-Land'); here again Buntu (whose name means 'Humaneness') briefly recreates a number of typical incidents and assumes various roles as he does so. Sizwe Bansi on the other hand is the inexperienced country man unaware of the pitfalls of city life and in particular of the network of pass laws which threaten to trip him up at every step.

Besides its moments of pathos, anger and its intensity, the play is often extremely funny. Sixth formers (age 16–18) should find it a challenging play to study and to act. The themes of lost identity and of the depersonalized roles of bureaucracy operating within an oppressive regime link the play with novels such as Solzhenitsyn's *A Day in the Life of Ivan Denisovich* and Orwell's *1984*. As didactic drama the play could be compared with works by Shaw and Brecht. It also raises the question of the relation between art and propaganda and perhaps, unlike some South African protest literature, it succeeds on both counts.

Sizwe Bansi is Dead, Athol Fugard, John Kani and Winston Ntshona in *Statements: Three Plays* by Athol Fugard, Oxford University Press, 1974; 1980 paperback.

The authors

Athol Fugard was born and educated in South Africa. He became involved in Black theatre in Johannesburg and began to write, using as the material for his plays the experience of Black and Coloured people under apartheid.

The involvement with John Kani and Winston Ntshona which led to the collaborative *Sizwe Bansi is Dead* and *The Island* grew from his work at the Serpent Players of New Brighton township, Port Elizabeth.

Kani and Ntshona, who first met at school, have acted together for a number of years. In their early careers they suffered from the limitations imposed on the free expression of Black art and artists in South Africa. For instance, when they and the Serpent Players began to work with Fugard they could only ply their trade as actors by being registered as his employees. They acted in the performances of *Sizwe Bansi is Dead* and *The Island* at the Royal Court Theatre in 1974 and in the BBC Television production of *Sizwe Bansi*. Since then Kani and Ntshona have enjoyed considerable success in film as well as dramatic productions. Ntshona has starred in *Full Frontal* – a film about the National Front – and both acted in *The Wild Geese*. Fugard, Kani and Ntshona all have major roles in the film *Marigolds in August*, written by Fugard and directed by Ross Devenish. Although now internationally known all three men live and work in South Africa.

The setting

The pass laws

(See Unit 4, *Tell Freedom*, p.30)
The action of the play revolves around these cumbersome and repressive laws which control the movement of Black people in South Africa. The nature in which they operate becomes apparent in the course of the play itself. See for instance Buntu's speech, 'Burn that book? Stop kidding yourself, Sizwe . . .' (pp.24–6)

Bantustans

The Bantustans, or Black Homelands as they are sometimes known, are in theory the only parts of South Africa where blacks belong. Elsewhere they are theoretically only temporary residents; they are citizens not of South Africa but of whichever Bantustan they are assigned to by virtue of their prescribed ethnic group. The Bantustans, with the exception of the Transkei, consist of separate blocks of land under a single administration. They are in general badly overcrowded, unproductive and economically unviable. The Ciskei, which is referred to with great scorn several times in the play, is one of these Bantustans.

Black theatre in South Africa

The growth of Black consciousness in South Africa throughout the 1970s has been accompanied by a resurgence of interest in the theatre as a medium of artistic and political expression. BBC Television extracts of plays in performance at Johannesburg's Market Theatre and at more clandestine venues (BBC 2, *Arena*, March 1980) show that the new theatre uses Zulu and Xhosa as well as English. Also, unlike Fugard's work, the plays use images of the heroic past in their language and visual effects. This past is viewed not with nostalgia but is seen as a source of inspiration for the present.

Classroom use

Level of use

The play would be most usefully studied at sixth form level. **Age 16–18.**

Parts could also be used as models for improvisation work with fourth or fifth years (age 14–16), on the themes of work (the Ford Plant section), religion (the preacher interlude, p.41) or encounters (the Studio customers/the police raid).

Teaching resources are listed at the end of the unit.

Points for focus and emphasis:

1 *The Ford Plant*:
the façade
the reality

2 *Style's studio shop*:
setting it up
customers: 'the simple people' (p.12)
the arrival of Robert Zwelinzima

3 *The flashbacks*:
reminiscences: Styles at the Ford Plant
                  Styles starting up business
the letter home (pp.22, 29, 44)
meeting Buntu
events after leaving Sky's place

4 *The pass-book*:
the raid and the Labour Bureau (p.23)
'repatriation to home district' (p.24)
'Wherever you go it's that bloody book'
  (pp.39–41)

5 *Work*: See 1 and 2
Chief Messenger at Feltex (p.20)
future head of Feltex (p.21)
paytime at Feltex (p.38)
the Labour Bureau (p.24)
'on leave . . . for life' (p.37)

6 *Identity*:
'What is your name?' (p.17)
'I cannot lose my name' (p.36)
Becoming a 'ghost' (p.38)
your name *or* your security (p.43)

7 *The Images*:
Robert seated (p.20)
Robert in front of the City of the Future
  (pp.22, 44)
'look at me! I'm a man' (p.35)

8 *Comedy*:
The Ford Plant scene
Starting a studio: cockroaches
Styles and his customer (pp.17–22)
lost after leaving Sky's place
Buntu persuades Sizwe to change his name
  (pp.36–7)

Teaching suggestions

(a) Interpretation and appreciation

1 What do you think of the way the play

opens? (Note this section can be improvised in performance.)

2 'I was also given a new asbestos apron and
fire-proof gloves to replace the ones I had
lost about a year ago.' (p.6) What other
examples of irony are there in the Ford
Plant episode?

3 Describe relations between management
and workers at the Ford Plant.

4 What seem to you the funniest moments of
the Ford Plant episode?

5 What difficulties might there be in acting
the parts of both Styles and Bradley (see
p.7 for instance)? How would you overcome these difficulties if you were acting
Styles' part? Test the situation for yourself
by acting one episode. **D**

6 'Yessus, Styles, they're all playing your part
today.' (p.8) What is Styles saying about
himself and his position here?

7 'This is a strong room of dreams.' (p.12)
What serious point is Styles making here?
What does it emphasize about Fugard's
intentions and interests as a playwright?

8 At what point does the mood change
during the 'Family Card' enactment? What
causes the change?

9 Do you think Styles' mention of his father
is relevant or not (p.16–17)? Why?

10 What does Buntu mean when he says,
'There's no way out, Sizwe.' (p.26) In what
ways are Buntu and Sizwe different?

11 '. . . when a car passes or the wind blows up
the dust, Ciskeian independence makes
you cough.' (p.31) What political point is
being made here?

12 What do you think the play gains (and
intends) by direct address to the audience
(at for instance p.35), 'What is happening
in this world good people . . . ?'

13 How important are the swift changes of
mood in the play (for instance leaving Sky's
place and the macabre discovery)?

14 What theme of the play does the preacher's
sermon underline (p.28)?

15 Do you think the play suffers through
having only two actors? Would a large cast
have been better, for example, in acting out
the Ford Plant scene or the studio group

photograph? (Compared with Soyinka's flashback techniques in *The Lion and the Jewel* how effective are Fugard's in *Sizwe Bansi*?)

16 How important to the themes and movement of the play are the props: the newspaper, the letter, the pass-book, the hat?

17 'All I'm saying is be a real ghost if that is what they want.' (p.38) How does this relate to the theme of identity in the play?

18 What impressions does the play give of relations between Black and White people in South Africa?

19 'Good propaganda, poor art.' What is your reaction to this comment on *Sizwe Bansi is Dead*?

(b)   Creative

1 Imagine that you work in a factory (for example a car plant/cable factory/electronic component factory). It has just been announced that a senior official from the Department of Trade is coming to inspect the building. Work out as an improvisation what happens next. **D**

2 Write a short story or plan an improvisation around a day in the life of a man or woman who runs his/her own photographic studio. **D**

3 Act the opening of a play (to be set in Britain) using the same device as Fugard – a single character reading a newspaper . . . **D**

4 Plan and then act out a situation between two people – one is unemployed and the other who has a job is trying to be helpful . . . **D**

5 Imagine that you have found work in a large town far from home. Write to your family telling them how you found the job and what it is. (The job could be one they like or one which they would find rather odd/unsuitable/alarming.)

6 Think of a situation where you have to change identity to survive (to evade arrest, escape from a country and so on) –

'become' – for instance, a garage attendant/fisherman/coal miner/teacher/tourist/gardener/lawyer's clerk. Act out a conversation with a suspicious/inquisitive landlord/landlady or policeman **D**.

7 Have you seen a person publicly humiliated? Where? In a shop? At school? In town? What happened?

8 Improvise an address to workers/a meeting/a church congregation. Plan and discuss it first with others, then deliver it. Try tape-recording yourself first to hear how you sound. **D**

9 Describe the experiences of someone you know a) looking for work, or b) registering at a Job Centre, or c) being offered a job. Compare them with Sizwe Bansi's experiences.

10 Act the preacher and congregation scene. Use the text as a guide and improvise where you want to. **D**

(c)   Curriculum-linked

1 Would you argue for or against the view that 'apartheid' is a threat to world peace?

2 What relevance (if any) has this play to life in England at the present time?

Topics

Identity
Work
Racism
Bureaucracy
Repression

Passages for reading

A letter home (p.22)
The nervous client (pp.17–18)
Deciding to leave a job: 'I said to myself . . .' (pp.9–10)
Names and pride (p.43)
Losing your name (pp.36–7)
A shop of your own (pp.10–12)

Teaching aids

(See items listed under Unit 4 *Tell Freedom*)

Audio-visual

Film
Boesman and Lena
Time: 102 mins   Colour   Distributor: Contemporary   Hire: £30
The screen version of Fugard's play, directed by Ross Devenish. A Cape-Coloured couple are evicted from their shanty, the man has lost all self-respect but Lena will not be crushed.
Marigolds in August
Time: 87 mins   Colour   Distributor: Contemporary   Hire: £40
Written by Athol Fugard, directed by Ross Devenish, 1979. Three men face unemployment and starvation. All are victims yet their responses are sharply varied.
Abaphuciwe, *The Dispossessed*
Time: 40 mins   Colour   Distributor: The Other Cinema   Hire: £25
Directors: G and A Yonge, 1980
Shows enforced removals of Blacks, pass raids, life in removal camps, interviews with men and women living under such conditions.

Photographic
Family Life and Migrant Labour in South Africa, A Christian Aid illustrated fact sheet. Available CWDE (order no. L-3) 20p.
Would be an excellent introduction to themes in *Sizwe Bansi*.

Background reading
Shula Marks, 'South Africa, the myth of the empty land' in *History Today*, January, 1980, pp.1–13.
Counters official argument that Black and White reached South Africa at the same period; questions ethnic fragmenting of Black peoples. Illustrated.
R.W. Johnson, *How long will South Africa Survive?*, Macmillan, 1977.

Critical studies
Stephen Gray (ed.), *Athol Fugard*, McGraw-Hill (Southern African Literature Series), 1981.
A thorough coverage of all Fugard's work to date. A section of reviews and articles by established critics and playwrights. Also contains a bibliography.
Robert J. Green, 'The Drama of Athol Fugard' in C. Heywood (ed.), *Aspects of South African Literature*, Heinemann, 1976, pp.163–73.
Peter Rosenwald, 'Separate Fables', *The Guardian*, London, 8 January 1974. An interview with John Kani and Winston Ntshona.
Dennis Walder, 'Athol Fugard, *Sizwe Bansi is Dead*' in *The Varied Scene*: Aspects of Drama Today (Units 27–30 of the Open University Drama Course, OU Press Milton Keynes), 1977, pp.67–79.
York Notes on Selected Plays of Athol Fugard, Longman, 1980.

Covers the three plays in *Statements*: 'Sizwe Bansi is Dead', 'The Island' and 'Statements after an arrest under the Immorality Act'. Useful critical analysis and helpful background information.

Reading links
Other plays by Athol Fugard

'The Blood Knot', 'Hello and Goodbye' and 'Boesman and Lena' in *Three Port Elizabeth Plays*, London and Cape Town, OUP, 1974.

Samuel Beckett, *Waiting for Godot*, Faber, 1956.
Links: similarities in dramatic technique and interest in the poor and the dispossessed.
Charles Dickens, *Little Dorrit*, Penguin, 1967.
The description of the circumlocation office. Link: another view of unwieldy officialdom.
Athol Fugard, *Tsotsi*, Ad Donker/Quagga Press, 1981.
This was written in the 1960s when Fugard as a young man was also writing *The Blood Knot*. A brilliant study of a young outcast existing on the fringes of city life.
Franz Kafka, *The Castle*, Penguin Modern Classics, 1970.
The bewildering maze of bureaucracy which traps the individual could be a link point.
M. Matshoba, 'Three Days in the Land of a Dying Illusion' in *Call Me Not a Man*, Ravan, 1979, Longman (Drumbeat 42) 1981.
The author visits a friend in the Transkei and vows 'never again'.
M. Mzamane, *My Cousin Comes to Jo'burg and other stories*, Longman (Drumbeat 41), 1982.
Black city life, pithy and humourous.
George Orwell, *Nineteen Eighty-Four*, Penguin Modern Classics, 1954.
Link could be emphasis on repressive bureaucracy.
Alexander Solzhenitsyn, *A Day in the Life of Ivan Denisovich*, Penguin Modern Classics, 1963.
The loss of personal freedom could serve as a common focal point.

Unit 12 *African Oral Poetry*

Increasing attention is being paid nowadays to African oral poetry. A great deal of oral poetry is functional and is at the same time aesthetically pleasing, conforming to the artistic conventions of the particular poetic tradition to which it belongs. Much oral poetry is sung and is sometimes accompanied by dance and by musical instruments. Obviously if such poetry is to be widely read in translation and used in schools a great deal of the original musical and performing context of the poetry is lost. The rhythm, alliteration and assonance of the original disappears as well. Nevertheless, much oral poetry remains very good teaching material, rich in figurative language, often humorous and often displaying an understanding of human nature which stretches across cultural divides. The fact that such poetry is meant to be spoken (or sung) means that it is particularly useful for dramatic and choral work.

The strong tradition in African poetry of public performance and public relevance also points out the link between African and Caribbean artistic traditions. The Barbadian poet Edward Kamau Brathwaite, for instance, frequently reads his poetry in public and each reading is in a very real sense a performance. The Black British poet, Linton Kwesi Johnson, also frequently performs in public and uses his poetry as a vehicle for social comment thereby underlining another common element in the Afro-Caribbean poetic tradition. Reggae and Calypso with their emphasis on topical, often satirical, comment provide a further link with the tradition of social comment in African poetry, found particularly in some work songs and in topical and political songs.[1]

Oral poetry in the classroom

Of the wide range of types of oral poetry the following could be experimented with and possibly used alongside written poetry or poems from the English oral tradition, such as ballads.

Praise poems

Praise poetry is widely used in Africa. Particularly when it is addressed to rulers and leaders, it is often elaborately structured and highly metaphorical. This is the case for instance with the Zulu, Sotho, Tswana and Shona praise poems of Southern Africa. The poem of a particular leader tends to focus on his exploits, his character and his ancestry. He himself is often personified in a series of striking images. Praise poems or extracts from them could be included in work on war or heroes and could also be compared with Irish and Welsh bardic poetry.

The following extract from the praises of the early nineteenth-century Zulu king, Shaka, still recited by present-day Zulu bards describes his ruthless treatment of opponents and his success in war:

I saw The Grey Hawk swoop like a bolt on the
    cattle of Macingwana
The Blazing Fire of Mjokwane's son,
The devastating rush of fire,
That burnt out the Buthelezis like owls.
Shaka, I fear to speak the name of Shaka.
For Shaka was King of the people of
    Mashobane.
Raving mad he ravened among the
    homesteads
Until dawn they called to one another.
He seized firmly the assegais of his father,
He who was like the maned lion.
(from J. Cope and U. Krige, (eds).
The Penguin Book of South African Verse,
p.290)

The lines above use the metaphor of fire to suggest the destructive force of Shaka; he is also called 'The Grey Hawk', a metaphorical praise name suggesting aggression, speed and grace. In its use of metaphor to express particular attributes and denote particular individuals Southern African praise poetry could be compared with Anglo-Saxon poetry with its stylized, richly metaphorical 'kennings' where, for instance, the sea is alluded to as 'the whale's road' or 'the swan's path' and a king is 'shield of the fighting-men'.

The Southern African praise poetry, though, also includes praises of ordinary people and animals and of inanimate objects such as bicycles and trains. Often the qualities of the person or thing are pithily described as in this brief haiku-like Hurutshe poem in praise of a bicycle:

My frail little bicycle,
The one with the scar, my sister Seabelo.
Horse of the Europeans, feet of tyre,
Iron horse, swayer from side to side.[2]

A Sotho praise of an owl is simply

Owl, crevice sitter
When it rains where do you sit?[3]

Classes might enjoy composing such compact praise poems on animals and objects familiar to them such as sparrows, buses and bicycles, and so on! In some societies composing praise poems begins when one is very young. When children compose their own praise poems they often include autobiographical details and use accepted popular imagery to highlight their own real or imagined qualities.

It seems that Busangokwakhe Xulu, the young composer of the next Zulu praise poem which I recorded in 1976, was caught with his brother while illicitly milking his neighbour's cow – only his brother, unlike himself, managed to escape.

Busangokwakhe, who was known to his friends as 'Pepper Bush', gives himself the praise names, 'Stealthy Milker' and 'Bush Warbler', after a small bird. He also alludes to the milk event with its unpleasant consequences! In the second part of his praise poem he boasts about himself, giving himself more metaphorical praise names which he has probably heard young men use in their praises:

'Bushes of the Pepper Plant', 'Powerful Rhinoceros Horn', 'Bull of a young man':

I am The Stealthy Milker, the Bush Warbler,
Bush Warbler of the finished business – Hit-hit, finish the business
My mouth was swollen.
Whilst you, Mduduzi – how did you get out?
You were at the back of the hut then 'wheet' – gone!

I am the Bushes of the Pepper Plant – ah they're bitter.
The (Powerful) Rhinoceros Horn at the back of the hut.
O little girls do grow up!
Black as pitch are the lightning sticks of the sky.
(I am) The Bull of a young man – the Angry One,
I said to them, "Just you dare throw me into the forest
I'll wake up a madman!"

This poem of the hyena cryptically recreates the animal's hazardous life. It focus on the four main points of danger in lines which combine repetition and variation, a technique common to much oral poetry and known as parallelism. In some ways the hyena's song, which is more like a lament, seems remarkably contemporary in its apt expression of the difficulties of life and the trials of parent-child relationships!

Hyena's song to her children
The fire threatens
the sling-stone menaces me
the assegais threaten me
the gun points death at me
yet you howl around me for food
my children!
Do I get anything so easily?[4]

Both the above poems could perhaps serve as models for children's own writing. Some might enjoy writing their own praise poems and trying to fit in compact autobiographical details, others might enjoy turning the hyena's song into a modern 'Parents' song' or alternatively 'A child's song to its parents'.

Elegaic and religious verse

Elegaic and religious verse are two other categories of African oral poetry where teachers might find poems which could interest classes, stimulate discussion on the language and ideas of the examples used and possibly serve as models for creative writing. Contrasting attitudes to death, to life after death and to the supernatural could be discussed as an introduction to the poems. Questions could be asked such as: Do western attitudes help to push the memory of the dead out of the way as soon as possible? How important are funerals? How important is it to comfort bereaved people? I remember that one of the features of the broadcasting week in Freetown, Sierra Leone, was the announcement of the week's deceased, their relations, where the funeral would be, and so on. The same was true of the Zulu broadcasts I listened to in 1976. What attitudes to death does this sort of media coverage reveal? Funeral wakes are important among the Creoles of Sierra Leone and among the Cape-Coloured community in South Africa. Do they happen here? In the West Indies? Among other communities? Examples of elegaic and religious poetry could be placed in the context of this kind of discussion conducted perhaps over several lessons.

In the first poem below a sharp sense of the insubstantiality of death is conveyed in the words, 'My brother blows like the wind', and the phrase 'the chief of youth' conveys a sense of the boy's untimely death. In the second poem loss is expressed through suggesting the presence of the deceased in a very concrete way and so achieving a sharp contrast between the past and the present:

1 *Acholi funeral dirge (Uganda)*
I wait on the pathway in vain,
He refuses to come again.
Only one, beloved of my mother oh,
My brother blows like the wind;
Fate has destroyed the chief of youth completely
I wait on the pathway in vain.[5]

2 *Ewe lament (Ghana)*
Mother dear,
Mother you freely give of what you have,
Fresh food and cooked meals alike.
Mother, listen to me:
The crying child will call after its mother.
Why don't you answer, Mother, when I call?
Are we quarrelling?[6]

The third poem from the Akan (i.e. the Ashanti and Fante) of Ghana illustrates how oral composers often work with stock expressions and do not constantly have to strive after originality to be appreciated. Also, of course, the way a poem is sung or recited is very important and can make or mar a performance. In the following example the woman soloist includes the conventional metaphor, comparing the duration of life to the time a market woman takes to sell her goods. Again, as convention demands, the mourner expresses sorrow and loss through particular concrete images rather than by using general statements about death.

3 *Akan funeral dirge (Ghana)*
Your death has taken me by surprise.
What were your wares
That they sold out so quickly?
When I meet my father, he will hardly recognize me:
He'll find me carrying all I have:
A torn old sleeping mat and a horde of flies.
The night is fast approaching.
The orphan is dying to see its mother.[7]

The following two poems on death are from Beier's anthology *African Poetry* (1966). The strong sense of separation between the dead and the living dominates the first poem, whereas the second expresses an attitude more widespread in Africa: that the dead remain close to the living. Both poems illustrate the use of the particular kind of repetition which is found so often in African and other oral poetry, namely parallelism. The second poem for instance, makes use of parallelism in lines 1 and 2, where the grammar and ideas remain the same but key words, needle/razor, piercing point/trenchant blade are varied.

4 *Prayer before the dead body (Pygmy? Congo)*

The gates of the underworld are closed.
Closed are the gates.

The spirits of the dead are thronging together
like swarming mosquitoes in the evening,
like swarming mosquitoes.

Like swarms of mosquitoes dancing in the
  evening,
When the night has turned black, entirely
  black,
when the sun has sunk, has sunk below,
when the night has turned black
the mosquitoes are swarming
like whirling leaves
Dead leaves in the wind.

Dead leaves in the wind,
they wait for him who will come
for him who will come and say:
'Come' to the one and 'Go' to the other
and God will be with his children.
And God will be with his children.[8]

5 *Death (Kuba, Congo)*

There is no needle without piercing point.
There is no razor without trenchant blade.
Death comes to us in many forms.

With our feet we walk the goat's earth.
With our hands we touch God's sky.
Some future day in the heat of noon,
I shall be carried shoulder high
through the village of the dead.
When I die, don't bury me under forest trees.
I fear their thorns.
When I die, don't bury me under forest trees,
I fear the dripping water.
Bury me under the great shade trees in the
  market.
I want to hear the drums beating
I want to feel the dancer's feet.[9]

The following poem from Malawi is both
religious and elegaic in its sentiments. It is
known to be old and was originally sung at
marriages but is now also used at church meetings and on other occasions. The Ngoni people
of Malawi, where the song was recorded by
Margaret Read in the 1930s, may have brought

it with them in their long journey from the
south which they left during the Shakan period
(i.e. c.1820). As Finnegan points out in her
discussion of the poem, the refrain, 'The earth
does not get fat', is a reference to the way in
which the earth constantly receives and so
'eats' the dead but is never satisfied:[10]

The earth does not get fat. It makes an end of
  those who wear the head plumes
We shall die on the earth.
The earth does not get fat. It makes an end of
  those who act swiftly as heroes.
Shall we die on the earth?
Listen O earth. We shall mourn because of
  you.
Listen O earth. Shall we all die on the earth?
The earth does not get fat. It makes an end of
  the chiefs.
Shall we all die on the earth?
The earth does not get fat. It makes an end of
  the women chiefs.
Shall we die on the earth?
Listen O earth. We shall mourn because of
  you.
Listen O earth. Shall we all die on the earth?
The earth does not get fat. It makes an end of
  the nobles.
Shall we die on the earth?
The earth does not get fat. It makes an end of
  the royal women.
Shall we die on the earth?
Listen O earth. We shall mourn because of
  you.
Listen O earth. Shall we all die on the earth?
The earth does not get fat. It makes an end of
  all the common people.
Shall we die on the earth?
The earth does not get fat. It makes an end of
  all the beasts.
Shall we die on the earth?
Listen you who are asleep, who are left tightly
  closed in the land.
Shall we all sink into the earth?
Listen O earth the sun is setting tightly.
We shall all enter into the earth.

The tone of the above is solemn and the regular
verses register the inevitable end of each individual in each social group. Like earlier

examples the poem makes great use of repetition and of parallelism as it lists in successive verses those who will sink into the earth which, like a rapacious monster, is seen to consume all living things. Not only would this poem be useful for choral work, it would fit very well into a wider topic on mortality or age and youth. Its very regularity and its copious use of repetition might also be a point of controversy: some class members might argue that the repetition is intensely boring and monotonous, others might say that if it were sung or recited this monotony would not be felt. Others, yet again, might argue that with the repetition and the slight changes in some lines a great momentum is built up leading to the climax of the last verse. Ballads, with their use of repetition as well as some hymns would be useful for comparison in the course of such a discussion. Writers of Caribbean origin, such as Edward Kamau Brathwaite, James Berry and Fred Williams, also make frequent use of repetition, and their work could be referred to here.

No examples have been given here of the *oriki* (praises) to the various members of the pantheon of Yoruba divinities. These religious poems, often couched in obscure and paradoxical language, yet containing startling juxtapositions and powerful images would appeal to many readers. The *oriki* of Ogun and Sango might particularly interest pupils who wish to follow through Yoruba cultural influences in Caribbean art forms and religious expression.[11] Two examples of *oriki* to Yoruba divinities are included in Section 2, p.127.

Love poetry

The compact and intense poems below should dispel any lingering notions pupils might have that 'love' is in some way a western phenomenon. The three examples, from Somali poetry are from a *genre* known as the *balwo*. A huge number of these cryptic, highly metaphorical love poems circulate in Somalia, particularly in towns, and are sung to a far smaller number of widely used *balwo* tunes:

1 Woman, lovely as lightning at dawn,
   Speak to me even once.

I long for you, as one
Whose dhow in summer winds
Is blown adrift and lost,
Longs for land, and finds –
Again the compass tells –
A grey and empty sea.

2 If I say to myself 'Conceal your love!'
   Who will conceal my tears?

   Like a tall tree which, fallen, was set alight,
   I am ashes.

3 My heart is single and cannot be divided,
   And it is fastened on a single hope; Oh you
      who might be the moon.[12]

Anger and sorrow at lost love are expressed in this Zulu poem. The composer, Ntombi Dlamini, a domestic worker who led her own singing group in Durban pours scorn on her faithless and worthless lover. She contrasts the present reality with her past illusions. The poem may have no obvious metrical or rhyme pattern yet it is built up around paired contrasts in the first four lines. A further contrast between 'pillow' and 'armpit' adds both a sting and balance to the latter lines. Classes could be asked to compare the sentiments and expression of the poem with popular songs on a similar theme. A useful follow-up might be to investigate how many modern pop singers write their own lyrics? Do groups have one singer/composer member? Do they always give the same version of a song or improvise in performance, add new phrases, discard others and so on?

I thought you loved me,
Yet I am wasting my time on you.
I thought you would be parted only by death,
But today you have disappointed me.
You will never be anything.
You are a disgrace, worthless and unreliable.
Bring my things. I will put them in my pillow.
You take yours and put them under your
   armpit.
You deceived me.[13]

Some available anthologies

In most cases teachers will probably not set oral poetry in a separate category for classroom work. It is useful, though, to know where texts can be found:

Anthologies of oral poetry

U. Beier (ed.), *African Poetry: an anthology of traditional African poems*, Cambridge University Press, 1966.
U. Beier (ed.), *Yoruba Poetry: an anthology of traditional poems*, Cambridge University Press, 1970.
R. Finnegan (ed.), *The Penguin Book of Oral Poetry*, Allen Lane, 1978.
Maina wa Kinyatti, *Thunder from the Mountains: Mau Mau Patriotic Songs*, Zed Publishers, London, 1980.
Short poems which express the aspirations, suffering and heroism of the Mau Mau fighters. Three categories are used: Mobilization Songs; Detention Songs; Guerrilla Songs.

Anglo-Saxon poetry

M. Alexander (trans.), *The Earliest English Poems*, Penguin, 1966.
Beowulf, Penguin, 1973.

Anthologies with oral poetry included

S.K. Akivaga and **A.B. Odaga** (eds), *Oral Literature: A School Certificate Course*, Heinemann, (Nairobi and London), 1982.
Contains poetry, oral tales, proverbs, riddles and lucid discussion of forms of oral literature. Mainly East African material.
Noel Machin (ed.), *African Poetry for Schools*, Books 1 and 2, Longman, 1978.
Designed for African schools at junior secondary level. Illustrated with photographs and line drawings. Contains a few Caribbean poems and a good selection of oral poems. Brief notes and questions are included. Already in use in a few British schools.
K.E. Senanu and **T. Vincent** (eds), *A Selection of African Poetry*, Longman, 1976.

Designed for use at upper secondary level in Africa. Contains information on each poet or *genre* of oral poem, a commentary, questions and brief notes on poems.
Jack Cope and **Uys Krige** (eds), *The Penguin Book of South African Verse*, Penguin, 1968.
Considered by some reviewers to be conservative in its selection. Nevertheless it contains a number of interesting and representative oral poems in its African section, also poems in translation by such giants as the Xhosa poet S.E.K. Mqhayi and the Zulu poet B.W. Vilakazi.
Wole Soyinka (ed.), *Poems of Black Africa*, Heinemann (African Writers Series 171), 1975.
Contains an introduction by Soyinka. Oral poems included in a number of the eighteen thematic sections.

Taped collections of poetry

African oral poetry. There is to my knowledge no tape or video-tape of an anthology of such poetry commercially available. However, listening facilities are available at The National Sound Archive, 29 Exhibition Road, London SW7. Copies of selected extracts of oral poetry for educational use may also be available on request. For an appointment or further information contact NSA. Tel. 01-589-6603/4.
The following are commercially available:
English Speaking Africa, Cassette 10, Englang Enterprises, 6 Well Walk, London NW3. Cost: £8 + script. This includes brief excerpts of oral poetry.
The English Speaking Caribbean, Cassette 12, Englang Enterprises. Cost: £8 + scrip . The tape includes a number of calypsos and examples of other performed poetry.
Caribbean Anthology. A set of five books plus a teachers book and cassette. Produced by ILEA Learning Materials Service, Highbury Station Road, London N1 15B. Cost: £8 ILEA teachers; £12 others. Includes poems by Berry, Linton Kwesi Johnson and John Agard.

Notes

[1] For a full discussion of comment in topical and political songs see R. Finnegan, *Oral Literature in Africa*, Oxford University Press, 1970, ch.10. Anyone at all interested in African oral literature should consult this invaluable and pioneering work.

[2] D. van de Merwe, 'Hurutshe Poems', *Bantu Studies* 15, 1941, p.336.

[3] S.K. Lekgothoane, 'Praises of Animals in Northern Sotho', *Bantu Studies* 12, 1938, p.211.

[4] *Penguin Book of South African Verse*, p.254, from W.H.I. Bleek, 'Reynard the Fox in South Africa', 'Hottentot fables and tales', London, 1864.

[5] *Oral Literature in Africa*, p.150, from Okot p'Bitek, 'Oral Literature and its social background among the Acholi and Lango', B.Litt. thesis, University of Oxford, 1963, p.209.

[6] U. Beier (ed.), *African Poetry: an anthology of traditional African poems*, Cambridge University Press, 1966, p.28. See also G. Adali-Mortty's essay, 'Ewe Poetry' in Ulli Beier (ed.), *Introduction to African Literature*, Longman 1967, p.p3–11.

[7] *Oral Literature in Africa*, p.157. Finnegan's discussion is based on J.H.K. Nketia's classic work, *Funeral Dirges of the Akan People*, Achimota, 1955.

[8] Beier, *op. cit.*, p.26. Beier has it marked as 'Hottentot' (i.e. Khoisan) but it appears in his sources to come from an article on the Pygmies! (P. Trilles, *Les Pygmes de la Grande Sylve Ouest Equatoriale*.)

[9] Beier, *op. cit.* In his sources merely as from *Jeune Afrique*.

[10] See *Oral Literature in Africa*, pp.151–2 for a discussion of the poem. See the article by Margaret Read, 'Songs of the Ngoni People', *Bantu Studies* 11, 1937, pp.14–15.

[11] See U. Beier (ed.), *Yoruba Poetry: an anthology of traditional poems*, Cambridge University Press, 1970.

[12] See *Oral Literature in Africa*, p.254. For a detailed and fascinating account of Somali poetry see B.W. Andrzejewski and I.M. Lewis, *Somali Poetry, an introduction*, Oxford University Press, 1964.

[13] Quoted in *Oral Literature in Africa*, p.256. From H. Tracey, *Zulu Paradox*, Silver Leaf Books, Johannesburg, 1948, pp.58–9.

Unit 13   *African Written Poetry*

Some teachers might feel that the seemingly exotic nature of African poetry and its alien references make it extremely difficult to use with ease in British classrooms. In some cases the references to beliefs within a culture do require explanation before a poem makes sense. Thus the traditional Ijaw and Yoruba belief in spirit children born only to die and return to their spirit world provides a key to understanding the poems 'Abiku' by J.P. Clark and the similarly titled one by Soyinka. Similarly some poems use imagery derived from particular beliefs, from particular deities, or in some instances they assume a certain body of knowledge on the part of their readers. Thus, to use J.P. Clark as an example again, his poem 'Olokun' is in praise of a beautiful girl who is compared to the Yoruba sea-deity Olokun. The war poems of Clark, Okara and Okigbo assume that the reader is familiar with the main events of the Nigerian civil war of 1967–70. A poem such as David Rubadiri's 'Stanley Meets Mutesa' shows how African poets writing in English may combine the influence of the English literary tradition with commentary on African history and politics. Rubadiri's poem contains echoes of T.S. Eliot's 'Journey of the Magi'. It begins:

Such a time of it they had;
The heat of the day,
The chill of the night
And the mosquitoes that followed.
Such was the time and
They bound for a kingdom.[1]

Stanley's journey, however, had its own objectives and Rubadiri uses the poem to depict the first confrontation between an Imperial power and an unsuspecting East African monarch.

One of the distinctive features of African poets is their willingness to tackle important public and political issues in their poetry. Possibly this is due in part to the influence of oral poetry with its insistence on the public role of poetry and its use on important social and political occasions. It is interesting also that two major figures of contemporary African politics have also been poets. Léopold Sédar Senghor, until recently (1980) President of Senegal, is widely known as a francophone poet and an exponent of the concept of 'negritude'; Agostinho Neto (d.1980), the Angolan leader, acquired a reputation as a poet when he was still in exile fighting the Portuguese. The press release on Nigeria's former President Shagari included the information that he had a high reputation as a writer of Hausa poetry and Tanzania's President Nyerere has translated Shakespeare's *Julius Caeser* into Swahili.

The following two poems, the first translated from the French, illustrate two dominant themes of African political poetry: the concern for independence from the colonial powers and the conflict in Southern Africa. The Diop poem, written in the 1950s, presents the contrasting images of the past, the present and the future of Africa and ends on a note of sombre hope. The second poem is from the South African school of Soweto poets who seek to use poetry to raise popular Black consciousness and to register protest. It is cryptic and its wit has a cutting edge. Both poems to some extent make use of repetition to drive home a point. The first poem does so in the central section dealing with the experience of colonialism and it highlights 'blood', 'sweat', 'toil' and 'slavery' in this way. The poem by Serote focuses on the word 'crowd' (used as a verb) and he uses it to chart a change in attitude from passive acceptance to a more aggressive stance. A class could discuss to what extent the first poem is a romantic view of Africa. Opinion might be divided on the usefulness of political poetry.

Should it be attempted at all? Which British poets, popular verse-makers or song-writers — attempt to marry poetry and politics? What would the reaction be to the double image of the

'tree that grows
There splendidly alone among white and
    faded flowers?'

Example 1 *Africa*

Africa my Africa
Africa of proud warriors in the ancestral
    savannahs
Africa my grandmother sings of
Beside her distant river
I have never seen you
But my gaze is full of your blood
Your black blood spilt over the fields
The blood of your sweat
The sweat of your toil
The toil of slavery
The slavery of your children
Africa, tell me Africa,
Are you the back that bends
Lies down under the weight of humbleness?
The trembling back striped red
That says yes to the sjambok on the roads of
    noon?
Solemnly a voice answers me
Impetuous child, that young and sturdy tree
That tree that grows
There splendidly alone among white and
    faded flowers
Is Africa, your Africa. It puts forth new shoots
With patience and stubbornness puts forth
    new shoots
Slowly its fruits grow to have
The bitter taste of liberty.

David Diop (Senegal)[2]

Example 2 *The Growing*

If you crowd me I'll retreat from you
If you still crowd me I'll think a bit,
Not about crowding you but about your right
    to crowd me;
If you still crowd me, I will not, but I will
    think
About crowding you.

Wally Mongane Serote (South Africa)[3]

Another theme explored by African poets is that of the clash of cultures between Africa and the West. A number of Gabriel Okara's poems deal with this near-cliché subject in a complex and original way. His poem 'Piano and Drums' compares the conflicting associations evoked by:

jungle drums telegraphing
the mystic rhythm, urgent, raw
like bleeding flesh
. . . a wailing piano
solo speaking of complex ways
in tear-furrowed concerto.[4]

The poem sets out the conflict but does not give any easy answers to it.

Okara's 'You Laughed and Laughed and Laughed' and 'The Snowflakes Sail Gently Down' also explore what he regards as the fundamental differences in attitude between Africa and the West. Again he avoids clichés and generalities. The former poem sets out the conflict as a confrontation between two people, one a sceptical Westerner:

You laughed at my song
You laughed at my walk

and the poet whose own laughter:

is the fire
of the eye of the sky, the fire
of the earth, the fire of the air,
the fire of the seas and the
rivers fishes animals trees.[5]

'The Snowflakes Sail Gently Down' uses the device of a dream to introduce symbols of vitality which for the poet represent African values. Contrasted with the symbols of natural vitality are the flaccid 'uprooters' who value only the 'brightness of gold'. When he awakes, his awareness of the winter scene is coloured by the powerful symbols of his dream. He is able to see the landscape as a reflection of his own African sensibilities rather than a totally alien thing. The poem could fit into work with a senior class on 'culture clash' or 'the poet and landscape' where it might be compared with, for instance, poems by the Anglo-Welsh poet R.S. Thomas. It could be used in a discussion of how people react to a totally different environ-ment: do they feel total alienation, or adapt or begin to see that the place has unexpected similarities with their old· home? Okara's poetic techniques also provide plenty of scope for discussion: there is the comparison of his treatment of the winter scene in the first and third stanzas; his use of figurative language, including the daring dream symbolism; his use of alliteration and assonance and his control of his chosen medium, free verse.

Example 3 The Snowflakes Sail Gently Down

The snowflakes sail gently
down from the misty eye of the sky
and fall lightly on the
winter-weary elms. And the branches,
winter-stripped and nude, slowly
with the weight of the weightless snow
bow like grief-stricken mourners
as white funeral cloth is slowly
unrolled over deathless earth.
And dead sleep stealthily from the
heater rose and closed my eyes with
the touch of silk cotton of water falling.

Then I dreamed a dream
in my dead sleep. But I dreamed
not of earth dying and elms a vigil
keeping. I dreamed of birds, black
birds flying in my insides, nesting
and hatching on oil palms bearing suns
for fruits and with roots tending the
uprooters' spades. And I dreamed the
uprooters tired and limp, leaning on my
roots –
their abandoned roots –
and the oil palms gave them each a sun.
But on their palms
they balanced the blinding orbs
and frowned with schisms on their
brows – for the suns reached not
the brightness of gold!

Then I awoke. I awoke
to the silent falling snow
and bent-backed elms bowing and
swaying to the winter wind like

white-robed Moslems salaaming at evening
prayer, and the earth lying inscrutable
like the face of a god in a shrine.

Gabriel Okara (Nigeria) [6]

Poetry concerned with the seasons features frequently in contemporary writing and could be used as an independent African unit or included in a wider category of nature poetry. J.P. Clark's 'Night Rain' evokes not only the sensations of a storm during the West African rainy season but gives a clear impression of a village household caught in the rain's power. The poem is written from the viewpoint of a young boy. He hears rather than sees his mother:

Although it is so dark
I know her practised step as
She moves her bins, bags and vats
Out of the run of water
That like ants filing out of the wood
Will scatter and gain possession
Of the floor. Do not tremble then
But turn, brothers, turn upon your side
Of the loosening mats
To where the others lie. [7]

Other poems which evoke a strong sense of nature in an African context are the Ghanaian poet Kwesi Brew's 'The Dry Season' and David Rubadiri's 'An African Thunderstorm'.

In the work of a number of poets writing in English, French or Portuguese the influence of various oral traditions of poetry is strong. The Ugandan writer Okot p'Bitek has integrated Acholi imagery and even the words of Acholi songs into his long poem *Song of Lawino*. Heron gives the following lines as an example of Okot's borrowing from an Acholi song: Lawino is advising her husband on how to seek forgiveness from the ancestors once he has thrown off his churlish modern arrogance:

Beg forgiveness from them
And ask them to give you
A new spear
A new spear with a sharp and hard point
A spear that will crack the rock
Ask for a spear that you will trust.

Other poets incorporate into their work a familiar feature of oral poetry such as praise names. Thus the Ghanaian Kofi Awoonor includes in his poem 'My uncle the diviner-chieftain' a series of praise names to his uncle:

'the godlike ram of sacrifices,
the only tree of the homestead now, occupant
and regent of an ancient honour house.'

Other poets such as Kofi Anyidoho and Atukwei Okai of Ghana set great store on the performance of their own work, so stressing their links with oral poetry. Anyidoho has uncles who are poets working in the oral tradition and he is able to turn to them for advice on his own different yet related poetry.

Contemporary African poetry is therefore very much a two-pronged affair with both oral and written traditions contributing to its vigour. If teachers can include African material in classroom work it should expand pupils' awareness of the craft of poetry, it could also provide a chance to use music, African music, with poetry. Such poetry should also provide insight – sometimes an uncomfortable insight – into African experience.

Some useful anthologies

See the texts listed in Unit 12. Also:
E. Finnegan and **B. Mahoney**, *Essential Poetry, A Guided Course*, Heinemann, 1981.
An anthology of African and mainstream English poetry based on the West African exam syllabus. Includes careful analysis of poems. Very useful for British schools.
Gerald Moore and **Ulli Beier** (eds), *Modern Poetry from Africa*, Penguin, 1963.
A little dated now but still an excellent collection with translations from the French and Portuguese included.
Donatus Ibe Nwoga (ed.), *West African Verse: an Anthology*, Longman, 1967.
To some extent superseded by the wider-ranging Senanu and Vincent anthology (see Unit 12). It has helpful annotations and comment, though.
J. Reed and **C. Wake** (eds), *A Book of African Verse*, Heinemann (African Writers Series 8), 1964.
Includes a strong section on francophone poets, brief biographical details and notes.
English Speaking Africa Cassette 10. (See Unit 12) includes some poetry.

Notes

[1] From K.E. Senamu and T. Vincent (eds), *A Selection of African Poetry*, Longman, 1976, p.93.
[2] From Gerald Moore and Ulli Beier (eds), *Modern Poetry from Africa*, Penguin African Library, revised edition 1968, pp.63–4. Reprinted by permission of Penguin Books.
[3] From R. Royston (ed.), *Black Poets in South Africa*, Heinemann (African Writers Series 164), 1977, p.77.
[4] From Gabriel Okara, *The Fisherman's Invocation*, Heinemann (African Writers Series 183), 1978, p.20.
[5] Okara, *op. cit.*, pp.24–5.
[6] Okara, *op. cit.*, pp.30–31.
[7] K.E. Senamu and T. Vincent, *op. cit.*, p.139.
[8] K.E. Senamu and T. Vincent, *op. cit.*, p.155.

Dagoretti bus stop, Kenya (Ted O'Connor)

Section 2   Themes from African Literature: An Anthology

Herdsman with Ankole cattle, Uganda   (Vicky Unwin)

Relationships

Mother and son

The author sees his mother for the first time after the ceremony of circumcision.

By the third week, I was allowed to see my mother. When one of the younger men came and said my mother was at the door, I leapt to my feet.

'Here, not so fast,' he said, taking me by the hand. 'Wait for me.'

'All right, but hurry.'

Three weeks! Never before had we been separated from each other for so long. When I used to go on holiday to Tindican, I would seldom stay away longer than ten or fifteen days, and that was not to be compared with the length of our present separation.

'Well, are you coming?' I cried.

I was quivering with impatience.

'Listen,' said the young man. 'Listen first of all to what I have to say. You are going to see your mother, you are allowed to see her; but you must stand within the fence when speaking to her; you must not go beyond the fence.'

'I'll stay inside the fence,' I said. 'Just let me go.'

And I tried to shake off his hand.

'We'll go together,' he said.

He had not let go of my hand. We left the hut together. The gate in the fence was open. Several of the young men were sitting on the threshold; they signalled to me not to go beyond it. With a few swift strides I covered the few yards that separated me from the gate, and suddenly I saw my mother. She was standing in the dusty road a few steps away from the fence; she, too, was forbidden to come any closer.

'Mother!' I cried. 'Mother!'

And all at once I felt a lump in my throat. Was it because I could go no closer, because I could not hug my mother? Was it because we had already been separated so long, because we were still to be separated a long time? I do not know. All I know is that I could only say 'Mother!' and that after my joy in seeing her I suddenly felt a strange depression. Ought I to attribute this emotional instability to the transformation that had been worked in me? When I had left my mother, I was still a child. Now . . . But was I really a man now? Was I already a grown man? . . . I *was* a man! Yes, I was a grown man. And now this manhood had already begun to stand between my mother and myself. It kept us infinitely further apart than the few yards that separated us now.

'Mother!' I said again.

But this time I spoke it very low, like a lament, sadly, as if it were a lament for myself.

'Yes, here I am,' said my mother. 'I've come to see you.'

'Yes, you've come to see me.'

And suddenly I passed from sadness to joy. What was I worrying about? My mother was there. She was here in front of me. I only had to go a couple of steps and I would be at her side; I would certainly have done so if there had not been that absurd order forbidding me to go beyond the gate.

'I am glad to see you,' went on my mother. She smiled.

from *The African Child* by Camara Laye, translated from the French by James Kirkup, Collins (Fontana) 1965, p.108.

Boy on a Swing

Slowly he moves
to and fro, to and fro,
then faster and faster
he swishes up and down.

His blue shirt
billows in the breeze
like a tattered kite.

The world whirls by:
east becomes west,
north turns to south;
the four cardinal ponts
meet in his head.

Mother!
Where did I come from?
When will I wear long trousers?
Why was my father jailed?

© Mbuyiseni Oswald Mtshali 1971.
From *Sounds of a Cowhide Drum*, 1971.
Reprinted by permission of
Oxford University Press, 1971.

Mourning a dead child

Isatou died
When she was only five
And full of pride
Just before she knew
How small a loss
It brought to such a few.
Her mother wept
Half grateful
To be so early bereft.
And did not see the smile
As tender as the root
Of the emerging plant
Which sealed her eyes.
The neighbours wailed
As they were paid to do
And thought how big a spread
Might be her wedding too.
The father looked at her
Through marble eyes and said:
'Who spilt the perfume
Mixed with the morning dew?'

Lenrie Peters, *Selected Poetry*, Heinemann
(African Writers Series 238), 1981.

Lost and among strangers

*A small Yoruba boy finds himself in an
army barracks with an English officer and
a Hausa sergeant.*

I was tired, I was sure of that now. The
thought of running away at once when the
man looked up, saw me, pointed and said
something to the sergeant therefore remained
just a thought. I had no idea in which direction to run. The sergeant also looked up,
turned and began to march towards me. I
probably would have run then, tiredness and
all, but the white officer restrained him and
came forward himself, the sergeant following
close. Instinctively I backed one step towards
the gate, but the man smiled, held out both
hands in a gesture I did not quite understand,
and approached. When he had come quite
close, he bent down and, using the most unlikely accent I had ever heard asked,
'Kini o fe nibi yen?'[1]
I knew the words were supposed to be in
my own language but they made no sense to
me, so I looked at the sergeant helplessly and
said,
'I don't understand. What is he saying?'
The officer's eyes opened wide. 'Oh, you
speak English.'
I nodded.
'Good. That is venhrry clenver. I was asking,
what do you want? What can I doon for you?'
'I want to go home.'
He exchanged looks with the Sergeant.
'Well, that seems vum-vum-vum. And where
is home?'
I could not understand why he should
choose to speak through his nose. It made it
difficult to understand him all the time but by
straining hard, I could make sense of his
questions. I told him that I lived in Aké.
'It has a big church,' I added, 'just outside
our walls.'
'Ah-ah, near the church. Tell me, whazn-
name?' I guessed that he was asking what my
name was, so I told him. 'My name is Wole.'
'Wonlay. Good. And your father's name?'

[1] Literally: what do you want there?

'My father's name is Headmaster.'

'What?'

'My father's name is Headmaster. Sometimes his name is Essay.'

For some reason this amused him immensely, which I found offensive. There was no reason why my father's name should be the cause for such laughter. But the Sergeant has reacted differently. His eyes nearly popped out of his head. I noticed then that he was very different from the grown-ups whom I had seen around. He had long marks on his face, quite different from the usual kind we encountered in Aké. And when he spoke, his voice sounded like that of the Hausa traders who brought wares to our house for bartering with old clothes and strange assortments of items. It was a strange procedure, one which made little sense to me. They spread their wares in front of the house and I had to be prised off them. There were brass figures, horses, camels, trays, bowls, ornaments. Human figures spun on a podium, balanced by weights at the end of curved light metal rods. We spun them round and round, yet they never fell off their narrow perch. The smell of fresh leather filled the house as pouffes, handbags, slippers and worked scabbards were unpacked. There were bottles encased in leather, with leather stoppers, amulets on leather thongs, scrolls, glass beads, bottles of scent with exotic names – I never forgot, from the first moment I read it on the label – Bint el Sudan, with its picture of a turbanned warrior by a kneeling camel. A veiled maiden offered him a bowl of fruits. They looked unlike anything in the Orchard and Essay said they were called dates. I did not believe him; dates were the figures which appeared on a calendar on the wall, so I took it as one of his jokes.

Once or twice my father tried to offer money but the trader proved difficult. 'No, I can like to take changey-changey.' Out came old shirts, trousers, discarded jackets with holes under the armpit, yet Changey-changey – as we now called him – actually received these clothing derelicts in return for his genuine 'morocco' leather. 'Look 'am master, a no be lie. Look, genuine morocco leather. 'E fit you, big man like you must have leather brief-case for carry file. 'E be genuine. Put 'am one more shirt. Or torosa.'

Their voices were so similar that they could only be brothers. I was even more convinced of it when I heard him say, 'If na headmaster of Aké be in father, I sabbe the place. But what 'im doing here?'

They both turned to me. I had no answer to the question. Then the white man asked, 'Are you lost?'

'I followed the band,' I replied.

The officer nodded sagely, as if everything had fallen in place. He turned to the sergeant and asked him to get his bicycle. The man saluted and went off. Something continued to puzzle the officer however. He put his hand on my shoulder and guided me towards the office.

'How old are you?'

'I am four years and a half.'

He let out a loud 'What!', stopped, and looked at me again. 'Are you sure?' I nodded. He looked at me more closely, said, 'Yes of course. Of course. And you walked from Aké? Where did you start from?'

'At the cenotaph. There were other children, but they left me.'

We reached his office and he lifted me on to a chair. 'Are you thirsty?' already producing a bottle of orange squash. There was a jar of water on the table and he mixed me a drink in a glass. I drank it to the last drop.

'Do you want another glass?' He did not wait for the reply before mixing another and handing it to me. It followed its predecessor just as rapidly. I began to feel better. I looked round the office for the first time. I recognized a journal on it which came very week to my father. I looked at the man with greater interest.

'You are reading my father's paper.'

He looked startled, 'Which one?'

'That one. In Leisure Hours.'

'Really! You say it's your father's paper?'

'Yes. He has a new one every week.'

He opened it rapidly, looking for something on its pages. 'You mean he is the editor?

I could not understand him. I repeated, 'He has it every week.'

And then the man grinned and nodded. 'I see, I see.'

I was feeling drowsy. The Sergeant arrived with his bicycle. Half-awake, I felt myself lifted on to the cross-bar and the bumpy ride began. I barely sensed the arrival back home, hands lifting me up, passing me to other arms. My head appeared to weigh a ton when I tried to come awake and respond to the babble of voices I heard around me. I felt the immense expanse of the bed in mother's bedroom coming up to meet me, the room easily recognized by the smell of ori [1]-and-camphor. Then I dropped into oblivion.

> from *Aké, the Years of Childhood*,
> by Wole Soyinka, Rex Collings, 1981,
> pp.46–9.

Preparations for a marriage

Obierika's compound was as busy as an ant-hill. Temporary cooking tripods were erected on every available space by bringing together three blocks of sun-dried earth and making a fire in their midst. Cooking pots went up and down the tripods, and foo-foo was pounded by a hundred wooden mortars. Some of the women cooked the yams and the cassava, and others prepared vegetable soup. Young men pounded the foo-foo or split firewood. The children made endless trips to the stream.

Three young men helped Obierika to slaughter the two goats with which the soup was made. They were very fat goats, but the fattest of all was tethered to a peg near the wall of the compound. It was as big as a small cow. Obierika had sent one of his relatives all the way to Umuike to buy that goat. It was the one he would present alive to his in-laws.

'The market of Umuike is a wonderful place,' said the young man who had been sent by Obierika to buy the giant goat. 'There are so many people on it that if you threw up a grain of sand it would not find a way to fall to earth again.'

'It is the result of a great medicine,' said Obierika. 'The people of Umuike wanted their market to grow and swallow up the markets of their neighbours. So they made a powerful medicine. Every market-day, before the first cock-crow, this medicine stands on the market-ground in the shape of an old woman with a fan. With this magic fan she beckons to the market all the neighbouring clans. She beckons in front of her and behind her, to her right and to her left.' . . .

Early in the afternoon the first two pots of palm-wine arrived from Obierika's in-laws. They were duly presented to the women, who drank a cup or two each, to help them in their cooking. Some of it also went to the bride and her attendant maidens, who were putting the last delicate touches of razor to her coiffure and cam wood on her smooth skin.

When the heat of the sun began to soften, Obierika's son, Maduka, took a long broom and swept the ground in front of his father's *obi*. And as if they had been waiting for that, Obierika's relatives and friends began to arrive, every man with his goatskin bag hung on one shoulder and a rolled goatskin mat under his arm. Some of them were accompanied by their sons bearing carved wooden stools. Okonkwo was one of them. They sat in a half circle and began to talk of many things. It would not be long before the suitors came . . .

Very soon after, the in-laws began to arrive. Young men and boys in single file, each carrying a pot of wine, came first. Obierika's relatives counted the pots as they came in. Twenty, twenty-five. There was a long break, and the hosts looked at each other as if to say, 'I told you.' Then more pots came. Thirty, thirty-five, forty, forty-five. The hosts nodded in approval and seemed to say, 'Now they are behaving like men.' Altogether there were fifty pots of wine. After the pot-bearers came Ibe, the suitor, and the elders of his family. They sat in a half-moon, thus completing a circle with their hosts. The pots of wine stood in their midst. Then the bride, her mother and

[1] shea-butter

half a dozen other women and girls emerged from the inner compound, and went round the circle shaking hands with all. The bride's mother led the way, followed by the bride and the other women. The married women wore their best clothes and the girls wore red and black waist-beads and anklets of brass.

When the women retired, Obierika presented kola nuts to his in-laws. His eldest brother broke the first one. 'Life to all of us,' he said as he broke it. 'And let there be friendship between your family and ours.'

The crowd answered: *'Ee-e-e!'*

'We are giving you our daughter today. She will be a good wife to you. She will bear you nine sons like the mother of our town.'

'Ee-e-e!'

The oldest man in the camp of the visitors replied: 'It will be good for you and it will be good for us.'

'Ee-e-e!'

'This is not the first time my people have come to marry your daughter. My mother was one of you.'

'Ee-e-e!'

'And this will not be the last, because you understand us and we understand you. You are a great family.'

'Ee-e-e!'

'Prosperous men and great warriors.' He looked in the direction of Okonkwo. 'Your daughter will bear us sons like you.'

'Ee-e-e!'

The kola was eaten and the drinking of palm-wine began. Groups of four or five men sat round with a pot in their midst. As the evening wore on, food was presented to the guests. There were huge bowls of foo-foo and steaming pots of soup. There was also pots of yam pottage. It was a great feast.

As night fell, burning torches were set on wooden tripods and the young men raised a song. The elders sat in a big circle and the singers went round singing each man's praise as they came before him. They had something to say for every man. Some were great farmers, some were orators who spoke for the clan; Okonkwo was the greatest wrestler and warrior alive. When they had gone round the circle they settled down in the centre, and girls came from the inner compound to dance. At first the bride was not among them. But when she finally approached holding a cock in her right hand, a loud cheer rose from the crowd. All the other dancers made way for her. She presented the cock to the musicians and began to dance. Her brass anklets rattled as she danced and her body gleamed with cam wood in the soft yellow light. The musicians with their wood, clay and metal instruments went from song to song. And they were all gay. They sang the latest song in the village:

> 'If I hold her hand
> She says, "Don't touch!"
> If I hold her foot
> She says, "Don't touch!"
> But when I hold her waist beads
> She pretends not to know.'

The night was already far spent when the guests rose to go, taking their bride home to spend seven market weeks with her suitor's family. They sang songs as they went, and on their way they paid short courtesy visits to prominent men like Okonkwo, before they finally left for their village. Okonkwo made a present of two cocks to them.

From *Things Fall Apart*, by Chinua Achebe, Heinemann (African Writers Series 1), 1967, pp.80, 82–3.

Teach me to dance!

A ball marks the end of a week of wedding festivities and Safi learns to dance.

In preparation for the ball I shut myself up for hours on end in the boys' room, with Karim's belt round my waist, while my brothers taught me to dance. I don't know where they had learnt to do the bolero, the swing, the quick-step and the tango; it was certainly not in our house, but they were perfect dancers. The lesson often ended in tears; I was quite light on my feet but I was so impatient to learn that I mixed all the steps up. My brothers made fun of me.

'Instead of pulling your waist in like a wasp and waggling your hips like a duck, you'd do better to watch where your feet are going. You stump around without listening to the music. Try to follow the beat . . .'

These sessions became a torture, but I endured it all; I needed their expertise . . .

Early on the day of the dance the boys brought home a gramophone to try out the records. Then the concrete yard was thoroughly washed down, chairs set round and the bride's table decorated with flowers and cakes. I wondered who Ami would open the ball with; her husband was a marabout's disciple of the strict *Tijan* sect — he never wore European clothes and had nothing to do with 'modern' young people. There were many students on holiday from France, easily recognisable by their stiff collars, three-quarter length jackets and thick-soled, high-heeled shoes. Whether ugly or handsome, they played havoc with all the girls' hearts. It was a status symbol for a girl to have a 'sweetheart in France'. France was the distant *alma mater* of every Dakar schoolboy.

At five o'clock Ami had the first dance with one of my brother's friends. It was hot. Powdered faces began to stream with perspiration. Hair which had been straightened with hot irons, curled and plastered down with pomade, began to flop over the head like cold pancakes. Carefully waved coiffures were ruined as their owners sweated, and fanned themselves with their handkerchiefs. The boys in their starched collars, stiff as pokers, could hardly turn their heads and looked as if they were suffering from torticollis. We younger girls sat in a corner with Marie-Louise, passing remarks about some of the outfits and laughing our heads off at them. We tried to deduce the degree of romantic involvement of the couples, according to the more or less moony way they danced. My brother put on my favourite record, 'Habanera'. I was itching to dance; I could not keep my feet still. We had been warned: on no account were we to venture onto the dance floor. Still, I didn't look so young with my face made up and my waist drawn in with a tight sash. I could pass for the same age as some of my cousin's friends.

Mass, a friend of my brother's, who was studying in France, came up to us.

'Well, well! If it isn't Safi! How she has grown!'

I summoned up all my courage, pulled in my waist, poked out my flat chest on which two potatoes stuffed inside a scarf made up for my lack of bosom, and replied coquettishly, 'This is my favourite record. I want to dance with you.'

He took my hand and led me onto the dance floor. I can't describe my emotion. I bit my lip and concentrated hard, my legs stiff instead of supple, while perspiration ran down my thighs. I trembled in my partner's arms as I did my best to follow the music. My cousin's friends gazed at me with eyes like saucers.

When the record finished my partner led me gallantly back to my place, congratulating me on my dancing which, he said, 'was as good as the older girls'. It probably wasn't true, but the compliment made my evening for me.

About eight o'clock the guests left and the family had the floor to itself. I danced lightheartedly with Marie-Louise as none of the boys would dance with us. We were mere kids, they said. We took no notice of their sarcasm and gave ourselves over uninhibitedly to our own enjoyment.

from *A Dakar Childhood*, by Nafissatou Diallo, translated from the French by Dorothy Blair, Longman (Drumbeat 48), 1982, pp.68–70.

Education

A strict teacher

Once in school, we went straight to our seats, boys and girls sitting side by side, our quarrels over; and, as soon as we sat down, we became all ears, and sat absolutely still, so that the teacher used to give his lessons in an impressive silence. I should just like to have seen what would have happened if we had so much as stirred in our seats. Our teacher moved like quicksilver: he never remained long in the same place; he was here, there and everywhere. His flow of talk would have bewildered less attentive pupils. But we were remarkably attentive, and we found it no strain to be so. Young though we were, we all regarded our school work as something deadly serious. Everything we learned was strange and unexpected; it was as if we were learning about life on another planet; and we never grew tired of listening. Even if it had been otherwise, the silence could not have been more absolute under the strict discipline of a master who seemed to be everywhere at once and who would never have given us an opportunity to let our attention wander or to interrupt. But as I have said, an interruption was out of the question: it simply did not occur to us. And so we tried to attract the teacher's attention as little as possible: for we lived in constant dread of being sent out to the blackboard.

This blackboard was our nightmare. Its dark, blank mirror was the exact reflection of the amount of our knowledge. We knew very little, and the little we knew was very shaky: the slightest thing could upset it. Now if we did not want to be the recipients of several strokes of the cane, we had to go to the blackboard and take the chalk in our hands and pay our debt in kind. Here the tiniest detail was of the utmost importance: the wretched black-board magnified every mistake. If we made one of the downward strokes not exactly of the same height as the others, we were required either to do an extra lesson on Sunday, or we had to go to the teacher during break, and receive, in the class that was always known as the infants', an unforgettable beating on our bare backsides. Irregular downward strokes used to horrify our teacher: he would examine our exercise-books under a magnifying-glass, and for each irregularity he discovered we got a stroke. I remember him well, a man like quicksilver; and he wielded his stick with joyous abandon! . . .

from *The African Child*,
by Camara Laye, p.65.

Speech Day

The school was neat. And the people saw everything in it, the outcome of their own efforts, the symbol of their defiance of foreign ways.

They went round the school admiring the well-mudded building. Here and there on the compound were little flower gardens whose general immaculate look was the talk of all. The parents saw this as the fruits of their labour, their sweat and patience. Their children could speak a foreign language, could actually read and write. And this had been done in spite of Siriana's stern action in refusing to admit the children of those who would not abandon the ancient rites.

Waiyaki, along with his colleagues, was most attentive. He mixed with the people and took them to various places, outlining his plans, obviously campaigning for his schemes before the real test came. People admired him. They liked the way he so freely mingled and the way he talked. He had a word for everyone and a smile for all. He pleased many. But not everybody. At such moments jealousy and ill-will are bound to work . . .

The meeting was scheduled to begin early. But old men always took their time. So the meeting actually started in the afternoon. Waiyaki opened the proceedings amid great silence. Though his voice was calm, his heart beat inside him. He feared the number of eyes in front of him. After the first few words he announced that the children would sing some songs of welcome. Waiyaki had not made up the songs. He had first been taught them in Siriana by a boy from the country beyond. But to the parents and the teachers who gathered there that day they were something new, something that strangely stirred their hearts and said what they felt.

Father, mother
Provide me with pen and slate
I want to learn.
Land is gone
Cattle and sheep are not there
Not there any more
What's left?
Learning, learning.

Father, if you had many cattle and sheep
I would ask for a spear and shield,
But now –
I do not want a spear
I do not want a shield
I want the shield and spear of learning.

from *The River Between*,
by Ngugi wa Thiong'o, Heinemann
(African Writers Series 17), 1965, pp.91, 93.

Education and language: French versus the indigenous languages, and creole

Climbié, at school in the Ivory Coast, has been caught speaking N'zima on school premises and is given the token of disgrace, 'the little wooden cube'.

Around Climbié, who had just been given the 'token', Dahoman students mixed with their Eburnean comrades, and swaying their shoulders, sang:

You spoke Fanti, you get the token,
Ha! Ha! You get the token.
You spoke Agni, you get the token,
Ha! Ha! You get the token.

Some of them had hoops and satchels with shoulder-straps, and others carried their books in their hands; all of them, moving in and out, circling about him, blurted in his ears:

You spoke Baoulé, you get the token,
Ha! Ha! You get the token.

The Headmaster stood in the doorway, smiling. . .

The collective sabotage of the French language was indeed a terrible thing. Everywhere one heard pidgin versions of a language which is so refined, airy, and feminine, a language which is like down floating in the breeze or the words a sweetheart whispers in your ear, a language resembling the soft murmur of a madonna, a language which leaves behind it a memory of melody! Instead of this, in the conversations with natives, all along the social ladder from boy to interpreter – with scullion and cook, washerwoman, worker, *garde-cercle*, farmer – one constantly heard such barbarisms as:

Moi y a dis, lui y a pas content.
Ma commandant, mon femme, ma fils.

And also, words and expressions whose origin you could never hope to find in Littré or Larousse: '*Manigola . . . Foutou-moi la camp.*'

What sanction could be invoked against individuals who trifled so wantonly with a language as rich, flowing, and diplomatic as French? against those obstinate individuals who never conjugated verbs correctly and who refused to use the time-honoured gender? How many times a day did one hear '*Je partis*' for '*Je pars*', and '*le mangue*' for '*la mangue*'? . .

This distressing situation certainly could not continue. It only caused bitterness on both sides. A remedy had to be found. Hence the decision to outlaw the use of dialects in the primary schools. It was intended in that way, and quickly, to fashion true men, men who would keep true north in all weathers. Well-oriented men, with feet firmly planted in their homeland, but not weathercocks, shifting with the slightest breeze . . .

The decision was therefore made, and circulars were distributed to all corners of the bush and even to the smallest village schools. 'The speaking of dialects on school property is hereby forbidden.' It was precise. The zones were clearly demarcated. On that day was born the token – a piece of wood, a box of matches, anything. It was entrusted to the top student in the class, whose duty it was to give it immediately to anyone caught speaking his own dialect. From the day the token first appeared, a coldness settled over the school. The students sang as well at the beginning of classes as they did at the end, but without the same abandon, the same gusto, the same fire. And the breaks, once so happy and loud, the breaks waited for impatiently during a lesson poorly understood or when the mind wandered back to an unfinished game of ball, the breaks which reminded one of a bird-cage suddenly thrown open, they too, alas, felt the effects of the new rule. In place of the carefree mingling, the noisy revels and frantic chases, the fights during which dialect was spoken fluently, as if this gave courage, one now saw only small groups of boys whispering timidly, distrusting any person who passed nearby or sat next to them as if by chance. At such times it was always advisable to strike camp. This person would take the liberty of speaking in, say, the Agni dialect; whoever answered him would answer suspiciously in French.

But to a friend, without distrust, you spoke your own dialect. Cheerfully and at once, he would give you the token.

That afternoon Climbié was the first to return to school. Lying down in the sand, he pretended to be asleep. The others returned alone or in small, talkative groups. Climbié was lying in wait for a victim.

from *Climbié*, by Bernard Dadié, translated from the French by Karen Chapman, Heinemann (African Writers Series 87), 1971, pp.11–15.

Literacy classes and political action

A group of educated women in Abeokuta ('gown wearers') start self-help and literacy classes for their illiterate sisters ('wrapper wearers'), mostly market women, with unexpected results.

'Do you know the real trouble with the *aróso*?[1] They are illiterate. They don't know how to read and write, that is why they get exploited. If you set aside half an hour at these meetings, you could end up making all the women in Egbaland literate by the end of the year!'[2] He chuckled at his own wild optimism, strolled on.

The idea was taken. Mama Aduni and the handful of *aróso* who had by now joined the Group were told to spread the word. Slates and markers were bought, pencils and exercise books. When the trickle became a flood, they shifted into the courtyard. Each *onikaba*[3] took on a group which she coached intensely for half-hour to an hour at each meeting. Then, while the discussions continued on hygiene, community development, self-help programmes, market and commodity prices, they continued to copy the letters, the figures, pausing only to join in the talking. From the top of the balcony, one saw only a series of backs humped in concentration, topped by headties which showed in some cases, wads of white hair. For that first half-hour they worked in almost total silence with sudden outbursts of laughter, laboriously making one stroke, then another. Often it was Wild Christian's[4] bantering voice which caused the laughter. She would for instance, seize an agonized hand in hers and guide it along the slate, instructing loudly:

'Like this. Look, put down this stick, no no, make it a straight piece of wood like an electric pole not a crooked one. Or do you think it's your husband's leg you are drawing? Now, put something like a curving road on it

[1] Wrapper wearers
[2] Daouda Ransome-Kuti, Principal of Abeokuta Grammar School, is the speaker
[3] Gown wearers
[4] The author's mother

– no, no, not like that. Don't you even know what your belly looks like when you and your husband have been getting up to God knows what? En-hen. I knew that would do it. Now that is a "b". One electric pole, and your big belly resting at the bottom of it – "b" bente-bente . . . asikun bente-bente . . .bente-bente, asikun bente-bente . . .' moving smoothly into an improvised song-and-dance.

The courtyard erupted with laughter while Mama Aduni or the white-haired lady went and dragged her away complaining, 'For a teacher's wife, you are remarkably good at disrupting the concentration of pupils!'

They were keen pupils, mostly young, and it was these keen ones who set in motion in Igbein, the Great Upheaval that ended in Aké. They were always the first to arrive, they helped in setting up the benches and chairs, sweeping the yard when necessary, getting in an extra hour of practice to themselves before the others arrived. . . And then they stopped coming; even to the main session they would come late. Sometimes they never turned up at all. It was not only the eager pupils, there were others too, and not only from the suburbs. It was harvest time; these were mostly farmers' wives, so the leaders assumed for a while that the chores of the farms kept them away. They took their places with apologies, tried to catch up on their lessons as the meeting progressed. Finally however the right question was asked, or the leaders listened more keenly to those excuses that the late comers mumbled through an ongoing debate. The gatherings of mutual self-improvement changed character from that moment when one voice followed the other to explain:

'I was arrested by the Tax people.'

'The *Parakoyi*[5] took half of my farm produce for market toll. I went to the local councillors to seek their help.'

'We were waylaid on the way to the farm. The Local Police asked us to contribute one-fifth of every item as duty.'

'I tried to dodge the uniformed men. I turned into a path I thought I knew and got lost. Only God saved me or I would still be wandering in the forests.'

'They have no heart, those men. They look at you like they have no flesh and blood until you give them what they want.'

'We spent the night in a police cell. They seized all our goods and will continue to hold them until we bring them our Tax papers. But we have not even been to the market, how can we pay when they have taken the goods we are going to sell?'

'It is those chiefs. They are in this together. They set the *adana*[6] to do their dirty work because they daren't levy a toll on farm produce.'

'No, it's the Alake; I heard one of the *adana* say we shouldn't complain to him. "Go to Kabiyesi who sent us," he said.'

'Our own tormentors said it was the white man. He said the order came to the *ajele*[7] from his fellow white man in Lagos. They are just servants of the white man in Lagos.'

'ENOUGH!' . . .

'Enough!' Kemberi repeated and the murmurs of indignation began to subside. 'What you are all saying in so many words, is that the women of Egbaland are no longer free to walk the streets of their own land, or pursue their living from farm to home and farm to market without being molested by these blood-suckers – am I right?'

'What else have we been saying?'

She held up her hands, then turned to Mrs Ransome-Kuti. 'Beere, you heard them. What are we doing about it? You said, teach them ABD; we have been doing that. And we also said to them, give your children a clean home, and strain every bone in your body to give them a good education. And they have been doing that. It is because of these children that they refuse to sit at home, waiting for some idle drunkard of a husband to learn the same lesson. After all, the women of Egbaland are not unaccustomed to hard work. But now we gave them a new reason – their children. And they began to work and they gave their little

---

[5] Market wardens
[6] Agents who waylay farmers or market women
[7] An administering agent, thus, the District Officer

savings to the education of their children. And because of the little we have learnt together, these good-for-nothing children no longer come home and lie that they have come first in class when all they have been doing is staying away from school and scoring the round, fish-eye of Zero. At least, some of us now know the difference between 100 and Zero, between 1st and 34th. When the school report comes home, even if some of our women cannot read everything, they can read enough on that card to know if that child is wasting their money. And if they cannot read, they know where they can bring the card – right HERE!

'Now these same women are telling us that they can no longer come here freely. The streets of Egba are blocked by the very people against whom we have tried to give them protection. Tax! Tax on what? What is left after the woman has fed children, put school uniform on his back and paid his school fees? Just what are they taxing?'

A roar went up from outraged voices.

from *Aké, the Years of Childhood*,
by Wole Soyinka, pp.181–3.

The Land

Jeri refuses to plant yams, in spite of his sister, and prefers to trade in palm oil.

People had long given her the praise-name 'Adaobi,' which meant that among women, she was outstandingly well-bred and respectable. She had also retained her forthright speech, crying out hoarsely against those things that wounded her susceptibilities, of which her brother's oil trade was one. Onugo would want him to go and till the soil and plant yams year in year out, in the tradition of all the great families of Obange and around. Yams! Yams! Yams! With her, it was yams every time.

Had he not spent many years in the past cultivating that crop? And what had he in the end? Definitely not anything that would enable anybody to rear his children the way he was doing. And that, with all the labour which went into it! You cut the bush until your palms were scarred and gnarled and blistered. Next, you burnt and cleared the remains, and removed the stumps. Then came the most strenuous of all the farming activities, which was mound-making. Bending down into an arc, with the hoe between your feet, you made hundreds of mounds in a single day; your back ached and sweat dripped from all over your body and you smelt the acrid smell of damp earth. You planted the seedlings; you mulched, staked, and tended the vines. If you were unlucky, heavy rains would come in succession, washing off the richness of the soil, or a parasitic growth would sap the tubers, or beetles would burrow into them, or a long spell of dry weather would cause a premature withering of the leaves or decay of the tubers.

At each one of those stages you required labour — many hands, not just one man, or a man with only one wife. You engaged some stalwarts whom you must feast at the close of each day; and then, you worked for each of them in turn. Except, of course, if you had a large household of many wives and many children of whom the greater number were male. But that would not do for the harvest; the yams had to be conveyed home on adult, male heads, inside long rectangular baskets. Usually, the baskets were stuffed full to snapping point, with as many as twenty big tubers in each if you came from the fertile plain of Obezi. For the exercise, you required the strongest men available on the land. Their necks would be seen bulging under the weight while sweat streamed down their bodies; and they would ululate or groan, mostly in song, or call themselves inspiring names. At intervals, they would go into a trot. They would also adjust the weight on the pad from time to time in order to relieve the pressure on a particular part of the skull. And for most of the time, they would move with quick strides, supporting their aching necks with their forehands, so that their stomachs sank in while their chests swelled, and the ribs showed prominently and they looked like monstrous dragonflies . . . What came of it all in the end? Perhaps the mere satisfaction of having a rich harvest if you were lucky? Yam was the king of crops, they told you; therefore, you must plant it, even when you had very little land and the soil was known to be infertile, and you were perhaps not going to receive back from the earth much more than you had put into it. A thing like that would not do for a man who had to find a substantial amount of money regularly in order to keep his children — three children already and more to follow — at school. Let Onugo react the way she was doing; that was her nature after all.

from *Oil Man of Obange*, by John Munonye, Heinemann (African Writers Series 94), 1971, pp. 105–6.

Land, ownership, attachment

The different attitudes of two men, one an owner, the other a farm worker, to the same land.

Ngotho left early for work. He did not go through the fields as was his usual custom. Ngotho loved the rainy seasons when everything was green and the crops in flower, and the morning dew hung on the leaves. But the track where he had disturbed the plants and made the water run off made him feel as if, through his own fault, he had lost something. There was one time when he had felt a desire to touch the dew-drops or open one and see what it held hidden inside. He had trembled like a child but, after he had touched the drops and they had quickly lost shape melting into wetness, he felt ashamed and moved on. At times he was thankful to Murungu for no apparent reason as he went through these cultivated fields all alone while the whole country had a stillness. Almost like the stillness of death.

This morning he walked along the road — the big tarmac road that was long and broad and had no beginning and no end except that it went into the city. . . He passed through the African shops, near the barber's shop, and went on, on to the same place where he had now been for years, even before the second Big War took his two sons away to kill one and change the other.

Mr Howlands was up. He never slept much. Not like Memsahib who sometimes remained in bed until ten o'clock. She had not much else to do. There was something in Howlands, almost a flicker of mystery, that Ngotho could never fathom.

'Good morning, Ngotho.'

'Good morning, Bwana.'

'Had a good night?'

'Ndio Bwana.'

Ngotho was the only man Mr Howlands greeted in this fashion — a fashion that never varied. He spoke in the usual abstract manner as if his mind was preoccupied with something big. It was at any rate something that took all his attention. His mind was always directed towards the *shamba*. His life and soul were in the *shamba*. Everything else with him counted only in so far as it was related to the *shamba*. Even his wife mattered only in so far as she made it possible for him to work in it more efficiently without a worry about home. For he left the management of home to her and knew nothing about what happened there. If he employed someone in the house, it was only because his wife had asked for an extra 'boy'. And if she later beat the 'boy' and wanted him sacked, well, what did it matter? It was not just that the boys had black skins. The question of wanting to know more about his servants just never crossed his mind. . .

They went from place to place, a white man and a black man. Now and then they would stop here and there, examine a luxuriant green tea plant, or pull out a weed. Both men admired this *shamba*. For Ngotho felt responsible for whatever happened to this land. He owed it to the dead, the living and the unborn of his line, to keep guard over this *shamba*. Mr Howlands always felt a certain amount of victory whenever he walked through it all. He alone was responsible for taming this unoccupied wildness. They came to a raised piece of ground and stopped. The land sloped gently to rise again into the next ridge and the next. Beyond Ngotho could see the African Reserve.

'You like all this?' Mr Howlands asked absent-mindedly. He was absorbed in admiring the land before him.

'It is the best land in all the country,' Ngotho said emphatically. He meant it. Mr Howlands sighed. He was wondering if Stephen would ever manage it after him.

'I don't know who will manage it after me. . . .'

Ngotho's heart jumped. He too was thinking of his children. Would the prophecy be fulfilled soon?

'*Kwa nini Bwana*. Are you going back to – ?'

'No,' Mr Howlands said, unnecessarily loudly.

'. . . Your home, home. . . .'

'My home is here!'

Ngotho was puzzled. Would these people never go? But had not the old Gikuyu seer said that they would eventually return the way they had come? And Mr Howlands was thinking, Would Stephen really *do*? He was not like the other one. He felt the hurt and the pain of loss.

'The war took him away.'

Ngotho had never known where the other son had gone to. Now he understood. He wanted to tell of his own son: he longed to say, 'You took him away from me'. But he kept quiet. Only he thought Mr Howlands should not complain. It had been his war.

from *Weep Not, Child*, by Ngugi wa Thiong'o, Heinemann (African Writers Series 7), 1964, pp.29–32.

Questions to be answered

I Speak for the Bush

When my friend sees me
He swells and pants like a frog
Because I talk the wisdom of the bush!
He says we from the bush
Do not understand civilized ways
For we tell our women
To keep the hem of their dresses
Below the knee.
We from the bush, my friend insists,
Do not know how to 'enjoy':
When we come to the civilized city,
Like nuns, we stay away from nightclubs
Where women belong to no men
And men belong to no women
And these civilized people
Quarrel and fight like hungry lions!

But, my friend, why do men
With crippled legs, lifeless eyes,
Wooden legs, empty stomachs
Wander about the streets
Of this civilized world?

Teach me, my friend, the trick,
So that my eyes may not
See those whose houses have no walls
But emptiness all around;

Show me the wax you use
To seal your ears
To stop hearing the cry of the hungry;

Teach me the new wisdom
Which tells men
To talk about money and not love,
When they meet women;

Tell your God to convert
Me to the faith of the indifferent,
The faith of those
Who will never listen until
They are shaken with blows.

I speak for the bush:
You speak for the civilized –
Will you hear me?

Everett Standa, in *Poems from East Africa*, ed. D. Cook and D. Rubadiri, Heinemann (African Writers Series 96), 1971.

The barren land

A superior young man pays a farewell visit to his family, who are peasant farmers in Zimbabwe.

The sudden transition from the rolling ranches of Hampshire Estates, with their tall dry grass and the fertile soil under that grass, into the scorched nothing-between-here-and-the-horizon white lands of Manyene Tribal Trust Land, with the inevitable tattered scarecrow waving a silent dirge in an empty field, makes a funereal intrusion into the bus. And those who have been singing all the way from Salisbury with the drunken excitement of going home seem to be regretting their having come at all.

The last beer has been drunk just before crossing the last fence into Manyene and now the empty beer bottles and empty plastic gallon containers roll unheeded on the dusty floor of the bus as the people lean out of the windows to point out homes in a uniformly dead landscape. Except for the heat. The heat and the oasis-like clumps of gumtrees through which the shadow-dappled white walls of a school can be seen.

This is our country, the people say with a sad familiarity. The way an undertaker would talk of death, Lucifer thinks.

. . . And they are all covered with dust. Dust, dust, dust. It rises from the floorboards, swirls and eddies up to hit the roof, then curls and spreads downwards, creating a confusion of currents and counter-currents. Each time someone in front turns his face towards him, Lucifer holds back laughter. Their faces look like a child's drawing of a face on a grey wall – without any other lines, just dark circles for the main features: the two eyes, the nostrils and the mouth.

. . . The bus passes on, going east. It turns sharply south a mile farther on towards Chambara township. And the first disagreeable thing Lucifer sees in his home country, after an absence of two years, is an ox-drawn cart on the western skyline, barely moving, and the sound of wailing.

A funeral, he knows, but he can't bring himself to say it out loud.

At Chambara the bus stops again. Most people get down to buy cold drinks. Lucifer remains on the bus. He recognizes familiar faces but they seem much older. He can't fit any names to the faces, they remain just familiar anonymous faces. He is ashamed. He is supposed to know their names but he doesn't. An uneasiness – a feeling of not belonging – assails him. He lowers his head so that if anyone below should raise their heads, they won't see him.

The place looks deserted. And most of the buildings seem to have been pulled down. Or is it because of the absence of people? The butchery still stands – a cloud of flies circling it – so does the grinding mill and the two stores. But where are the people? From the bus, through the double doors of one of the shops, he can see the shopkeeper, alone in the middle of his assorted empire of hardware, cloth, food – fanning himself with a soiled handkerchief.

And further to the west is another building Lucifer hasn't seen before. The building is not yet complete but from its dull and blurred appearance, Lucifer knows that it has weathered one or two seasons of rain. He wonders whether it will survive this coming season.

A few words in the sun, with the engine idling, and the bus groans on.

Not until you cross Chambara River into the old village with roofless huts and gaping doorways and the smell of dog-shit and burnt rags are you at home. And then the signature of time truly appears in the work-scarred body of an abandoned oxcart with its shaft pointing an accusing finger at the empty heavens, and the inevitable stray dog – all ribs and the fur worn down to the sore skin – rummaging for something to eat among the ruins.

Not until you look towards the east and see the tall sun-bleached rocks of Manyene Hills casting foreboding shadows over the land beyond like sentinels over some fairy-tale land of the dead, are you really at home.

And here now the bus turns west, following the line of the old village, and you look across Suka – which has given up flowing – and see the line of the new village stretching like an interminable snake in the sun from the southern bank of the river, on and over the rim of the earth to the other end of the world, with the Ancient Rain Tree – now impotent – standing guard in an empty landscape.

Then, once more, the bus turns south and the driver switches off the engine for the mile-long roll into Suka. And now, with the engine off, you can hear just how the old thing shakes and rattles and always dust, dust and more dust, so that you see the heads of those sitting in front like figures appearing in a mist, silently, except for the coughing and sneezing, not complaining, resigned. 'It's been a long journey from the city and we are all so tired now and we are thinking of home as we get nearer and nearer but home seems to get farther and farther as one approaches. Lucifer's head sings.

. . . Lucifer pulls the bellrope.

The conductor, who had fallen asleep in the incredibly short run between this stop and the last one, opens his bloodshot eyes, yawns and asks as if he has got a grudge against Lucifer:

'Anything on top?'

'No.'

Lucifer looks ahead at the seemingly hundred-miles-long road and sees a figure frantically waving, signalling the bus to stop. And in the middle of the road too! And suddenly Lucifer recognizes his father. He strangles an impulse to tell the driver to move on to the next stop.

Not till the very last minute does this crazy figure jump off the road, all teeth and rolling eyes. The bus screeches to a stop.

The driver leans out of his window and shouts: 'Tired of living – heh, Mudhara?'

'You have got my son on this bus, haven't you?'

The driver doesn't answer, someone giggles, and a minute later Lucifer and his father are standing on the dust-clearing road in the strange silence following the departure of the bus in a dead country and the awkwardness of a long-due reunion: the son looking at a dust-cloud going farther and farther away from him, and the father stretching a work-abused hand in welcome.

from *Waiting for the Rain*, by
Charles Mungoshi, Heinemann
(African Writers Series 170), 1975,
pp.39–42.

Harmony

The rice harvest at Tindican

When the signal had been given, the reapers used to set out, and I would fall into step with them, marching to the rhythm of the tom-tom. The young men used to toss their glittering sickles high in the air and catch them as they fell, shouting aloud for the simple pleasure of hearing their own strong young voices, and sketching a dance step or two on the heels of the tom-tom players. I suppose I should have done well to follow my grandmother's advice and to keep at a safe distance from those lively jugglers. But there was such a vivid freshness in the morning air, such scintillating vivacity in their juggling feats, in the spinning sickles that in the rising sun would blaze and flash with sudden brilliance, and there was such irresistible alacrity in the rhythm of the tom-tom that I could never have kept myself away from them.

Besides, at that particular season it was impossible not to want to join in everything. In our December, the whole world is in flower and the air is sweet: everything is young and fresh; the spring seems linked with the summer, and the country-side that for so long has been drenched in rain and shrouded in baleful mists now lies radiant; the sky has never seemed so blue, so brilliant; the birds are ecstatically singing; there is joy all round us — its gentle explosions are echoed in every heart. It was this season, this beautiful time of every year, that was stirring me so deeply, and the beat of the tom-tom and the festive air of our little procession moved me also. It was the best time of the year, the summer and all it stands for, all it holds and cannot hold — for how could it contain so much profusion? — and it made my heart leap with joy.

When they had arrived at the first harvest-field, the men would line up at the edge, naked to the loins, their sickles at the ready. Then my Uncle Lansana or some other farmer — for the harvest threw people together and everyone lent a hand in each other's harvesting — would invite them to begin work. At once the black torsos would bend over the great golden field, and the sickles would begin the reaping. Now it was not only the breeze of morning that was making the whole field sway and shiver, but the men also, with their sickles.

These sickles kept rising and falling with astonishing rapidity and regularity. They had to cut the stalk between the bottom joint and the lowest leaf, so that only the leaf was left behind; well, they hardly ever missed. Of course, such a degree of accuracy depended on the reaper: he would hold the ear with one hand and incline the stalk to receive a clean blow from the sickle. He would reap the ears one by one, but the swift rise and fall of the sickle was nevertheless amazing. Besides, each man made it a point of honour to reap as accurately and as swiftly as possible; he would move forward across the field with a bunch of stalks in his hand, and his fellow-workmen would judge his skill by the number and size of his sheaves . . .

from *The African Child*, by Camara Laye, pp. 46–7.

The harmony of the agricultural year

Yam, the king of crops, was a very exacting king. For three or four moons it demanded hard work and constant attention from cock-crow till the chickens went back to roost. The young tendrils were protected from earth-heat by rings of sisal leaves. As the rains became heavier the women planted maize, melons and beans between the yam mounds. The yams were then staked, first with little sticks and later with tall and big tree branches. The women weeded the farm three times at definite periods in the life of the yams, neither early nor late.

And now the rains had really come, so heavy and persistent that even the village rain-maker no longer claimed to be able to intervene. He could not stop the rain now, just as he would not attempt to start it in the heart of the dry season, without serious danger to his own health. The personal dynamism required to counter the forces of these extremes of weather would be far too great for the human frame.

And so nature was not interfered with in the middle of the rainy season. Sometimes it poured down in such thick sheets of water that earth and sky seemed merged in one grey wetness. It was then uncertain whether the low rumbling of Amadiora's thunder came from above or below. At such times, in each of the countless thatched huts of Umuofia, children sat around their mother's cooking fire telling stories, or with their father in his *obi* warming themselves from a log fire, roasting and eating maize. It was a brief resting period between the exacting and arduous planting season and the equally exacting but light-hearted month of harvests.

from *Things Fall Apart*, by Chinua Achebe, p.24.

Harmony and a social event: the wrestling competition

The whole village turned out on the *ilo*, men, women and children. They stood round in a huge circle leaving the centre of the playground free. The elders and grandees of the village sat on their own stools brought there by their young sons or slaves. Okonkwo was among them. All others stood except those who came early enough to secure places on the few stands which had been built by placing smooth logs on forked pillars.

The wrestlers were not there yet and the drummers held the field. They too sat just in front of the huge circle of spectators, facing the elders. Behind them was the big and ancient silk-cotton tree which was sacred. Spirits of good children lived in that tree waiting to be born. On ordinary days young women who desired children came to sit under its shade.

There were seven drums and they were arranged according to their sizes in a long wooden basket. Three men beat them with sticks, working feverishly from one drum to another. They were possessed by the spirit of the drums.

The young men who kept order on these occasions dashed about, consulting among themselves and with the leaders of the two wrestling teams, who were still outside the circle, behind the crowd. Once in a while two young men carrying palm fronds ran round the circle and kept the crowd back by beating the ground in front of them or, if they were stubborn, their legs and feet.

At last the two teams danced into the circle and the crowd roared and clapped. The drums rose to a frenzy. The people surged forwards. The young men who kept order flew around, waving their palm fronds. Old men nodded to the beat of the drums and remembered the days when they wrestled to its intoxicating rhythm. . .

The drummers took up their sticks again and the air shivered and grew tense like a tightened bow.

The two teams were ranged facing each other across the clear space. A young man from one team danced across the centre to the other side and pointed at whomever he wanted to fight. They danced back to the centre together and then closed in.

There were twelve men on each side and the challenge went from one side to the other. Two judges walked around the wrestlers and when they thought they were equally matched, stopped them. Five matches ended in this way. But the really exciting moments were when a man was thrown. The huge voice of the crowd then rose to the sky and in every direction. It was even heard in the surrounding villages.

The last match was between the leaders of the teams. They were among the best wrestlers in all the nine villages. The crowd wondered who would throw the other this year. Some said Okafo was the better man; others said he was not the equal of Ikezue. Last year neither of them had thrown the other even though the judges had allowed the contest to go on longer than was the custom. They had the same style and one saw the other's plans beforehand. It might happen again this year. . .

The wrestlers were now almost still in each other's grip. The muscles on their arms and their thighs and on their backs stood out and twitched. It looked like an equal match. The two judges were already moving forward to separate them when Ikezue, now desperate, went down quickly on one knee in an attempt to fling his man backwards over his head. It was a sad miscalculation. Quick as the lightning of Amadiora, Okafo raised his right leg and swung it over his rival's head. The crowd burst into a thunderous roar. Okafo was swept off his feet by his supporters and carried home shoulder-high. They sang his praise and the young women clapped their hands:

'Who will wrestle for our village?
   Okafo will wrestle for our village.
Has he thrown a hundred men?
   He has thrown four hundred men.
Has he thrown a hundred Cats?
   He has thrown four hundred Cats.
Then send him word to fight for us.'

from *Things Fall Apart*, pp.34–6.

Work and harmony: the goldsmith

Then he would take the clay pot that was kept specially for the smelting of gold and pour in the grains; thereupon he would cover the gold with powdered charcoal, a charcoal which he obtained by the use of plant juices of exceptional purity; finally he would place a large lump of the same kind of charcoal over the whole thing. . .

On a sign from my father, the apprentices would start working the two pairs of sheepskin bellows which were placed on the ground at each side of the forge and linked to it by earthern pipes. These apprentices remained seated all the time, with crossed legs, in front of the bellows; at least the younger did, for the elder would sometimes be allowed to take part in the craftsmen's work and the younger – in those days it was Sidafa – only had to work the bellows and watch the proceedings while awaiting his turn to be elevated to less rudimentary tasks. For a whole hour they would both be working the levers of the bellows till the fire in the forge leapt into flame, becoming a living thing, a lively and merciless spirit.

Then my father, using long pincers, would lift the clay pot and place it on the flames.

Immediately all work would more or less stop in the workshop: actually while the gold is being melted and while it is cooling all work with copper or aluminium is supposed to stop, for fear that some fraction of these less noble metals might fall among the gold. It is only steel that can still be worked at such times. But workmen who had some piece of steel work in hand would either hasten to finish it or would openly stop work to join the other apprentices gathered round the forge. In fact, there were often so many of them at these times pressing round my father that I, the smallest, would have to get up and push my way in among them, so as not to miss any of the operation.

It might happen that, feeling he had too little room to work in, my father would make his apprentices stand well away from him. He would merely raise his hand in a simple gesture: at that particular moment he would never utter a word, and no one else would, no one was allowed to utter a word, even the go-between's voice would no longer be raised in song; the silence would be broken only by the panting of the bellows and by the faint hissing of the gold. But if my father never used to utter actual words at this time, I know that he was uttering them in his mind; I could see it by his lips that kept working while he bent over the pot and kept stirring the gold and the charcoal with a bit of wood that would keep bursting into flame, and so had to be constantly replaced by a fresh bit.

What were the words my father's lips were forming? I do not know; I do not know for certain: I was never told what they were. But what else could they have been, if not magical incantations? Were they not the spirits of fire and gold, of fire and air, air breathed through the earthern pipes, of fire born of air, of gold married with fire – were not these the spirits he was invoking? Was it not their help and their friendship he was calling upon in this marriage of elemental things? Yes, it was almost certainly those spirits he was calling upon, for they are the most elemental of all spirits, and their presence is essential at the melting of the gold. . .

from *The African Child*, by Camara Laye, pp.25–6.

Yoruba doorpost carved in honour of Sango (John Picton)

Change

New masters and old masters

A young Ghanaian doctor spends the night at a rest house up-country, and is dismayed.

'Massa, I must go to market now. I say I wan' get good meat. What you go chop?'

'I'll eat anything you cook.'

'Massa, you tink you go like fried fillet of calf? Or a braised lamb liver? Yes, here a good one. An escalope of veal with onions and fried potatoes.'

'Zirigu, whom did you say you were going to cook for?'

'Yourself, Massa.'

'But that is not the food I eat.'

'But 'e be white man chop.'

'Zirigu, I no be white man. And that is the second time this morning I've told you that. And if you do it again, I'll pack up and leave.'

Jesus, isn't there anywhere on this bloody land one can have some blinking peace? Jesus . . . Lord I am sweating . . . God . . . see how I'm sweating. Jesus see how I'm sweating.

'Massa, why you sweat so?'

'It gets hot here early.'

'Yes, make I open them windows.'

Jesus!

'Massa, I beg. Don't make so. I no wan' vex you. This here chop, 'e be white man's chop. 'E be the chop I cook for all massas, for fifteen years. The Ministars, the party people who stay for here, the big men from the Ministries, the Unifartisy people, the big offisars from the army and police. . . . 'E be same chop, they chop, this white man chop.'

'Zirigu, can't you cook any food of the land? Don't they sell things in that market with which you could make the food of this land?'

'Yes. But I no fit cook your kind food. No, I no fit cook food of your area.'

'How about the food of your area? Your food?'

'I no fit cook that.'

'Jesus. And you've been a cook steward here for all these years?'

'Yes. But Massa. I know my job. Massa, don't com' make trouble for me. O, look, my hair don' gone white. I no fit find another job. Who go look for my pickin'? I know how to cook, Massa, white man's chop.'

from 'For Whom Things Did Not Change'
in *No Sweetness Here* and other stories,
by Ama Ata Aidoo, Longman (Drumbeat 16),
1979, pp.16–17.

Squalor, affluence and an interview

A young journalist waits for an interview in down-town Lagos.

Sagoe, awaiting the arrival of the full complement of the Board of Interview, made his first tour of the premises. The area had been chosen, according to Mathias, for reasons of pure political strategy. Every loud city has its slums, and Isale-Eko symbolized the victory of the modern African capital over European nations in this one aspect of civilisation. A few foreigners seeking off-beat local colour found it always in Isale-Eko; daring its dark maze they admitted that their experience was unique, there was hop-scotch to be played among garbage heaps, and the faint-hearted found their retreat cut off by the slop from housewives' basins. *Independent Viewpoint* owned a large building in the slum; the paper itself was a party organ, its location meant easy patronage of local thugs, and Isale-Eko was rich spawning ground. . .

Sagoe looked through the rear window. The wall dropped sheer on to a canal which led water into the lagoon. This water was stagnant, clogged, and huge turds floated in decomposing rings, bobbing against the wall. He turned to Mathias, 'How do you work in this stench?'

'Ah, na so everybody dey say first time. But make you look me now, I just dey grow fat for the smell.'. . .

It came to his turn half an hour later and Sagoe thought – how right that Dehinwa sometimes is, we only despise the small criminal. The room into which he was ushered could be a banqueting room. A plush carpet swallowed all shoes below a three-inch soling, contradicting the building itself which had been hurriedly buttressed to pass a second examination by a bribed slums inspector. The boardroom, a different world, contradicted all evidence of other offices. To it belonged the only air-conditioner in the building, and the walls were wood-panelled; hidden behind the panelling was powdering mortar, and there were small curtains to match the wall which screened the cooling machines when they were not in use.

Each seat was a swivelling tilt-back armchair, the table was the best mahogany; a pin scratch on it would have shown up like a bleach mark. A gold-edged pad lay at each place, at scrupulous angles to the table edge. In one corner, an apoplectic radiogram, but no records, only the radio was ever used, and that just for the news. The radio had nine winking lights, all differently coloured, although no one had yet discovered what they proved. This was the pride of the Managing Director. On his visit to Germany on his eleventh round-the-world mission, the grandeur of the thing hit him on the apple and he could only mutter, 'It has class, it has class.' The sales fraulein complimented him on his taste and he paid on the spot with travellers' cheques. 'By the way,' he said, 'do come to my hotel and show me how it works.'

from *The Interpreters*, by Wole Soyinka, Heinemann (African Writers Series 76), 1970, pp.71–2.

A man of the people?

There was a time when Nderi wa Riera was truly a man of the people. He used to play darts and draughts in small and big places, punctuating his playing with witty light-hearted comments and threats to unnerve his opponents: you will know me today . . . You think I was in Manyani for nothing! It used to be said that he had chosen his offices in the Market Street to be near Camay which was then a renowned centre for darts and draughts and roasted goat meat and beer. Camay had in fact thrown up first-rate African darts players like Waiguru and Parsalli who, on reaching the thrilling finals staged at the Brilliant Night Club in what used to be an exclusively Asian and European pastime, had become household names in dart-playing circles all over Nairobi. He was in those days also one of the most vocal and outspoken advocates of reform in and outside Parliament. He would champion such populist causes as putting a ceiling on land ownership; nationalisation of the major industries and commercial enterprises; abolition of illiteracy and unemployment and the East African Federation as a step to Pan-African Unity.

Then he was flooded with offers of directorships in foreign-owned companies. 'Mr Riera, you need not do anything: we do not want to take too much of your busy and valuable time. It is only that we believe in white and black partnership for real progress.' The money he had collected from his constituents for a water project was not enough for piped water. But it was adequate as a security for further loans until he bought shares in companies and invested in land, in housing and in small business. He suddenly dropped out of circulation in small places. Now he could only be found in special clubs for members only, or in newspapers – photographed while attending this or that cocktail party. As if to reinforce his new social standing, he took a huge farm in the Rift Valley. But his most lucrative connection was with the tourist industry. He owned a number of plots and premises in Mombasa, Malindi and Watamu and had been given shares in several tourist resorts all along the coast. Soon he began talking of 'the need for people to grow up and face reality. Africa needed capital and investment for real growth – not socialist slogans'. But he remained a strong advocate of African culture, African personality, Black authenticity: 'If you must wear wigs, why not natural African or Black wigs?' He insisted on most of the companies of which he was chairman or director dropping their European names and taking names like Uhuru, Wananchi, Taifa, Harambee, Afro, Pan-African, which would give the enterprises a touch of the soil.

Nderi wa Riera was the envy of most of his parliamentary peers. His areas were so remote from the city that he was hardly ever troubled by endless complaints from his constituents. A happy contented lot your people are, they would tell him, and he would receive the compliment with a beaming smile. An MP's political freedom! And it was true that the chairs and the carpets in his office would have gathered dust had their cleanliness depended on visits from Ilmorog. The arrival of the delegation from his area became instant news among his parliamentary friends. They eagerly waited for him in his night haunts to find out the outcome of this unexpected confrontation.

from *Petals of Blood*, by Ngugi wa Thiong'o,
Heinemann (African Writers Series 188),
1977, pp.174–5.

Modern marriage

LAKUNLE
When we are wed, you shall not walk or sit
Tethered, as it were, to my dirtied heels.
Together we shall sit at table
– Not on the floor – and eat,
Not with fingers, but with knives
And forks, and breakable plates
Like civilized beings.
I will not have you wait on me
Till I have dined my fill.
No wife of mine, no lawful wedded wife
Shall eat the leavings off my plate –
That is for the children.
I want to walk beside you in the street,

Side by side and arm in arm
Just like the Lagos couples I have seen
High-heeled shoes for the lady, red paint
On her lips. And her hair is stretched
Like a magazine photo. I will teach you
The waltz and we'll both learn the foxtrot
And we'll spend the week-end in night-clubs
    at Ibadan.
Oh I must show you the grandeur of towns
We'll live there if you like or merely pay visits.
So choose. Be a modern wife, look me in the
    eye
And give me a little kiss – like this.
[*Kisses her.*]

© Wole Soyinka 1963. From *The Lion and the Jewel* by Wole Soyinka, 1963. Reprinted by permission of Oxford University Press, 1963.

A view of progress

BAROKA
I do not hate progress, only its nature
Which makes all roofs and faces look the
    same.
And the wish of one old man is
That here and there,
[*Goes progressively towards Sidi, until he bends over her, then sits beside her on the bed.*]
Among the bridges and the murderous roads,
Below the humming birds which
Smoke the face of Sango, dispenser of
The snake-tongue lightning; between this
    moment
And the reckless broom that will be wielded
In these years to come, we must leave
Virgin plots of lives, rich decay
And the tang of vapour rising from
Forgotten heaps of compost, lying
Undisturbed . . . But the skin of progress
Masks, unknown, the spotted wolf of
    sameness . . .
Does sameness not revolt your being,
My daughter?

© Wole Soyinka 1963.
From *The Lion and the Jewel*, p.52.

The wife speaks to her husband

Ocol says
He does not love me any more
Because I cannot play the guitar
And I do not like their stupid dance,
Because I despise the songs
They play at the ball-room dance
And I do not follow the steps of foreign
    songs
On the gramophone records.
And I cannot tune the radio
Because I do not hear
Swahili or Luganda.

What is all this?

My husband refuses
To listen to me,
He refuses to give me a chance.
My husband has blocked up my path
    completely.
He has put up a road block
But has not told me why.
He just shouts
Like house-flies
Settling on top of excrement
When disturbed!

My husband says
He no longer wants a woman
With a gap in her teeth,
He is in love
With a woman
Whose teeth fill her mouth completely
Like the teeth of war-captives and slaves.

Like beggars
You take up white men's adornments,
Like slaves or war captives
You take up white men's ways.
Didn't the Acoli have adornments?
Didn't Black People have their ways?

Like drunken men
You stagger to white men's games,
You stagger to white men's amusements.

Is *lawala*[1] not a game?
Is *cooro*[2] not a game??
Didn't your people have amusements?
Like halfwits
You turn to white men's dances.
You turn to musical instruments of foreigners
As if you have no dances;
As if you have no instruments!

And you cannot sing one song
You cannot sing a solo
In the arena.
You cannot beat rhythm on the half-gourd
Or shake the rattle-gourd
To the rhythm of the *orak* dance!
And there is not a single *bwola* song
That you can dance,
You do not play the drum
Or do the mock-fight;
At the funeral dance
Or at the war dance
You cannot wield the shield!

And so you turn
To the dances of white people,
Ignorance and shame provoke you
To turn to foreign things!

Perhaps you are covering up
Your bony hips and chest
And the large scar on your thigh
And the scabies on your buttocks;

You are hiding
Under the blanket suit
Your sick stomach
That has swollen up
Like that of a pregnant goat.

And the dark glasses
Shield the rotting skin around your eyes
From the house-flies,
And cover up
The husks of the exploded eye balls.

from 'Song of Lawino' in *Song of Lawino
and Song of Ocol* by Okot p'Bitek, East
African Publishing House, 1972, pp.60–2;
Heinemann (African Writers Series 266)
1984

[1] *Lawala* is a hunting game.
[2] *Cooro* is a board game.

The Experience of Migrant Workers

The flow of men to the south (of Ghana)

An old woman in Northern Ghana gains a grandson but is about to lose a son who steels himself to tell her that he too is about to go south.

In twenty years Fuseni's has been the only pregnancy and the only birth ... twenty years, and the first child and a male! In the old days, there would have been bucks and you got scolded for serving a woman in maternity a duicker. But these days, those mean poachers on the government reserves sneak away their miserable duickers, such wretched hinds! Yes, they sneak away even the duickers to the houses of those sweet-toothed southerners.

In the old days, how time goes, and how quickly age comes. But then does one expect to grow younger when one starts getting grandchildren? Allah be praised for a grandson.

The fire was still strong when she returned to the room. ... M'ma Asana put the nuts down. She craned her neck into the corner. At least those logs should take them to the following week. For the rest of the evening, she set about preparing for the morrow's marketing.

The evening prayers were done. The money was in the bag. The grassland was still, Hawa was sleeping and so was Fuseni. M'ma came out to the main gate, first to check up if all was well outside and then to draw the door across. It was not the figure, but rather the soft rustle of light footsteps trying to move still more lightly over the grass that caught her attention.

'If only it could be my husband.'
But of course it was not her husband!
'Who comes?'
'It is me, M'ma.'
'You Issa, my son?'
'Yes, M'ma.'
'They are asleep.'
'I thought so. That is why I am coming now.'

There was a long pause in the conversation as they both hesitated about whether the son-in-law should go in to see Hawa and the baby or not. Nothing was said about this struggle but then one does not say everything.

M'ma Asana did not see but she felt him win the battle. She crossed the threshold outside and drew the door behind her. Issa led the way. They did not walk far, however. They just turned into a corner between two of the projecting pillars in the wall of the kraal. It was Issa who stood with his back to the wall. And this was as it should have been, for it was he who needed the comforting coolness of it for his backbone.

'M'ma, is Fuseni well?'
'Yes.'
'M'ma, is Hawa well?'
'Yes.'
'M'ma please tell me, is Fuseni very well?'
'A-ah, my son. For what are you troubling yourself so much?' 'Fuseni is a new baby who was born not more than ten days. How can I tell you he is very well? When a grown-up goes to live in other people's village ...'
'M'ma.'
'What is it?'
'No, Please it is nothing.'
'My son, I cannot understand you this evening. Yes, if you, a grown-up person, goes to live in another village, will you say after the first few days that you are perfectly well?'
'No.'

from 'Certain Winds from the South' in *No Sweetness Here*, by Ama Ata Aidoo, pp.48–9.

Men as labour chattels: from Mozambique to the gold mines of the south

Mamparra M'gaiza[1]

The cattle is selected
counted, marked
and gets on the train, stupid cattle.

In the pen
the females stay behind
to breed new cattle.

The train is back from "migoudini"[2]
and they come rotten with diseases, the old
    cattle of Africa
oh, and they've lost their heads, these cattle
    "m'gaiza"

Come and see
the sold cattle have lost their heads
my god of my land
the sold cattle have lost their heads.

Again
the cattle is selected, marked
and the train is ready to take away meek
    cattle.

Stupid cattle
mine cattle
cattle of Africa, marked and sold.

> José Craveirinha, translated from the
Portuguese, in *When Bullets begin to Flower*,
ed. Margaret Dickinson, East African
Publishing House, 1981.

[1] M'gaiza (also magaiça) is a Mozambican expression for a man just returned from the mines, his pockets full of money and his health broken.
[2] Dialect for the mines.

From 'Amagoduka' at Glencoe Station

The poet sits in the 'non-European Males' waiting room with a group of 'Amagoduka', countrymen going to work for a time on the mines of the Witwatersrand.

. . . One of them picked up a guitar
plucked it with broken finger nails
caressed its strings with a castor oil bottle –

it sighed like a jilted girl.
"You play down! Phansi! Play D" he
    whispered.

Another joined in with a concertina,
its sound fluttered in flowery notes
like a butterfly picking pollen from flower to
    flower.

The two began to sing,
their voices crying for the mountains
and the hills of Msinga, stripped naked of
their green garment.

They crossed rivers and streams,
gouged dry by the sun rays,
where lowing cattle genuflected
for a blade of grass and a drop of water
on riverbeds littered with carcasses and
    bones.

They spoke of hollow-cheeked maidens
heaving drums of brackish water
from a far away fountain.

They told of big-bellied babies
sucking festering fingers
instead of their mothers' shrivelled breasts.

Two cockroaches
as big as my overcoat buttons
jived across the floor
snatched meat and bread crumbs
and scurried back to their hideout.

The whole group joined in unison:
curious eyes peered through frosted windows
"*Ekhaya bafowethu!* – Home brothers!"

We come from across the Tugela river
we are going to EGoli! EGoli! EGoli![1]
where they'll turn us into moles
that eat the gold dust
and spit out blood.

We'll live in compounds
where young men are pampered
into partners for older men.

We'll visit shebeens
where a whore waits for a fee
to leave your balls burning
with syphilitic fire.

If the gods are with us –
Oh! beloved black gods of our forefathers
What have we done to you
Why have you forsaken us –
We'll return home
to find our wives nursing babies –
unknown to us
but only to their mothers and loafers.

© Mbuyiseni Oswald Mtshali, 1971.
From *Sounds of a Cowhide Drum*, 1971.
Reprinted by permission of
Oxford University Press, 1971.

[1] The Zulu name for Johannesburg.

Fast food stall in Bonthe, Sierra Leone (Mike Gunner)

The Difficulties of Urban Life

Homeless in the city

'What did you begin to say?'

Somewhere in blind air, a loud rending, the agony of pitch-soaked beams torn against the grain, and they all waited for the crash of zinc. It was very near and they strained over the low roofs of the courtyard towards the sound. But Sekoni's were the cat's eyes. 'Th-there, it is over th-th-there.' And immediately the crash came, a damp thud of bricks, and later the higher-pitched collapse of rusted sheets.

'One tooth,' Egbo announced. 'The sky-line has lost a tooth from its long rotted gums.' Sekoni stammered worse than ever. 'Th-th-they will b-b-be homeless to . . .n-night. P-p-p-perhaps we should stop there and see if wwwe can h-h-h-help.'

from *The Interpreters*, by Wole Soyinka, p.16.

A campaign and its results

The shimmering circles of dim light coming from the stationary bus, focused with oblique haziness on the side of the road, caught in their confusion what seemed to be a small pile of earth with a sort of signboard standing nonsensically on top of it. As the man got closer, the mound assumed a different shape and the signboard acquired the dimensions of a square waste box.

The thing had been a gleaming white sign when it was first installed, and that was not so very long ago. Now even the lettering on it was no longer decipherable. It was covered over thickly with the juice of every imaginable kind of waste matter. But once the letters had said in their brief brightness:

K.C.C. RECEPTACLE FOR DISPOSAL OF WASTE

That was printed in blue. Underneath, in bolder capitals executed in lucent red, was the message:

KEEP YOUR COUNTRY CLEAN
BY KEEPING YOUR CITY CLEAN

The box was one of the few relics of the latest campaign to rid the town of its filth. Like others before it, this campaign had been extremely impressive, and admiring rumours indicated that it had cost a great deal of money. Certainly the papers had been full of words informing their readers that dirt was undesirable and must be eliminated. On successive days a series of big shots had appealed to everybody to be clean. The radio had run a program featuring a doctor, a Presbyterian priest, and a senior lecturer brought down from the University of Legon. The three had seemed to be in agreement about the evil effects of uncleanliness. People were impressed. Judging by the volume of words printed and spoken, it was indeed, as the Principal Secretary to the Ministry of Health stated at the durbar held to round it off, the most magnificent campaign yet.

It was at the durbar that the little boxes had been launched. In the words of the principal secretary, they would be placed at strategic points all over the city, and they would serve, not just as containers for waste matter, but as shining examples of cleanliness.

In the end not many of the boxes were put out, though there was a lot said about the large amount of money paid for them. The few provided, however, had not been ignored. People used them well, so that it took no time at all for them to get full. People still used them, and they overflowed with banana peels and mango seeds and thoroughly sucked-out oranges and the chaff of sugarcane and most of all the thick brown wrapping from a hundred balls of *kenkey*. People did not have to go up to the boxes any more. From a distance they aimed their rubbish at the growing heap, and a good amount of juicy offal hit the face and sides of the box before finding a final resting place upon the heap. As yet the box was still visible above it all, though the writing upon it could no longer be read.

from *The Beautyful Ones are Not Yet Born*, by Ayi Kwei Armah, Heinemann (African Writers Series 43), 1969, pp.7–8.

City Johannesburg

This way I salute you;
My hand pulses to my back trouser pocket
Or my inner jacket pocket
For my pass, my life,
Jo'burg City.
My hand like a starved snake rears my pockets
For my thin, ever lean wallet,
While my stomach groans a friendly smile to hunger
Jo'burg City.
My stomach also devours coppers and papers
Don't you know?
Jo'burg City, I salute you;
When I run out, or roar in a bus to you,
I leave behind me, my love –
My comic houses and people, my donga and my ever whirling dust,
My death,
That's related to me as a wink to the eye.
Jo'burg City
I travel on your black and white and roboted roads,
Through your thick iron breath that you inhale
At six in the morning and exhale from five noon.
Jo'burg City
That is the time when I come to you,
When your neon flowers flaunt from your electrical wind,
That is the time when I leave you,
When your neon flowers flaunt their way through the falling darkness
On your cement trees.
And as I go back, to my love,
My dongas, my dust, my people, my death,
Where death lurks in the dark like a blade in the flesh,
I can feel your roots, anchoring your might, my feebleness

In my flesh, in my mind, in my blood
And everything about you says it,
That, that is all you need of me.
Jo'burg City, Johannesburg,
Listen when I tell you,
There is no fun, nothing, in it,
When you leave the women and men with such frozen expressions,
Expressions that have tears like furrows of soil erosion,
Jo'burg City, you are dry like death,
Jo'burg City, Johannesburg, Jo'burg City; . . .

Mongane Wally Serote
from *Black Poets in South Africa*
(Heinemann African Writers 164)
ed. Robert Royston, 1974 (pp. 20–1).

Violence

The child who was shot dead by soldiers at Nyanga[1]

The child is not dead
the child lifts his fist against his mother
who shouts Afrika! shouts the breath
of freedom and the veld
in the locations of the cordoned heart

The child lifts his fists against his father
in the march of the generations
who shout Afrika! shout the breath
of righteousness and blood
in the streets of his embattled pride

The child is not dead
not at Langa or at Nyanga
not at Orlando nor at Sharpeville
nor at the police station at Philippi
where he lies with a bullet through his brain

The child is the dark shadow of the soldiers
on guard with rifles saracens[2] and batons
the child is present at all assemblies and law-
givings
the child peers through the windows of
houses and into the hearts of mothers
this child who just wanted to play in the sun
at Nyanga is everywhere
the child grown to a man treks through all
Africa
the child grown into a giant journeys through
the whole world

Without a pass[3]

from *Selected Poems*, by Ingrid Jonker,
edited and translated from the Afrikaans by
Jack Cope and William Plomer,
Jonathan Cape, 1968.

[1] Nyanga is a Black township adjoining Langa and Guguletu, outside Capetown. The shooting was in 1960 after the Sharpeville massacre.

[2] Armour-plated police vehicles.
[3] See p.30. The pass laws, and Unit 11.

Religious and Spiritual Values in a Society

Praises of two Yoruba deities

Oriki Obatala – the praises of Obatala, the creator.

He is patient, he is not angry.
He sits in silence to pass judgement.
He sees you even when he is not looking.
He stays in a far place – but his eyes are on
  the town

The granary of heaven can never be full.
The old man full of life force.

He kills the novice.[1]
And wakens him to let him hear his words.
We leave the world to the owner of the world.
Death acts playfully till he carries away the
  child.[2]
He rides on the hunchback.[3]
He stretches out his right hand.
He stretches out his left hand.

He stands by his children and lets them
  succeed.
He causes them to laugh – and they laugh.[4]
Ohoho – the father of laughter.
His eye is full of joy,
He rests in the sky like a swarm of bees.

We dance to our sixteen drums that sound
  jingin, jingin,
To eight of the drums we dance bending
  down,
To eight of the drums we dance erect.
We shake our shoulders, we shake our hips.
Munusi, munusi, munusi,
We dance to your sixteen drums.

Those who are rich owe their property to him.
Those who are poor, owe their property to
  him.
He takes from the rich and gives to the poor.
Whenever you take from the rich – come and
  give it to me!

Obatala – who turns blood into children.
I have only one cloth to dye with blue indigo.
I have only one headtie to dye with red
  camwood.
But I know that you keep twenty or thirty
  children for me
Whom I shall bear.

[1] Initiates go through a rite of symbolical death and resurrection in most 'orisha' cults.
[2] Obatala is the kindest of the orisha (deities) – but he too can kill.
[3] Obatala created men out of clay. One day he was drunk on palm-wine and then he created hunchbacks, albinos and blind men. These are sacred to him.
[4] 'He causes them to laugh' refers to the giving of breath after creation.
See Unit 10 Setting, for notes on the Yoruba deities.

from Oriki Shango – the praises of Sango[1]

When the elephant wakes up in the morning
He must pay his respects to his new wife.
When the guinea fowl wakes up in the
  morning
It must prostrate to the lord of the forest.
If it fails to greet him thus,
It will be killed by the hunter.
He will carry it home on his back.
He will sell it in the market
And use the money to make charms.
If the antelope wakes in the morning
And does not bow to the lord of the forest
The hunter will come and eat its head with
  pounded yam.
Shango, I prostrate to you every morning,
Before I set out to do anything.

[1] Yoruba 'sh' is now written 's'.

The dog stays in the house of its master
But it does not know his intentions.
The sheep does not know the intentions
Of the man who feeds it.
We ourselves follow Shango
Although we do not know his intentions.
It is not easy to live in Shango's company.
Crabs' feet are confusion.
The parrot's feet are crooked.
When the crab leaves its hole.
We do not know which direction it is taking.
Shango went to Ibadan and arrived at Ilorin.

Rain beats the Egungun mask, because he
   cannot find shelter.[2]
He cries: 'Help me, dead people in heaven,
   help me!'
But the rain cannot beat Shango.
They say that fire kills water.
He rides fire like a horse.
Lightning – with what kind of cloth do you
   cover your body?
With the cloth of death.
Shango is the death that drips to, to, to,
Like indigo dye dripping from a cloth.

Shango is the death who kills money with a
   big stick.
The man who lies will die in his home.
Shango strikes the one who is stupid.
He wrinkes his nose and the liar runs off.[3]
Even when he does not fight, we fear him.
But when war shines in his eye
His enemies and worshippers run all the
   same.
Fire in the eye, fire in the mouth, fire on the
   roof.
He walks alone, but he enters the town like a
   swarm of locusts.
The leopard who killed the sheep and bathed
   in its blood.
The man who died in the market and woke
   up in the house.

from *Yoruba Poetry* by B. Gbadamosi and
Ulli Beier, Ministry of Education, Nigeria,
1959, p.14.

Spiritual authority

The chief priest Ezeulu at the new pumpkin festival.

The *ogene* sounded again. The Ikolo began to salute the Chief Priest. The women waved their leaves from side to side across their faces, muttering prayers to Ulu, the god that kills and saves.

Ezeulu's appearance was greeted with a loud shout that must have been heard in all the neighbouring villages. He ran forward, halted abruptly and faced the Ikolo. 'Speak on,' he said to it, 'Ezeulu hears what you say.' Then he stooped and danced three or four steps and rose again.

He wore smoked raffia which descended from his waist to the knee. The left half of his body – from forehead to toes – was painted with white chalk. Around his head was a leather band from which an eagle's feather pointed backwards. On his right hand he carried *Nne Ofo*, the mother of all staffs of authority in Umuaro, and in his left he held a long iron staff which kept up a quivering rattle whenever he stuck its pointed end into the earth. He took a few long strides, pausing on each foot. Then he ran forward again as though he had seen a comrade in the vacant air; he stretched his arm and waved his staff to the right and to the left. And those who were near enough heard the knocking together of Ezeulu's staff and another which no one saw. At this many fled in terror before the priest and the unseen presences around him.

As he approached the centre of the market place Ezeulu re-enacted the First Coming of Ulu and how each of the four Days put obstacles in his way. . .

By now Ezeulu was in the centre of the market place. He struck the metal staff into the earth and left it quivering while he danced a few more steps to the *Ikolo* which had not paused for breath since the priest emerged. All the women waved their pumpkin leaves in front of them .

---

[2] Sango worshippers control rain. The ceremony of the Egungun masqueraders may be spoiled by rain if they are not on good terms with the Sango worshippers.

[3] These are idiosyncrasies of Sango. The Yoruba deities are not moral beings. Sango dislikes liars – he equally dislikes the stupid.

Ezeulu looked round again at all the men and women of Umuaro, but saw no one in particular. Then he pulled the staff out of the ground, and with it in his left hand and the *Mother of Ofo* in his right he jumped forward and began to run round the market place.

All the women set up a long, excited ululation and there was renewed jostling for the front line. As the fleeing Chief Priest reached any section of the crowd the women there waved their leaves round their heads and flung them at him. It was as though thousands and thousands of giant, flying insects swarmed upon him.

Ugoye who had pushed and shoved until she got to the front murmured her prayer over and over again as the Chief Priest approached the part of the circle where she stood:

'*Great Ulu who kills and saves, I implore you to cleanse my household of all defilement. If I have spoken it with my mouth or seen it with my eyes, or if I have heard it with my ears or stepped on it with my foot or if it has come through my children or my friends or kinsfolk let it follow these leaves.*'

She waved the small bunch in a circle round her head and flung it with all her power at the Chief Priest as he ran past her position. . .

from *Arrow of God*, by Chinua Achebe, Heinemann (African Writers Series 16), 1965, pp.70 and 72.

A desecration

The spiritual authority of the clan's ancestors is openly challenged.

It happened during the annual ceremony which was held in honour of the earth deity. At such times the ancestors of the clan who had been committed to Mother Earth at their death emerged again as *egwugwu* through tiny ant-holes.

One of the greatest crimes a man could commit was to unmask an *egwugwu* in public, or to say or do anything which might reduce its immortal prestige in the eyes of the uninitiated. And this was what Enoch did.

The annual worship of the earth goddess fell on a Sunday, and the masked spirits were abroad. The Christian women who had been to church could not therefore go home. Some of their men had gone out to beg the *egwugwu* to retire for a short while for the women to pass. They agreed and were already retiring, when Enoch boasted aloud that they would not dare to touch a Christian. Whereupon they all came back and one of them gave Enoch a good stroke of the cane, which was always carried. Enoch fell on him and tore off his mask. The other *egwugwu* immediately surrounded their desecrated companion, to shield him from the profane gaze of women and children, and led him away. Enoch had killed an ancestral spirit, and Umuofia was thrown into confusion.

That night the Mother of the Spirits walked the length and breadth of the clan, weeping for her murdered son. It was a terrible night. Not even the oldest man in Umuofia had ever heard such a strange and fearful sound, and it was never to be heard again. It seemed as if the very soul of the tribe wept for a great evil that was coming – its own death.

from *Things Fall Apart*, p.133.

Reconciling two sets of beliefs

Obi's homecoming.

After the first four hundred handshakes and hundred embraces, Obi was able to sit down for a while with his father's older kinsmen in the big parlour. There were not enough chairs for all of them to sit on, so that many sat on their goatskins spread on the floor. It did not make much difference whether one sat on a chair or on the floor because even those who sat on chairs spread their goatskins on them first.

'The white man's country must be very distant indeed,' suggested one of the men. Everyone knew it was very distant, but they wanted to hear it again from the mouth of their young kinsman.

'It is not something that can be told,' said Obi. 'It took the white man's ship sixteen days

– four market weeks – to do the journey.'

'Think of that,' said one of the men to the others. 'Four market weeks. And not in a canoe, but a white man's ship that runs on water as a snake runs on grass.'

'Sometimes for a whole market week there is no land to be seen,' said Obi. 'No land in front, behind, to the right and to the left. Only water.'

'Think of that,' said the man to the others. 'No land for one whole market week. In our folk stories a man gets to the land of spirits when he has passed seven rivers, seven forests and seven hills. Without doubt you have visited the land of spirits.'

'Indeed you have, my child,' said another old man. 'Azik,' he called, meaning Isaac, 'bring us a kola nut to break for this child's return.'

'This is a Christian house,' replied Obi's father.

'A Christian house where kola nut is not eaten?' sneered the man.

'Kola nut is eaten here,' replied Mr Okonkwo, 'but not sacrificed to idols.'

'Who talked about sacrifice? Here is a little child returned from wrestling in the spirit world and you sit there blabbing about Christian house and idols, talking like a man whose palm-wine has gone into his nose.' He hissed in disgust, took up his goatskin and went to sit outside.

'This is not a day for quarrels,' said another old man. 'I shall bring a kola nut.' He took his goatskin bag which he had hung from his chair and began to search its depths. As he searched, things knocked against one another in it – his drinking horn, his snuff-bottle and a spoon. 'And we shall break it in the Christian way,' he said as he fished out a kola nut.

'Do not trouble yourself, Ogbuefi Odogwu,' said Okonkwo to him. 'I am not refusing to place a kola nut before you. What I say is that it will not be used as a heathen sacrifice in my house.' He went into an inner room and soon returned with three kola nuts in a saucer. Ogbuefi Odogwu insisted on adding his kola nut to the number.

'Obi, show the kola nut round,' said his father. Obi had already stood up to do so, being the youngest man in the room. When everyone had seen he placed the saucer before Ogbuefi Odogwu, who was the eldest. He was not a Christian, but he knew one or two things about Christianity. Like many others in Umuofia, he went to church once a year at harvest. His only criticism of the Christian service was that the congregation was denied the right to reply to the sermon. One of the things he liked particularly and understood was: 'As it was in the beginning, is now and ever shall be, world without end.'

from *No Longer at Ease*, by Chinua Achebe, Heinemann (African Writers Series 3), 1963, pp.46–7.

A pilgrim returns from Mecca

Father sent us a picture postcard of Kaaba.[1] 'The pilgrimage is going well,' he wrote, 'but it's exceptionally hot here. Many people have died. Be extra zealous in your prayers. Give generously to the poor. Be good to the children.'

Father's whole personality was in those last words. He was the only one in the family who would be able to worry about us children from such a great distance. 'Be good to them,' said the postcard which was passed from hand to hand and which delighted us youngsters.

At last the end of the pilgrimage was approaching and we prepared to welcome back the traveller. The day of his arrival two rams were slaughtered and several kilos of millet were ground and made into couscous. Relatives and friends sent crates of lemonade. The house was cleaned till it shone; immaculate sheets covered all the beds; we were dressed in our best clothes.

We children were not allowed to go to the airport as there was always such a crush on these occasions when pilgrims returned in large numbers. We waited quietly at home,

[1] The big, black stone in Mecca which is central to the pilgrimage.

getting more and more excited every time we heard the noise of a car approaching.

Finally there came the cry, 'Here he is! He's here!'

With beating heart I raced to the door and saw my father, majestic in his new pilgrim's attire: he wore a huge cloak embroidered with gold thread and the lamé turban of a 'Hadj' on his head. He lifted me off my feet and nearly suffocated me in his embrace. Tears of joy streamed down my cheeks. Generally we were very undemonstrative and kept our feelings of love buried deep in our hearts; to show affection was considered ill-bred, westernised. In my heart of hearts I cursed the way we were brought up, with this strictness, all these scruples and taboos.

That morning my heart overflowed with gratitude to God for bringing Father home safe and sound. Grandmother was in the seventh heaven, trotting briskly hither and thither and petting the pilgrim like a child. To tell the truth Father looked as if he could do with a bit of spoiling and feeding up; he had lost a good deal of weight. This, he said, was quite normal; you were supposed to leave some of your weight behind in Mecca as a symbol of *asaka*, that is the charity to be given to the poor.

The traveller's luggage was unpacked. The jars of *zem-zem* that he had brought back were emptied into basins of water placed outside all the bedrooms. Then we recited verses from the Koran, as laid down for this ritual, made our wishes and drank the goblets full of this mixture of holy water from Mecca and Dakar tap-water.

Dressed in our best clothes we waited for the arrival of our visitors whom we welcomed with gifts of dates and sticks of incense. We kept a good look-out for the ones who came for the *ziara*, the pilgrimage, and made a bee-line for them before they even had time to greet anyone.

Father welcomed everyone with a smile. Some of the visitors embraced him; others held his hand in a long grasp, to obtain the benefit of his *baraka*, his spiritual plenitude.

From time to time he turned to us to congratulate us on our progress or give us a word of encouragement which warmed our hearts. He personally handed us our share of dates and incense, while our aunts darted disapproving glances at him; if they had been left to share out our dates they would have counted them out one by one. Father always knew who he was dealing with, what was the right thing to do or say, making his presence felt by small gestures, such as giving us children a larger share like this. Naturally he knew that the children always had the worst deal when it came to sharing things out, and that was why we often had recourse to helping ourselves.

Father waited till all the neighbours had left, each one going off with his little packet of incense, then he brought out the presents for the family. The boys got skull-caps which they wore later for the important Korité and Tabaski prayers. For my grandmother and the aunts there were shawls, rosaries and jars of *tusngel*. We girls received necklaces, rings and sandals made out of plaited gold thread.

We dug mercilessly into the sacks of dates which the aunts tried every trick to hide from us. We regularly drank our *zem-zem* water in the belief that we were saturating our bodies with holiness. And we felt that this would promote the fulfilment of the wishes that we made.

But I haven't told you about my special supply of *zem-zem*. On the very day of Father's return, in the confusion created by the unpacking, I abstracted from his luggage a jar of the holy Mecca water to keep all for myself, wishing to obtain all its undiluted virtues.

Not finding any other place to drink it without being seen, I locked myself in the lavatory, broke open the top with a knife, coughing hard to cover the noise, fervently pronounced my wishes and drank the bitter liquid down in one gulp. For the next two days I had the most appalling diarrhoea.

from *A Dakar Childhood*, Nafissatou Diallo, pp.57–9.

Section 3   Resources

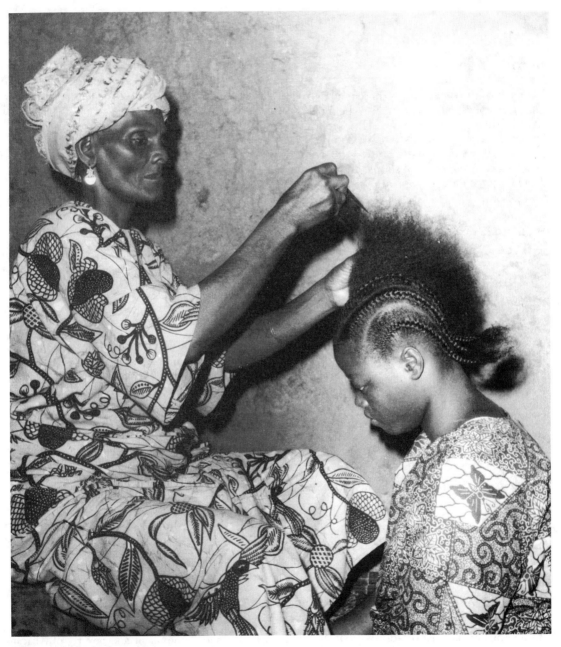

The art of African hairstyling

Part A   *Audio-visual Resources*

Introduction

For each of the twelve units there is a list of the audio-visual resources thought to be most useful for that particular unit. This section includes a more general list, also a complete list of the addresses of the distributors referred to, as well as museums, bookshops, and so forth. The layout of Part A is as follows:

The Resource List (1) is divided into *four* main sections:
Southern Africa
East
West
General

Each section lists in order:
Films, with name of distributor, hiring charge when available (conditions vary), and a short note on each film.
Other resources: books, booklets, posters, photographs, slides.

Film distributors (2) is an alphabetical list of distributors, with some information (very brief) on their hiring conditions.
Recorded sound (3) gives the names of tapes, distributors and records of African and Caribbean music and poetry.

Other useful addresses (4) includes, in alphabetical order:
– all the addresses for obtaining the audio-visual aids *other than films* described in the text.
– resource centres
– libraries
– museums
– addresses for music workshops
– permanent exhibitions
Bookshops (5) is a list of addresses of stockists of African and Caribbean literature.

NB *All prices are correct at time of going to press, but may get out of date. It is worth checking with all distributors before ordering.*

Resource list

Southern Africa

Films

Let My People Go
23 mins   B/W   Concord   £7.60
A film on apartheid, which uses drama and newsreel Commentary by James Cameron, music by Michael Tippett. Directed by John Krish, 1961.

A World of Strangers
92 mins   B/W   Concord   £15.20
A film based on Nadine Gordimer's novel about a young man who goes to work in South Africa, and makes friends among the different groups there. Directed by Henning Carlsen, 1962.

Cry the Beloved Country
103 mins   B/W   Connoisseur Films   £20
From the novel by Alan Paton. A humble Zulu priest leaves his native village to seek his son and a daughter who have left him to live in Johannesburg. He finds them, degraded by the surrounding squalor – the boy a thief and murderer, the girl a prostitute.

Katutura
37 mins   Colour   Contemporary Films   £10
'Katutura' means total insecurity. The film presents a wealth of detail and history about South Africa in a factual and direct way, appealing to the intellect rather than the heart. Produced in co-operation with various missionary groups.

The Dumping Grounds
25 mins   B/W   Concord (Oxfam)   £3.00
A Granada 'World in Action' programme, made in 1970. It shows the plight and poverty of Africans who have been evicted from 'white' areas.

A Luta Continua
32 mins Colour Other Cinema £14
A film and record of the experiences of a black American film crew who joined Frelimo's guerrilla army and travelled around Mozambique.

Chimurenga (The War in Zimbabwe) £25
1977 51 mins Colour Contemporary Films
Made by Morena Films in 1977. It concentrates on the view of ordinary people – on the Smith regime, and the effects of the war.

Malawi – The Women
15 mins Colour Concord £6.20
Film showing the varying life styles and employment of Malawian women in a village, a city and a city suburb. Shows the contrasts in women's work in city and village.

Malawi – Two Young Men
15 mins Colour Concord £6.20
The film deals with the problems of employment faced by young people in an African state. Two young men try unsuccessfully to become middlemen in the fish trade in Malawi.

From Rhodesia to Zimbabwe
19 mins Colour Concord £11
UN 1981. Film covering the history of what is now Zimbabwe – the early Shona states, the arrival, conquests and settlement by the Ndebele, by Cecil Rhodes and the Europeans, the nationalist struggle and independence.

Zimbabwe – the Struggle for Health
60 mins Colour Concord £20.40
Central TV 1983. Explores the role of doctors in a developing country and the role of the government in extending the health service. Many doctors see their task as promoting health as well as curing disease.

Zimbabwe – from Swords to Ploughshares
20 mins Colour Concord £4.40
UN 1981. Shows the programme of humanitarian assistance aimed at helping refugees and those whose lives were violently disrupted by the 1971–80 war.

Bitter Melons
30 mins Colour Royal Anthropological Institute Film Library £9
From the San (Bushman) series by John Marshall. Extremely interesting and beautifully filmed account of the daily life of the Gwi San of Botswana.

The following films are described in Unit 11 (Sizwe Bansi)

Boesman and Lena
Marigolds in August
Abaphuciwe: The Dispossessed.

Slides

From Rhodesia to Zimbabwe
80 slides CAFOD £4
A slide cassette programme produced since independence.

Lesotho: Thaba Khupa Farm Institute
18 slides CWDE(S-12) £5.00 + VAT
About training young boys and girls in farming techniques. Also notes on general background and on problems of life in Lesotho.

Books

AUBREY ELLIOTT, *Sons of Zulu*, Collins, 1978.
The text of this is patronizing and full of disparaging generalizations. The photography is good.

Magubane's South Africa, Secker and Warburg, 1978.
Text and photographs by Peter Magubane (see Unit 4).

JOYCE SIKAKANE, *A Window on Soweto*, IDAF, 1977.
An autobiography.

PATRICIA VINNICOMBE, *People of the Eland: Rock Paintings of the Drakensberg Bushmen as a Reflection of their Life and Thought*, University of Natal Press, 1976.
Illustrations include numerous colour plates; also maps. Widely recognised as a classic. A tribute to the art and life of the San people who once roamed widely over Southern Africa.

J.D. LEWIS WILLIAMS, *The Rock Art of Southern Africa*, Cambridge University Press, 1983.
Extremely informative and superbly illustrated.

Booklets, resource collections, photographs

The following are available from CWDE:

Botswana: Country and People An Oxfam Resource Wallet. £1.90 + VAT (PA-5).
Has a background paper, list of materials for teachers and pupils, a day in the life of village people in Botswana, cattle herding, a recipe, a story, three biographies of families and photographs.

Botswana CWDE (B-114) £2.50
A collection of pupil and teacher material for 15–16 year-olds.

Portrait of an African Village CWDE (L-123) 12p
A brief account of a Botswanan village, with particular mention of educational changes.

Lesotho – Children of the Mountains (OXFAM) CWDE (B-28) 65p
Nine children from Lesotho write about themselves and their families. Suitable for middle schools and above.

Black Women in Zimbabwe CWDE (B-181) 65p
Photo-illustrated booklet published by the Zimbabwe Women's Bureau. Based on numerous interviews in 1980 with a range of women; includes notes on position of women.

Profile: Zimbabwe (CAFOD 1982) CWDE (B-163) 40p
Photo-illustrated booklet giving basic facts on history, post-war situation, agriculture, health and education.

Country Factsheets, A4 booklets, available from Commonwealth Institute, 30p each + 20p postage.
  Botswana (L-67)
  Lesotho (L-71)
  Malawi (L-72)
  Zambia (L-77)

CAFOD Campaign 1983, Families Divided: Migrant labour in South Africa, includes: Families Divided, £1.00; South Africa Profile, 50p; Poster map, 50p; Family life and migrant labour in South Africa, 20p.
From: 2 Garden Close, Stockwell Road, London SW9 9TY.

East Africa

Films

African Odyssey: Two Worlds of Musembe
For ages 10 upwards 15 mins Colour Rank Aldis £9.95
The two worlds of 11-year-old Musembe from Kenya are the two worlds of twentieth century Africa: the modern city and the primitive village. The dramatic thrust of the film comes from his journey 'home' from modern Nairobi to the village where his father was born – it reflects the pull of tribalism versus the growing sense of nationalism.

Black Man's Land: Images of Colonialism and Independence in Kenya
1973 3 × 50 mins Colour The Other Cinema
£45 for three, or £20 each if hired separately
A series of three films about Kenya, about colonialism, about Mau-Mau, and finally about Jomo Kenyatta (see Unit 3 *Weep Not, Child*).

Freedom Railway
1974 45 mins Colour Contemporary Films
£20
Made by Felix Greene, who is internationally acclaimed as a maker of documentary films. It is about the Tan-Zam Railway which the Chinese helped to build along 1900 kilometres of jungles, mountains and swamps, from Dar es Salaam in Tanzania to Kapiri Mposhi in Zambia.

Horizon: A Fair Share of What Little We Have
45 mins Colour Distributor: Concord £16.40
About Tanzania's 'front-line' doctors – an army of 3000 rural medical aides who, though trained for only three years at a cost of £600, treat 85% of diseases much more cheaply but as competently as western doctors.

Films from Kenya High Commission Colour No charge
Personal collection is preferred.
 1 *Annual Film Magazine* 1960, 63, 64 15 mins each
   About East African Railways and Harbours, and contemporary events of this period.
 2 *Kahawa* (Coffee) 15 mins
 4 *Cotton* 15 mins
 7 *Kenya Becomes a Nation* 30 mins Achievements since independence.
 9 *Magadi Soda* 15 mins Excavation of soda at Lake Magadi including processing and bi-products.
11 *Permanent Way* 45 mins The building of the railway in East Africa.
12 *Safari to Kenya* 30 mins A guided tour around Nairobi, the coast, game parks, etc.
13 *Samaki* (Fish) 25 mins Fishing in rivers and on the coast.
16 *Victoria* 20 mins The building of a steamer, now in service in Lake Victoria.

34 mm filmstrips

Kenya (Parts 1 and 2)
33 and 29 frames Colour Drake Educational Productions £6.50 each
These show the wildlife in Kenya as well as the agricultural work of the people, and aspects of their traditional life.

A School in Kenya 1979 20 slides plus detailed notes £5.50 + VAT (CWDE Order No. S-9).

Leaflets

From Kenya High Commission, 45 Portman Place, London W1N 4AS.

Posters and Handbooks

From Kenya Tourist Office, 13 New Burlington Street, London W1.

Books

Kenya (Peoples First Series), published by World Vision Educational Resources, 1978. Attractive photo-illustrated paperback – includes background, history, rural development, urban drift, details of slum clearance project in Nairobi, Nakuru street boys. £2.

Booklets and photographs

Country Fact Sheets, A4 booklets, available from Commonwealth Institute, 30p each + 20p postage.
  Kenya (L-70)
  Tanzania (L-76)
  Zambia (L-77)

Ujamaa in Tanzania
Commonwealth Institute Topic Series, 30p + 20p postage. Description of an ujamaa village.

Omari and Thadea Two Boys in Tanzania
20 A3 B/W photographs, notes, CWDE (P-5) £1.80 + VAT.

Choices in Development CWDE (PA-37) £4.50 + VAT
Set of 34 A3 B/W photographs; teacher's booklet with ideas for activities, discussion and inter-disciplinary work.

Women in development in Kenya. People and Work No.273, 40p.
From: CAFOD office: 2 Garden Close, Stockwell Road, London SW9. Tel: 01-735-9041.

West Africa

Films

My Brother's Children
47 mins Colour Concord £9.80
An unusual film in the style of a Yoruba folk-opera, actually made for a Nigerian audience to contrast the way of life of a better-off family with fewer children with another large poor family. It is acted in the authentic traditional style.

After the Drought
3 films each 30 mins Colour Concord £11.20 each
(A Nomad Family in West Africa, A Peasant Family in West Africa, and an Urban Family in West Africa).
About Upper Volta — the drought, exploitation of natural resources, and economic dependence. Each film looks at a West African family in different circumstances.

The Parched Land
1975 48 mins Colour Contemporary £15
About the shortage of water and severe drought in the Sahel region of Africa, and in particular one small village in Senegal. The film shows various relief projects, but allows us to draw our own conclusions as to their effectiveness.

Xala
123 mins Colour Contemporary Films £30
A film by the internationally known Senegalese film-maker, Sembène Ousmane, made in 1975. It is a satire on the role of the rich middle class now in Senegal. It concerns a powerful trader, El Hadji Abdou Kadar Beye, newly elected to the all-African Chamber of Commerce. He takes a third wife who is to be set up with a big house, servants, and a car. But on their wedding night El Hadji is impotent. Someone has bestowed on him a *Xala* – a curse of impotence. By the end the story has become a parable on Senegal – and it has a shocking finish.

Other films by Sembène Ousmane are:
(from The Other Cinema):

Borom Sorret
1964 20 mins B/W £20
About a young man trying to make a living with his horse and cart in Dakar, Senegal – the cart is confiscated by the police . . .

Black Girl
1965   60 mins   B/W   £30
A story of exploitation and alienation. A young girl leaves Senegal to work as a domestic servant in France, with tragic consequences.

The Money Order
1968   90 mins   Colour   £40
A bitter comedy. The receipt of a money order from his nephew in France leads the innocent Ibrahim Dieng into a maze of false friends, bureaucracy and corruption.

Taaw
1970   26 mins   Colour   £24
A day in the life of a 20 year old youth, who cannot find a job, is thrown out by his father . . .

Emitai (Lord of the Sky)
1972   103 mins   Colour   £35
Also available from BFI in two 15-minute extracts designed for school showings. Set at the end of the Second World War, centred on the Diola people, whose menfolk have been pressured into French military service – a film about what leads to revolution.

Life on the River Shari
1962   19 mins   (Oxfam)   Concord   £4.20
This film describes one day in the life of a fishing village in the country of Chad – which borders on Lake Chad at the north-west corner of Nigeria.

Bozo Daily Life
16 mins   Edward Patterson Associates   £9.50
One of a series of films on the Bozo, a river people of Mali. It is beautifully photographed and there is a natural sound track – the sounds of the river, voices, etc.

Gambia: River of the Ancestors
15 mins   Colour   Concord   £4
Juffereh, the village in Alex Haley's *Roots* is revisited and its past and present explored. Current UNICEF projects are concerned with the search for clean water supplies and the setting up of health clinics.

Films available from Ghana High Commission are listed in Unit 11 *Anowa*. Titles are:

1 *This is Ghana*	2 *Panoply of Ghana*
4 *Wealth in Timber*	5 *Ghana at a Glance*
8 *Ghana Dances*	10 *Deer Hunt Festival*
11 *Ghana Builds –*	12 *Volta River Project*
Parts 1 and 2	15 *Industrial Develop-*
14 *Ghana – Gateway*	*ment in Ghana*
to Africa	20 *Independence*
	Celebration

Posters

From CWDE at £1.20 + VAT the set of two, with notes. Published 1979:
Photoposter 1: Woman selling eggs (Nigeria)
Order No. P-11
Photoposter 2: Girl selling bread (Nigeria)
Order No. P-12

Slide sets (all in colour)

From CWDE, all accompanied by notes (order number in brackets):

Nigeria in Change
No. 1 – *Modern Nigeria*, 1979 (S-1)
20 slides   £5.50 + VAT
No. 2 – *Traditional Nigeria* – Oyo (S-2)

Kwadjo of Ghana
1978   32 slides   £6.45 + VAT   (S-6)
About the daily life of teenage Kwadjo, son of a tax collector.

Town and Village in Northern Ghana
1973   12 slides   £3.25 + VAT

Any Old Scrap
1981   30 slides   £6.45 + VAT   (S-5T)
Focuses on ingenious use of scrap material in the Sahel as well as recycling in UK.

From Audio-Visual Library Services, Powdrake Street, Grangemouth, Stirlingshire, K3 9UT, Scotland:
Ashanti Gold Weights by M. McLeod   12 slides and commentary   £3.25

From the Museum of Mankind:
Slides of West African Art and Artefacts (e.g. Ashanti gold weights, masks and pottery) – catalogue on request £2.

Available for loan at Northamptonshire teachers centres: produced by P. Jones and F. Bourne:
6 Slide sets of Ghana: 1. Kumasi; 2. A journey through Ghana; 3. The Coast of Ghana; 4. Ghana – Traditional Culture and Crafts; 5. Tema and the Volta River Scheme; 6. Accra and the Accra Plains.

Books

VICTOR ENGELBERT, *Camera on Ghana: The World of A Young Fisherman*, Harcourt, Brace, Jovanovich (N.Y.), 1971.
Excellent photographs of Ashanti life.

MICHAEL GREEN, *Through the Year in West Africa*, Batsford, 1982.
A vivid account of life in a small town in north-west Cameroon. Excellent photographs. Available CWDE (B-223) £5.95.

MYLENE REMY, *Ghana Today*, Jeune Afrique, Paris, 1977.
Covers different regions and cultures of Ghana, their agriculture and urban life.

Resource collections and booklets

All the following are available from CWDE (order numbers in brackets):

Ghana (H-18), 1979. Class materials about Ghana and Ghanaian life, including maps, £2.

Ghana – The Road to Wonoo (B-26). Booklet on life in a weaving village, 50p.

Country Fact Sheets, published by Commonwealth Institute. A4 booklets, 30p each + 20p postage.
Nigeria (L-73)
Sierra Leone (L-74)
The Gambia (L-68)
Ghana (L-69)

Commonwealth Institute Topic Booklets. 30p each + 20p postage.
Two Savannah Villages in Northern Ghana (B-98)

Nigeria in Change. Each set has 16 A4 B/W photos, separate notes. £1.60 + VAT.
Women and Children in Nigeria (P-2)
Health in Nigeria (P-3)

Sierra Leone (P31-35). £2 per pack.
5 resource packs for 'O' and 'A' Level.
1 Case Studies in Colonialism
2 Political Development
3 Agricultural Development
4 Urban Development
5 Development Strategies

From British Museum Publications, Ltd:
The Yoruba and their Gods, by Ben Burt, booklet, 60p.

Published by Oxford University Press:
Section C of 'Living Together', Schools Council Integrated Studies Project, The Mandingo of West Africa, OUP, 1974. A folder containing 6 sets of 10 sheets with Teachers' Notes, a separate tape and 24 slides.

The 10 sheets cover geography, history, daily life, family life, music, art, towns and markets, and education. The text includes many extracts from contemporary documents, rewritten for simplicity – it is all very simply written. There are pictures and maps and an extract from Alex Haley's *Roots*, and the tape has his voice recounting the Mandingo praise singer who knew his family well. The kit includes a sheet on music, which illustrates the instruments used on the tape.

General

Films

The Ancient Africans
27 mins Colour Edward Patterson Associates £11.50
A fascinating kaleidoscope view of Ancient Africa, using a wide range of techniques: animation, modern film, reconstruction, and stills.

Kentu
28 mins Colour Concord £14.20
Part of a series 'Africa the Transitional Society' by Congolese Film Production 1975. Film focuses on a group of Congolese women who prefer independence with their children to the restrictions of customary marriage, yet they retain what they consider to be the best features of their own customs and combine these with some Western values.

Mukissi
25 mins Colour Concord £14.20
Part of the series 'Africa the Transitional Society'. Film depicts a crisis of mental illness in the life of a young women and the community's response to this. Interesting comparison of African and Western attitudes to mental health and ways of cure.

Partnership for Prosperity
29 mins Colour Central Film Library £10.50
Focuses on interdependence of North and South. Relationship between primary producers (three examples from Africa and the Caribbean) and final markets shown. Lomé Convention and EEC relations discussed.

Multi-Cultured Swap Shop 25 mins Concord £13.20
Number 1 of a series called Multi-Racial Britain. About how teachers can help prepare the next generation to live in a multi-racial society. The film shows how schools in Bradford and West Bromwich are responding to pupils of Asian and West Indian origin.

Black Children, White Schools
25 mins   Colour   Concord   £14.20
The film argues that a completely new school system is needed in Africa to reflect more the cooperative orientated society which is traditional in Black Africa. Schools at present teach the western idea of competition and individual success.

Black Man's Burden
50 mins   B/W   Concord   £11
Probably the best film available on the problems encountered by poor countries. Is the aid supplied by richer countries really aid – or is it to the long-term benefit of the 'investors'? Julius Nyerere of Tanzania discusses his own country. Thames TV, 1971.

Notes for an African Oresteia   Connoisseur films
75 mins   £25
Directed by Pier Paolo Pasolini, 1969. Commentary in English. The film consists of a series of visual notes intercut with interviews and discussions with black students of the University of Rome. It is a personal essay on democracy and on the condition of black humanity today. He interprets present-day Africa in terms of the classic tragedy, *Oresteia*, by Aeschylus.

African Sanctus
1975   50 mins   Colour   Concord   £14
A BBC 'Omnibus' programme in which David Fanshawe, composer and explorer, went to Africa in search of traditional music, which he incorporated into his *Sanctus*. The vitality of the music and the brilliant photography show the cultural richness of traditional Africa.

Recorded sound

English Speaking Africa Cassette 10. England Enterprises, 6 Well Walk, London N3. (Tel: 01-435-4323)
Interviews, readings, debates on apartheid; also useful dramatization from Equiano's account of his Atlantic passage as a slave.

Books, Booklets, Resource Packs

The following are available from CWDE (Order numbers in brackets).

M. KILLINGRAY, *African Studies: A Handbook for Teachers* £3 (H-15)
1979 production of the SOAS Extramural Division. Second ed. 1983.

African Beliefs and Customs Booklet 20p (B-23)

Africa – Patterns of Development Booklet published by Commonwealth Institute in 1978   50p (B-24)
An attractive illustrated survey of the African past, and present development, costumes, music and dance, etc.

Learning about Africa £2 (H-16)
1979 account and evaluation of a teachers' in-service study visit to Ghana – with photos, drawings, and material suitable for group work.

Why the Spider Lives in Corners £1.85 (B-33)
Collection of African 'facts and fun' on five countries: Ghana, Liberia, Congo, Uganda, Zambia. (1971).

The Development Puzzle £2.85 (H-1)
1979 revised edition of best-selling sourcebook for teachers – includes introductory information, resources, ideas for teaching.

From British Film Institute Publications

African Film: The Context of Production, by Angela Martin, BFI Dossier 6. £2.60 inc. p. & p.

Film distributors

This section lists the address of each film distributor together with information on the hire prices which are quoted in the refrences to films.
All the films listed are available as 16 mm films with optical sound track.

BFI (British Film Institute):
Enquiries concerning film, video, or study extract hire to BFI Film and Video Library, 9 Chapone Place, Dean Street, London W1 (Tel: 01-437-4355). Extracts on film or video are £3 a day + VAT + carriage.

Central Film Library, Chalfont Grove, Gerrards Cross, Bucks SL9 TN (Tel. 02-407-4111)
Prices shown are for hire for one day and exclude VAT and carriage. 14–16 days notice required, free Securicor return for 2 or more films hired at once.

Concord: Concord Films Council Ltd., 201 Felixstowe Road, Ipswich, Suffolk, IP3 9BS. Bookings and Accounts (Tel: 0473-76012) Film Despatch (Tel: 0473-77747)

Prices shown are for hire for one day, and do not include VAT and carriage. Subsequent days are at 25% of first day's hire, per day.

Connoisseur: Bookings and enquiries to Harris Films Ltd., Glenbuck Road, Surbiton, Surrey KT6 6BT (Tel: 01-399-0022)
Details on hire charges from Connoisseur, 167 Oxford Street, London W1R 2DX (Tel: 01-734-6555/6).

Contemporary: Contemporary Films Ltd., 55 Greek Street, London W1V 6DB (Tel: 01-434 2623)
Prices for one day hire and exclude VAT and carriage. 15% discount available for schools.

Drake Educational Productions Ltd, St Fagans Road, Fairwater, Cardiff (Tel: 0222-245-02).

Office of the High Commissioner for Ghana, 13 Belgrave Square, London SW1 (Tel: 01-434-2623)
Films lent free of charge, on condition that they are returned immediately after use by registered post.

Kenya High Commission, 45 Portland Place, London W1 (Tel: 01-636-2371/5)
Conditions as for Ghana High Commission.

Other Cinema: The Other Cinema, 79 Wardour Street, London W1V 3TH (Tel: 01-734-8508)
Prices shown do not include carriage. Hire period three days.
Films sent out by Securicor, and should be returned the same way. The cost of this is pre-paid, and is about £8.50.

Edward Patterson Associates, Treetops, Canongate Road, Hythe, Kent (Tel: 0803-64195), CT21 5PT.
Prices do not include VAT or carriage. Hire period one day or weekly. Free educational catalogue available.

Rank Aldis: Rank Aldis, P.O. Box 70, Great West Road, Brentford, Middlesex TW8 9HR (Tel: 01-568-9222).
Film hire (Tel: 01-560-0762/3) Hire period two days.

Royal Anthropological Institute Film Library, c/o Scottish Film Library, Dowanhill, 74 Victoria Crescent Rd, Glasgow G12 2JN. Hire period: two days. Prices exclude VAT and carriage.

Recorded sound

National Sound Archive, 29 Exhibition Road, London SW7 (Tel: 01-589-6603/4)
This houses a large collection of African recorded material including poetry and song, African popular music and interviews with and talks by contemporary African writers. Listening facilities are available. Copies of selected tapes for educational use may be made on request. Tapes of the BBC Schools Broadcast 1981 series on the writers Ngugi, Achebe and Soyinka, linked to the London 'A' level Special Paper 2 option are also housed here.

Collet's Record Shop, 180 Shaftesbury Ave., London WC2 (Tel: 01-240-3969)
Stocks a collection of popular and traditional African music and some Caribbean.

Other useful addresses

Africa Resource Centre
38 King Street, London WC2 (Tel: 01-836-1973)
A basic reference collection of books and journals on all parts of Africa, which includes some school materials. An information service is available to the public.

African Arts in Education Project
Administrator and Education Officer: Jane Grant, c/o 2nd floor, Coburg School, Coburg Road, London SE5 0JD (Tel: 01-836-1973) and Director: E. Josiah c/o L101 Odhams Walk, London WC2 (Tel: 01-836-2103)
A project aiming to integrate visits by West African musicians, artists and teachers to London schools, into the wider curriculum in a multi-cultural and development education context. A report together with supportive audio-visual material has been produced for ILEA Learning Materials Service. Anyone interested in participating is invited to contact either E. Josiah or J. Grant at the addresses above.

African and Asian Resource Centre
Newman College, Bartley Green, Birmingham B32 (Tel: 021-476-1181). Has a large supply of reference material on Iran, for consultation. Also runs courses and seminars on African and Caribbean literature, and history.

African and Caribbean Educational Research Project Library
Centre for Learning Resources, 275 Kennington Lane, London SE11 (Tel: 01-582-2771)
A multi-media collection of publications with an African and Caribbean perspective or which refer to the Black experience in societies such as Britain or the USA. Includes a substantial collection of children's literature, reference books and works on multicultural education. Visitors are welcome.

The Aklowa Centre for Traditional African Drumming and Dancing
Takeley, Bishops Stortford CM22 6QR
Organizes courses in African music, dance, folk stories; cultural expeditions, special events. Group membership £20 per annum.

The Association for the Teaching of Caribbean and African Literature (ATCAL)
An association of teachers and others concerned to promote African, Caribbean and Black British writing at all levels of education. Resource lists available from: Robert Bush, 8 Tylecroft Road, London SW16.

Birmingham Development Education Centre
Selly Oak Colleges, Birmingham B29 6LQ (Tel: 021-472-4231)

Black People's Information Centre – Library
301 Portobello Road, London W10 (Tel: 01-969-4123)
A reference collection of books and journals on the history, culture, politics, etc. of Black people all over the world – includes also a collection of slides on Caribbean history and slavery.

City of Bristol Museum and Art Gallery
Queen's Road, Bristol BS8 1RL (Tel: 0272-299771)
The museum has an extensive ethnographical collection of art and everyday objects from Africa, though these are too precious to be sent out to schools. There are however occasional exhibitions.

British Film Institute Publications
81 Dean Street, London W1V 6AA

British Museum Publications Ltd
6 Bedford Square, London WC1B 3RA

CAFOD (Catholic Fund for Overseas Development)
2 Garden Close, Stockwell Road, London SW9 9TY (Tel: 01-735-9041)
Publishes a Resources Catalogue, an educational newsletter and provides speakers on CAFOD projects. Excellent material on South Africa.

CIIR
Educational Dept., Catholic Institute for International Relations, 1 Cambridge Terrace, London NW1 (Tel: 01-487-4431)

Centre for Language in Primary Education – Library
Ebury Teachers' Centre, Sutherland Street, London SW1 (Tel: 01-821-8012)
A reference library of Caribbean and Asian books suitable for teaching and easily available in the UK. The staff are also happy to give critical advice on books they consider inappropriate for teaching. The Centre publishes a journal, *Language Matters*.

Centre for Urban Educational Studies – Library
Robert Montefiore School, Underwood Road, London E1 5AD (Tel: 01-377-0040)
A reference collection of multi-ethnic fiction and general books for primary and secondary schools. A file of bibliographies and reading lists on various aspects of multi-ethnic education is available for consultation.

CWDE
Centre for World Development Education, 128 Buckingham Palace Road, London SW1W 9SH (Tel: 01-730-8332/3)
An agency funded mainly by the Overseas Development Administration of the Foreign and Commonwealth Office.

The Children's Rights Workshop (CRW)
4 Aldebert Terrace, London SW8.
Issues a termly journal *Children's Literature Bulletin* with articles, news, and reviews about children's literature with particular reference to content. Please send a stamped addressed envelope for replies.

CA Publications
Christian Aid, P.O. Box 1, London SW9
Has published extremely useful map of the world (The North and South Map) giving a fairer impression of the relative size of continents. Useful teaching aid.

Commission for Racial Equality
The Education Department, The CRE, Elliott House, 10–12 Allington House, London SW1 (Tel: 01-828-7022)
The education department has materials and advice on multi-cultural education.

Commonwealth Institute, Library and Resource Centre
Kensington High Street, London W8 (Tel: 01-602-3252 extension 242)

A collection of books, journals and audio-visual materials for reference and loan on the way of life, culture, development, etc. of the countries of the Commonwealth and other aspects such as multi-ethnic education, race relations, world religions. The collection is one of the largest in the UK for contemporary Commonwealth literature and includes a large number of children's books, many of them published overseas. Reading lists and bibliographies on Commonwealth countries are also available.

Community Relations Commission
15–16 Bedford Street, London WC2E 9HX

CEWC, Council for Education in World Citizenship
Cobham House, Blackfriars Lane, London EC4 6EB (Tel: 01-236-0348)

Ekomé Arts
36 Argyle Road, St Pauls, Bristol BS2 8UY.
Nationally known for their music and dance group. Formed to promote arts of Africa and the Caribbean in education.

English Centre
Ebury Teachers' Centre, Sutherland Street, London SW1 (Tel: 01-821-8012)
This centre includes a small collection of multicultural books suitable for secondary schools. It is also active in publishing and has issued multi-ethnic story books, bibliographies, and anthologies, some of which are devoted to Caribbean writing. Visitors by appointment.

The Ghana Union
The Project Officer, Ghana Union Community Centre, St Andrews Church, Salusbury Road, London NW6.
Formed in 1978, it has among its objectives to establish a resource centre, to give courses on African studies, to create greater awareness of African cultures among UK children and professional groups. It is a possible source of speakers on Ghana.

Office of the High Commissioner for Ghana
13 Belgrave Square, London SW1
(Tel: 01-235-4142/7)
For films and posters.

History and Social Sciences Teachers Centre, ILEA
377 Clapham Road, SW4 near Clapham North tube (Tel: 01-733-2935)

Horniman Museum
London Road, Forest Hill, London SE23 3PQ (Tel: 01-699-4911/2339/1872)
Has a large ethnographic section which includes African material, particularly musical instruments.

Has talks, demonstration material, films and slides available on:
Traditional crafts of Africa
African Rural Life
Tribal Beliefs and Ritual
Other talks may be arranged.

IDAF
Canon Collins House, 64 Essex Road, London N1 (Tel: 01-326-6181)
Has a wealth of well-produced educational material on South Africa. It takes a strong anti-Government view on South Africa.

ITDG, Intermediate Technology Development Group
9 King Street, London WC2 (Tel: 01-836-9434)

Kenya High Commission
45 Portland Place, London W1 (Tel: 01-636-2371/5)
For films, information and leaflets.

Kenya Tourist Office
13 New Burlington Street, London W1
For posters and handbooks.

Minority Arts Advisory Service (MAAS)
Beauchamp Lodge, 2 Warwick Crescent, London W2 (Tel: 01-286-1854) Directory available: cost £5. Magazine: *Artrage* ed. Fay Rodrigues.

Multi-cultural Education Centre
Bishopston School, Bishop Road, Bishopston, Bristol 5, Avon

Multi-ethnic Curriculum Development Unit
Centre for Learning Resources, 275 Kennington Lane, London SE11 5QS (Tel: 01-582-4509)

The Museum of Mankind
The Ethnography Department of the British Museum, 6 Burlington Gardens, Piccadilly, London W1 (Tel: 01-437-2224)
Permanent Exhibition: Yoruba Religious Cults (Nigeria)

The Museum of Mankind has a students' room with reference material for consultation. Bibliographies on particular topics (for example, Yoruba Art) are also available on request. There is also a wide selection of postcards, posters, and slides for purchase.

National Association for Multi-Racial Education (NAME)
c/o Ms Madeleine Blakeley, General Secretary, 86 Station Road, Mickleover, Derby DE3 5FP (Tel: 0332-511751)
(Please send a stamped addressed envelope)

ODI, Overseas Development Institute
10–11 Percy Street, London W1P 0JB (Tel: 01-580-7683)
Orders for lists and publications to Research Publications Services Ltd., 11 Nelson Road, London SE10 (Tel: 01-858-1717). Include payment with order. (Public welcome to use the library.)

ODA
Information Department, Overseas Development Administration, Room E920, Eland House, Stag Place, London SW1 (Tel: 01-213-4953)

OXFAM
Education Dept., Oxfam, 274 Banbury Road, Oxford (Tel: 0865-56777)

Resources for Learning Development Unit
Redcross Street, Bristol 1

Public Libraries – various
Some have substantial collections of Afro-Caribbean literature and have appointed specialist librarians in charge of those collections.

SCF, Save the Children Fund
157 Clapham Road, London SW9 0PT (Tel: 01-582-1414)

Secondary Curriculum Development Unit
Centre for Learning Resources, 275 Kennington Lane, London SE11 5QS
(Tel: 01-633-2738/9)
Advisory teachers working for the ILEA Multi-ethnic Inspectorate on development within ILEA secondary schools across the curriculum.

School of Oriental and African Studies (SOAS), Extramural Division – Resource Centre
Malet Street, London WC1 (Tel: 01-637-2388)
A reference collection of books, audio-visual materials, and journals on Africa and Asia which are easily available in the UK. Includes a card index of audio-visual materials commercially available for hire or sale.

School of Oriental and African Studies (SOAS) Library
Malet Street, London WC1 (Tel: 01-637-2388)
The African section of the Library covers books on African and European languages and includes a growing collection of books on African literature. Visitors are welcome.

Steel and Skin Dance Group
Runs workshops in schools, teaches dance steps, also a dance group. Specializes in dancing from Ghana, Dahomey, Nigeria.

Contact: Genge Dzikunu, 143B Abbey Road, London NW6 (Tel: 01-328-5233)

South Africa House
Trafalgar Square, London WC2 (Tel: 01-930-4488)
Visual material and information available which presents South Africa in a favourable light.

UNICEF
46–47 Osnaburgh Street, London NW1 (Tel: 01-388-7487)

USPG
United Society for the Propagation of the Gospel, 15 Tufton Street, London SW1P 3QQ (Tel: 01-222-4222)
Its shop stocks a range of books on Africa plus teachers' packs and slide sets on countries or African dioceses. The quarterly magazine *Network* is full of information.

WDM (World Development Movement)
26 Bedford Chambers, London WC2 (Tel: 01-836-3672)

WOW (War on Want)
467 Caledonian Road, London N7 (Tel: 01-609-0211)

Bookshops specializing in Caribbean, African and Black American books

London

African Book Centre, 38 King Street, London WC2 (Tel: 01-240-2666)
A permanent exhibition of English-language books on Africa suggested by publishers. Some titles of low-priced fiction by African authors are also available for sale. Will shortly include books on the Caribbean and by Caribbean authors.

Archway Development Education Centre, 173 Archway Road, London N6 (Tel: 01-348-3030)
Stockist of Third World books with a limited supply of artefacts, films, slides. Mainly development education.

The Bookplace, 13 Peckham High Street, London SE15 (Tel: 01-701-1757)
Publish some works by Caribbean writers and literacy students; mainly children's books but some books for adults, cards, posters, etc. are also stocked.

Centreprise, 136 Kingsland High Street, London E8 (Tel: 01-254-9632)
A community bookshop with sections on African, Black American and Caribbean culture and literature, children's books, Black British writing and adult literacy books. Stocks mainly paperbacks and books published in the UK.

Dillon's University Bookshop, 1 Malet Street, London WC1 (Tel: 01-636-1577)
The African Department of the shop includes an African literature section of books for adults published in Africa and in Britain and also a few titles by Caribbean authors.

Global Book Resources Ltd, 109 Great Russell Street, London WC1B 3NA (Tel: 01-580-2633)
All Ad Donker and David Philip publications are available here.

Grassroots Storefront, 61 Golbourne Road, London W10 (Tel: 01-969-0687)
Specializing in Caribbean and African books for adults and children; also stock posters, art and crafts, post cards.

Headstart Books and Crafts, 25 West Green Road, London N15 (Tel: 01-802-2838)
Specializing in books on Africa, Black America and the Caribbean. African crafts are also available.

Kegan Paul, Trench, Trubner, 39 Store Street, London WC1 (Tel: 01-636-1252)
Useful for the arts, culture and anthropology of Africa and Asia. The shop includes a growing stock of African literature published in Britain.

New Beacon Books, 76 Stroud Green Road, London N4 (Tel: 01-272-4889)
Specializing in Caribbean, African and Black American Literature. A large selection of children's books especially Caribbean school books. Also publishes Black British books.

Sabarr Books, 378 Coldharbour Lane, London SW2 (Tel: 01-274-6785)

Specializing in Caribbean African and Black American books. They also stock works about other ethnic minorities, cards, posters and art.

Soma Books (Independent Publishing Co.), 38 Kennington Lane, London SE11 (Tel: 01-735-2101) and at the Commonwealth Institute, Kensington High Street, London W8.
Originally stocked books from the Indian Sub-continent, recently extended their stock to include Afro-Caribbean books.

Ujamaa Bookshop, 14 Brixton Road, London SW9 (Tel: 01-582-2068)
Third World Development Education books, posters, cards, artefacts are stocked. They also organize meetings and suggest the use of materials for schools.

Walter Rodney Book Shop (formerly Bogle L'Ouverture Bookshop), 5a Chigwell Place, London W13 (Tel: 01-579-4920)
Publishers and stockists of Caribbean African and Black American books, periodicals, journals and newspapers from the Caribbean. A large selection of Caribbean school books.

This list compiled by Christiane Keane and Beryl Thomas for ATCAL (Association for the Teaching of Caribbean and African Literature)

Birmingham

Harriet Tubman Bookshop, 27–29 Grove Lane, Handsworth, Birmingham B21 9ES (Tel: 021-554-8479/5323)
Specializes in African and Caribbean fiction and non-fiction.

Third World Publications, Head Office, 151 Stratford Road, Birmingham B11 1RD (Tel: 021-773-6572)
Wide selection, catalogue on request. Suppliers for Ravan Press, Johannesburg.

Part B *Bibliographies*

Texts: Lower secondary

First–third year. (Age 11–14)
P = Also suitable top primary, **D** = Drama,
Po = Poetry

CHINUA ACHEBE, *Chike and The River*, Cambridge University Press, 1966.
Chike's life with his uncle in Onitsha, south-east Nigeria. Covers school, masqueraders at Easter, finding an English pen-friend, a bicycle accident, car thieves. **P**

ELECHI AMADI, *Isiburu*, Heinemann Secondary Readers, 1973.
Set in pre-colonial Igboland, south-east Nigeria. A wrestler dies suddenly and is miraculously restored to life. Focus on wrestling competition, visit to sacred grove. A lot of drumming. **D**

PEGGY APPIAH, *Ring of Gold*, André Deutsch, 1976.
Set in Ghana. Children need money for their school library. They find a ring, trace the owner and manage to raise the necessary funds. Style on the dull side.
Tales of an Ashanti Father, André Deutsch, 1967.
Folk tales from Ghana for young children. Very well illustrated by Mora Dickson.
The Pineapple Child and Other Tales from the Ashanti, André Deutsch, 1969.
A Smell of Onions, Longman, 1971, Longman (Drumbeat 10), 1976.
A series of stories of village life based around the genial figure of Kwaku Hoampam. Covers setting up a post-office, a better road, problems at school, a robbery, and the resulting court case.

KATHLEEN ARNOTT, *African Fairy Tales*, Muller, 1967.
A collection from Southern, East and West Africa. Covers magic, mystery and morality. Author manages to retain vigour and liveliness of original oral performance. Bibliography. Illustrated.
Auta the Giant Killer and other Nigerian Folk stories, Oxford University Press, 1971.
Stores from the Hausa, Yoruba, Tiv and Igbo. Good for reading aloud. Well illustrated; map and information. **P**

MARTIN BALLARD, *The Speaking Drums of Ashanti*, Longman (Young Books), 1970.
Set in Ghana, historical, fast-moving narrative.

The Beauty of Being Black, Friendship Press (USA), 1971 (available CWDE).
Folk Tales, Poems and Art from Africa.
Well illustrated.

ANDRÉE CLAIR AND BOUBOU HAMA, *The Enchanted Savannah: Tales from West Africa*, Translated Oliver Jones, Methuen Children's Books, 1974.
The work of a distinguished collector of oral traditions and a well-known French children's writer. Five stories of adventure and courage rewarded. Excellent illustrations. **P**

J.V. CLINTON, *The Rescue of Charlie Kalu*, Heinemann Secondary Readers, 1971.
Set in the Niger delta. Charlie is kidnapped in Calabar by members of the Kamalu secret society. Private detective Okai Ata sets out to find him.

DOUGLAS COOMBES AND JOHN EMLYN EDWARDS, *Hassebu*, BBC Publications, 1974 teachers' and pupils' books.
Set in Zanzibar. A boy encounters the wise and powerful King of Snakes who helps him to save the Sultan's life and gain a rich reward. In the *Time and Tune Cantatas* series. Can be performed with narrator and chorus, in mime, or as a playlet. **P D**

MICHAEL CULLUP (ed.), *The Stomach and his Friends*, Heinemann Secondary Readers, 1973.
Stories, mostly from Western Kenya; legends of famous men, of migrations; many with a moral point some stressing value of, for example, courage, or quick wittedness.

SUSHEELA CURTIS, *Mainane – Tswana Tales*, Botswana Book Centre, Gaberone, 1975.
Twenty-eight tales recorded by the author in two villages in Southern Botswana. Full of magic and fantasy; often about human failings such as jealousy, rivalry. Useful notes.

JUNE O. DANKYI AND KITTY L. LAWRENCE, *Firelight Fables*, Longman, 1972.
A collection of traditional Ghanaian folktales. Illustrated.

GERALDINE ELLIOTT, *Where the Leopard Passes*, Routledge and Kegan Paul, 1949.
Eighteen animal stories; as so often in African tales, the animals are used as a device for exploring human nature. **P**

FIONA FRENCH, *Aio the Rainmaker*, Oxford University Press, 1975.
By well-known children's writer; superbly illustrated, useful for any work on masks. **P**

FREDERIC GUIRMA, *Tales of the Moglio*, Collier Macmillan (USA), 1974.
Stories from the Upper Volta, remembered and retold by author from his own childhood. Range of subjects. Illustrated.

HUMPHREY HARMAN, *Tales Told to an African King*, Hutchinson Junior Library, 1978.
Set in Uganda, in islands and mainland north-east of Lake Victoria. Uses historical/legendary figure of young king in exile. Includes tales and legends told to him and account of how he wins back his kingdom. Suspense, humour, good for reading aloud. **P**

SAMUEL KAHIGHA, *Lover in the Sky*, Heinemann, Spear, 1975.
Set in Kenya. A trainee pilot falls in love with an independent and beautiful girl who at first rejects him. Credible central characters, skilful use of recent history and urban themes.

GERALDINE KAYE, *Kofi and the Eagle*, Methuen Children's Books, Second ed. 1973.
About a little boy who is sold a young eagle. Slow-moving but a good story. **P**

DAVID KILLINGRAY, *Samori Touré Warrior King*, Hulton, 1973.
A simply told story of one of the most famous resisters of French rule in present-day Guinea. **P**

JEANNE NGO LIBONDO, *Joseph Haven't You Got Your Bicycle Yet?*, Heinemann Secondary Readers, 1973.
A comic-sad play about petty bureaucracy and one man's frustrated attempts to own a bicycle. Theme similar to Ousmane's *Money Order*. **D**

NOEL MACHIN, *African Poetry for Schools*, Books 1 & 2, Longman, 1978.
A rich collection covering oral and written poetry: proverbs, love songs, drinking songs, songs of protest, dirges, praise poems are included; the written poetry is wide-ranging in theme and form. Some Caribbean and Black American included. Questions. Teachers' notes. Photographs and line drawings. **Po**

ARTHUR MARKOWITZ, *The Rebirth of the Ostrich*, National Museum and Art Gallery, Gaberone, Botswana, 1971.
Poetry and stories. Useful for animal poems, the supernatural, nature and the elements, death; people in an intense relationship with living creatures and elemental forces. **Po**

R.E. MCDOWELL AND E. LAVITT, *Third World Voices for Children*, Allison and Busby, 1973.
Useful selection of prose and poetry; includes oral poetry and narrative but often omits country of origin. Illustrations. **Po**

JOHN MERCER, *The Stories of Vanishing Peoples*, Allison and Busby, 1982.
A good collection of stories, suitable for lower secondary. Includes some African material.

NAOMI MITCHISON, *Snake!*, Collins, 1976.
A little girl who thinks she has been bitten by a snake is taken to town and to hospital for the first time. Evocative Botswana atmosphere, good dialogue, accessible language. **P**
Ketse and the Chief, Nelson, Salamander, 1965.
A young boy meets his Chief in unusual circumstances. Emphasizes respect for traditional authority in Botswana; lively story. **P**
Sunrise Tomorrow: A Story of Botswana, Collins, 1973.
Interesting consideration of problems and choices facing young adolescents in Botswana: a training or marriage? School or herding? Modern or traditional? A combination? Individual or community first?
The Family at Ditlabeng, Collins, 1966.
Covers friendships of children, relationships with parents, hardships, aspirations, linking of economic conditions and family life; fathers away in South African gold mines.

THOMAS MOFOLO, *Chaka the Zulu*, Oxford University Press, English Readers Library, 1949. (See D. Kunene, Sixth form texts)

MUSA NAGENDA, *Dogs of fear*, Heinemann Secondary Readers, 1971.
A young Ugandan boy wants to do well at school and to please his traditionally minded father. Nagenda describes often conflicting values of school and village with vividness and an eye for detail.
The Ostrich Egg-Shell Canteen, Heinemann Secondary Readers 1973.
Story of a San (Bushman) girl who wishes to learn to hunt. Courage and initiative of girl, Khuana, and affection between her and her grandmother well conveyed.

MARTIN OWUSU, *The Story Ananse Told*, Heinemann Secondary Readers, 1971.
A poor hunter is given riches and a Kingdom by a young woman with magical powers – but there are conditions he must keep. Lively, humorous with message that a person is rarely satisfied with whatever he or she has. **D**

PEPETELA, *Ngunga's Adventures: A Story of Angola*, Young World Books, 1980. (c/o Liberation, 313–315 Caledonian Road, London N1.)
A realistic and simple account of a young boy's involvement in the war of liberation. Based on true accounts.

MARGUERITE POLAND and LEIGH VOIGT, *Mantis and the Moon*, Ravan, 1979.
Stories from Southern African folk-lore. Sense of place, atmosphere, well conveyed; precision in detail of birds, insects, beasts and their often recognizable human characteristics. Illustrated.

JENNY SEED, *The Sly Green Lizard*, Hamish Hamilton, Antelope series, 1973.
Three stories of Zulu princesses – includes journeys into an imaginary world, a trick, a change of identity. Well illustrated. **P**

ZULU SOFALA, *King Emene*, Heinemann Secondary Readers, 1974.
Set in mid-western Nigeria. The King disregards warnings that a crime in his own household must be revealed before the great festival. Dramatic contrasts and tensions rather understated. **D**

EFUA T. SUTHERLAND, *The Marriage of Anansewa*, Longman (Drumbeat 17), 1980.
Ananse's own plans misfire and only his daughter's death can save him. Use of song, dance and group interaction makes this a useful play for performing. **D**

DAVID SWEETMAN, *Queen Nzinga, the Woman who Saved her People*, Longman (Makers of African History Series), 1971.
A biography of the Angolan queen who resisted the early Portuguese invaders.

CHARITY WACIUMA, *Merry-Making*, East African Publishing House, Lioncub series, 1972.
Six short stories. Well illustrated. **P**

RICHARD WOOLLEY, *Shaka: King of the Zulu*, Longman (Makers of African History Series), 1973.
The herd-boy who founded a nation.

FRANK WORTHINGTON, *Kalulu the Hare* (simplified by M. West), Longman Supplementary Readers, 1937, 1963.

YOUNG WORLD BOOKS, *Tales from Mozambique*, Liberation, 313–315 Caledonian Road, London, 1980.
Mostly animal tales. Compiled for school use.

Texts: middle secondary

(Fourth and fifth year; age 14–16)
* = Also suitable at sixth form level; age 16–18

PETER ABRAHAMS, *Mine Boy*, Heinemann (African Writers Series 6), 1963.
One of the earliest explorations of the urban experience of a black worker in Johannesburg.
Wreath for Udomo See Unit 7.
Path of Thunder See Unit 7.

S.K. AKIVAGA and A.B. ODAGA (eds), *Oral literature* See Unit 12.

AMA ATA AIDOO, *No Sweetness Here* See Unit 11.
Dilemma of a Ghost **D** See Unit 11.

ELECHI AMADI, *The Concubine*, Heinemann (African Writers Series 25), 1966.*
A good and beautiful woman sees each of the men who love her die. What divine agency brings this about, and why?
The Great Ponds, Heinemann (African Writers Series 44), 1970.*
A feud between two villages in Eastern Nigeria over the rights to one of the Great Ponds brings victory to no one. Once again as in *The Concubine*, Amadi shows the gods at work amongst men.
An abridged edition also available in the Heinemann Guided Readers Series. Upper Level 7.

KOFI AWOONOR and G. ADALI MORRTY (eds), *Messages: Poems from Ghana*, Heinemann (African Writers Series 42), 1971.
Awoonor from the Eastern, Ewe region of Ghana, is known for the integration of traditional and modern techniques in his poetry. **Po**

MONGO BETI, *Mission to Kala*, translated from the French by Peter Green, Heinemann (African Writers Series 13), 1964.*
Medza has failed his French oral exams but instead of a rest, he spends his holiday on a mission to Kala to retrieve the runaway wife of a man from his own village. A comical and irreverent novel.
An abridged edition also available in the Heinemann Guided Readers Series Intermediate Level 17.

ULLI BEIER, *African Poetry* See Unit 12. **Po**

DONALD BURNESS, *Fire: Six writers from Angola, Mocambique and Cape Verde*, Three Continents Press, 1977.

GUY BUTLER and CHRISTOPHER MANN (eds), *A New Book of South African Verse*, Oxford University Press, 1979.
Both the editors are themselves poets. Mann has a particular interest in oral poetry. **Po**

ROBERT WELLESLEY COLE, *Kossoh Town Boy*, Cambridge University Press, 1960.
An autobiography of a Creole childhood in Freetown, Sierra Leone.

D. COOK and D. RUBADIRI (eds), *Poems from East Africa*, Heinemann (African Writers Series 96), 1971.
Still one of the most representative East African collections. **Po**

BERNARD DADIÉ, *Climbié*, translated from the French by Karen Chapman, Heinemann (African Writers Series 87), 1971.
A vivid account of a boy's youth on the Ivory Coast. Has parallels with Joyce's *Portrait of the Artist as a Young Man* and Camara Laye's *The African Child*.

NAFISSATOU DIALLO, *A Dakar Childhood*, translated from the French by Dorothy Blair, Longman (Drumbeat 48), 1982.
An autobiographical account of a young girl growing up in a large, stable Muslim family. Humorous and perceptive.

CYPRIAN EKWENSI, *People of the City*, Heinemann (African Writers Series 5), 1963.
Amusa Sango is a band-leader and journalist with a weakness for women. Set in Lagos, the story covers a city intrigue over money, wives, unfaithful husbands and good-time girls. Ending is moralistic.
Jagua Nana, Heinemann (African Writers Series 146), 1975.*
Jagua has made her living and her reputation as a successful prostitute of considerable standing. But marriage and real status elude her. A sympathetic portrait of a remarkable woman.

BUCHI EMECHETA, *The Bride Price*, Allison and Busby, 1976: Collins (Fontana), 1978.
A story focusing on the conflict between traditional Igbo marriage customs and personal choice.
The Slave Girl, Allison and Busby, 1977, Collins (Fontana), 1979.
Easily read story of an Igbo girl's experience of domestic slavery at the turn of the century, the effects of taxation on the Onitsha market women, and the girl's eventual marriage.

The Joys of Motherhood, Heinemann (African Writers Series 227), 1980.*
A harrowing account of a woman's exploitation as wife and mother. Realistic accounts of life in Lagos during the Second World War, written from a woman's perspective.

MICHAEL ETHERTON, *African Plays for Playing 1*, Heinemann (African Writers Series 165), 1975. **D**
African Plays for Playing 2, Heinemann (African Writers Series 179), 1976. **D**
Particularly useful is 'The Tragedy of Mr No Balance', by V.F. Masinga.

ATHOL FUGARD, *Tsotsi* See Unit 10.

ALEX LA GUMA, *A Walk in the Night, and Other Stories* See Unit 7.

MAFIKA GWALA, *No More Lullabies*, Ravan (Johannesburg), Staffrider Series 15, 1982.
Includes some fine poems from this pioneer Black Consciousness poet. **Po**

BESSIE HEAD, *The Collector of Treasures and other Botswana Village Tales*, Heinemann (African Writers Series 182), 1977.
Head writes about traditional and modern marriage in contemporary Botswana and explores the problems of rural people.

LOUIS BERNARDO HONWANA, *We Killed Mangy-Dog and other Mozambique Stories*, Heinemann (African Writers Series 60), 1969.
Title story frightening analysis of group violence from a child's point of view.

L. KIBERA and S. KAHIGA, *Potent Ash* (short stories) See Unit 3.

DORIS LESSING, *Nine African Stories*, Longman Imprint, 1968, 1978.
These brilliant stories from Lessing's early period deal with childhood in an African setting, issues of race and master-servant relationships.

MTUTUZELI MATSHOBA, *Call Me Not A Man* (short stories), Ravan (Johannesburg), 1979; Longman (Drumbeat 42), 1981.
Stories showing different aspects of the hectic, troubled and courageous existence of South Africa's black city-dwellers.

JOHN MUNONYE, *Obi*, Heinemann (African Writers Series 45), 1969.
A progressive Igbo couple return to their village to settle but in the end public opinion turns against them and they have to leave.

Oil Man of Obange, Heinemann (African Writers Series 94), 1971.
The depiction of a poor man's determined but doomed struggle to make a living and educate his family.

MBULELO MZAMANE, *The Children of Soweto*, Longman (Drumbeat 60), 1982.
My Cousin Comes to Jo'burg and other stories
See Unit 11.

NGUGI WA THIONG'O, *Secret Lives: Short Stories*, Heinemann (African Writers Series 150), 1975.
Covers the themes which dominate his novels: the land, false gods, loyalty and leadership.

GRACE OGOT, *The Promised Land*, East African Publishing House, 1966.
A story of Luo migration from Kenya to the north of Tanzania. Uncanny atmosphere of malevolence well created.

OKOT P'BITEK, *Song of Lawino and Song of Ocol*, East African Publishing House, 1966.
Satires on modernity by one of East Africa's leading poets. **Po**

A.M. OPPONG-AFFI, *Powers of Darkness*, Heinemann Secondary Readers, 1971.
A boy's interest in the occult leads him to try out a number of religious beliefs. Slow-moving. Also suitable for lower secondary.

ESSOP PATEL (ed.), *The Worlds of Nat Nakasa*, Intro. by Nadine Gordimer. Ravan Press/Bateleur Press, 1975.
Interesting because of his influence on figures such as Serote, Nkosi and Fugard, his insight into apartheid in the 1950s and his skill as an essayist.

ALAN PATON, *Cry the Beloved Country*, Penguin Modern Classics, 1958.
A priest from Zululand goes in search of his son and daughter who have gone to Johannesburg and never returned.
Debbie Go Home (short stories) See Unit 4.

J. REED and C. WAKE (eds), *A Book of African Verse*, Heinemann (African Writers Series 8), 1964. See Unit 13. **Po**

ROBERT ROYSTON, *Black Poets in South Africa* See Unit 13. **Po**

M. RUGYENDO, *The Barbed Wire* and other plays, Heinemann (African Writers Series 187), 1977.
Last play in book, on political instability, particularly recommended. **D**

MWANGI RUHENI, *Mystery Smugglers*, Heinemann (Spear), 1975.
Set in Nairobi – full of suspense with some good type characters: policeman, bar girls, con girls, and so on.
The Love Root, Heinemann (Spear), 1976.
A fast-moving account of the seamy side of life in Nairobi with the police in the role of tough-minded, patient individuals who don't give up.

TAYEB SALIH, *The Wedding of Zein* and other stories, translated from the Arabic by D. Johnson-Davie, Heinemann (African Writers Series 47), 1969.
The title story is a study of an eccentric but charismatic figure who at last finds a bride. Village setting skilfully evoked.

C. SEARLE (ed. and translator), *The Sunflower of Hope: poems from the Mozambican Revolution*, Allison and Busby, 1982.
Includes poems by Craveirinha and Noemia De Sousa. **Po**

K.E. SENANU and T. VINCENT, *A Selection of African Poetry* See Unit 13. **Po**

W. SOYINKA, *The Trials of Brother Jero* See Unit 10.
Aké: The years of childhood, Rex Collings, 1981; Hutchinson (Arena), 1983 (paperback)
Teeming with interest and useful for extracts with lower secondary or in full with senior classes.

EFUA T. SUTHERLAND, *Edufa*, Longman (Drumbeat 11), 1979. **D**
The Marriage of Anansewa, Longman (Drumbeat 17), 1980. **D**

J. LUANDINO VIEIRA, *Luaanda*, translated from the Portuguese by Tamara Bender, Heinemann (African Writers Series 222), 1980.
Three stories set in the slums of Luanda, Angola, in the 1940s and 1950s.

PAM ZABALA and CHRIS ROSSELL, *African Writing: a Thematic Anthology*, Collins, 1974.
Designed for use in African schools but adaptable to the British classroom. Includes Camara Laye, Achebe, Mugo Gatheru. Illustrated.

Texts: upper secondary

(Sixth form; age 16–18)

AMA ATA AIDOO, *Our Sister Killjoy: Reflections from a Black-eyed Squint*, Longman 1977; Longman (Drumbeat 35), 1981, see Unit 9.

CHINUA ACHEBE, *Arrow of God*, Heinemann (African Writers Series 16), second edition, 1974.
A proud but far-sighted Chief Priest stands alone against his clan and the white man. A penetrating study of personal and political conflict.
A Man of the People, Heinemann (African Writers Series 31), 1966.
A satirical portrait of a prosperous politician.

I.N.C. ANIEBO, *The Journey Within*, Heinemann (African Writers Series 206), 1978.
A study of two marriages, one Christian, one traditional, set in the bustling town of Port Harcourt before the Second World War.

AYI KWEI ARMAH, *The Beautyful Ones are Not Yet Born*, Heinemann (African Writers Series 43), 1969.
A satire on post-Independence Ghana.
Fragments, Heinemann (African Writers Series 154), 1974.
Baaka rejects the materialism of his family and of Accra society and finds himself an outcast.
The Healers See Unit 11.

MARIAMA BÂ, *So Long a Letter*, translated from the French by Modupé Bodé-Thomas, Heinemann (African Writers Series 248), 1981; Virago, 1981.
A novel focusing on the position of women in contemporary Africa.

ULLI BEIER, *Yoruba Poetry* See Unit 12. **Po**

MICHAEL CHAPMAN and ACHMAT DANGOR (eds), *Voices from Within: Black Poetry from southern Africa*, Ad Donker, Johannesburg, 1982.
The anthology ranges from early Khoisan poems to the Soweto poets of the 1970s. **Po**

J. PEPPER CLARK, *A Reed in the Tide* See Unit 13. **Po**
Casualties, Longman, 1970. **Po**
Poems written during the Nigerian Civil War.
A Decade of Tongues, Longman (Drumbeat 22), 1981.
Includes selections from the two above collections and previously unpublished work by this major Nigerian poet. **Po**

R. SARIF EASMON, *The Feud* (short stories), Longman (Drumbeat 29), 1981.
A collection from Sierra Leone. See Unit 10.

FARAAX M.J. CAWL, *Ignorance is the Enemy of Love*, translated from Somali by B.W. Andrzejewski, Zed, 1982.
Love is destroyed through the Dervish hero's illiteracy. A didactic novel with large sections of poetry.

NADINE GORDIMER, *Some Monday for Sure* (short stories), Heinemann (African Writers Series 177), 1976.
A selection from her writing over a number of years. Incisive, with perfect craftsmanship.

STEPHEN GRAY, *Modern South African Stories*, Ad Donker, Johannesburg, 1980.
An expanded and revised version of the 1974 *On the Edge of the World*. Includes work by established and lesser known writers.

CHUKWUEMEKA IKE, *Toads for Supper*, Fontana, 1965.
A university student falls in love with a girl from a different ethnic group and finds himself in trouble.

FESTUS IYAYI, *Violence*, Longman (Drumbeat 1), 1979.
Two families – one wealthy, the other poor, meet by chance. A powerful study of contemporary urban life in Nigeria.

DENYS JOHNSON-DAVIES (ed. and trans.), *Egyptian Short Stories*, Heinemann (African Writers Series 196), 1978.

GIBSON KENTE, AND OTHERS, *South African People's Plays*, Heinemann (African Writers Series 224), 1981.
Popular drama depicting the political struggle in South Africa. **D**

CAMARA LAYE, *The Radiance of the King*, translated from the French by James Kirkup, Fontana, 1965.
A brilliant allegorical novel of a European's journey of self-discovery in Africa.

DORIS LESSING, *The Grass is Singing*, Heineman (African Writers Series 131), 1973.
A classic story of loneliness and murder on a Rhodesian farm.

THOMAS MOFOLO, *Chaka*, translated from the Sotho by D.P. Kunene, Heinemann (African Writers Series, 229), 1981.
Mofolo's classic novel of the Zulu leader in a much-needed new translation.

EZEKIEL MPHAHLELE, *Down Second Avenue*, Faber, Second ed., 1971.
A classic autobiography of a South African childhood.

MBUYISENI OSWALD MTSHALI, *Sounds of a Cowhide Drum*, Oxford University Press, 1971.
South African poems. **Po**

CHARLES MUNGOSHI, *Waiting for the Rain*, Heinemann (African Writers Series 170), 1975.

Set in pre-Independence Zimbabwe – a family struggles to hold together, to hold onto shreds of belief. Bleak and powerful.

HAM MUKASA, *Sir Apollo Kagwa Discovers Britain*, ed. Taban Lo Liyong, Heinemann (African Writers Series 133), 1975.
A true account of a Ugandan Prime Minister's impressions of Britain and the British at the end of the last century.

MEJA MWANGI, *Going Down River Road*, Heinemann (African Writers Series 176), 1976.
Set in Nairobi. Not a particularly deep or thoughtful novel, but an attempt to capture the shallowness and harshness of fast city life.
Kill Me Quick, Heinemann (African Writers Series 143), 1973.
Describes the hardships of the young urban unemployed in bustling Nairobi.

NGUGI WA THIONG'O, *A Grain of Wheat*, Heinemann (African Writers Series 36), 1968.
A complexly structured account of the experience of Mau Mau and of the beginnings of Uhuru.
Petals of Blood, Heinemann (African Writers Series 188), 1977.
An epic novel: a small settlement becomes part of a new road but the prosperity does not extend to its original inhabitants.

ABIOSEH NICOL, *Two African Tales*, Cambridge University Press, 1965.
Two tales, one of the supernatural, the other of a fatal error of judgement, by a master of style and suspense.

D. NWOGA and R. EGUDU, *Igbo Traditional Verse*, Heinemann (African Writers Series 129), 1973.
A varied and stimulating collection of oral poetry. **Po**

GABRIEL OKARA, *The Voice*, Introduction by A. Ravenscroft, Heinemann (African Writers Series 68), 1970.
Okolo seeks for truth but in so doing does not conform and makes many enemies. Tries to keep Ijaw sentence patterns in his English – a successful experiment?
The Fisherman's Invocation, Heinemann (African Writers Series 183), 1978.
The only collection of his poetry. **Po**

ANTONIO OLINTO, *The Water House*, Nelson (Panafrica Library), 1981.
A Yoruba family returns from Brazil to Lagos after emancipation.

FEMI OSOFISAN, *The Chattering and the Song*, Ibadan University Press, 1977.
A critical look at the inane and the incongruous in contemporary Nigeria. **D**

FERDINAND OYONO, *Houseboy*, translated from the French by J. Reed, Heinemann (African Writers Series 29), 1966.
A young servant observes too well the double standards of his French employers, so they destroy him.
The Old Man and the Medal, translated from the French by J. Reed, Heinemann (African Writers Series 39), 1969.
Carefully wrought satire on French colonialism in Cameroon.

K. PIETERSON and A. RUTHERFORD (eds), *Cowries and Kobos: the West African Oral Tale and Short Story*, Dangaroo Press (Denmark), 1981.
An excellent selection of stories with useful critical introductions.

SOL PLAATJE, *Mhudi*, Heinemann (African Writers Series 201), 1978.
A historical novel by a politician and scholar, written in the 1930s. Set in the turbulent hinterland of South Africa where the beautiful and brave Mhudi encounters the Ndebele under Mzilikazi and the Boers.

OLA ROTIMI, *The Gods are Not to Blame*, Oxford University Press (Three Crowns), 1971.
A Yoruba version of *Oedipus Rex*. **D**

OLIVE SCHREINER, *The Story of an African Farm*, Penguin Modern Classics, 1971.
The classic tale of childhood and lost love, set in the lonely Karroo at the end of the nineteenth century.

L. SÉDAR SENGHOR, *Selected Poems/ Poésies Choisies*, Rex Collings, 1976 (p.6).
A bilingual text with English translations and an introduction by Craig Williamson. **Po**

SEMBÉNE OUSMANE, *God's Bits of Wood*, Translated from the French by Francis Price, Heinemann (African Writers Series 63), 1970.
A classic novel of a strike on the Dakar-Bamako railway in the 1940s.
Xala, Translated by Clive Wake, Heinemann (African Writers Series 175), 1976.
Satire on the new black 'aristocrats' of independent Senegal.
The Money Order with White Genesis, Translated by Clive Wake, Heinemann (African Writers Series 92), 1972.
Two stories, one showing the difficulties of cashing a large money order if you are illiterate, the second a grim tale of poverty and incest.

SIPHO SEPAMLA, *The Soweto I Love*, David Philip/ Rex Collings, 1977.
Poetry recording the events and experience of those involved in the 1976 uprising. **Po**
A Ride on the Whirlwind, Ad Donker, Johannesburg, 1981; Heinemann (African Writers Series 268) 1984.
An insider's novel of the Soweto uprising of 1976 presented through the experience of a group of young student radicals.

MONGANE WALLY SEROTE, *Selected Poems*, Ad Donker, Johannesburg, 1982.
A comprehensive selection from one of South Africa's leading poets. Introduced and selected by Mbulelo Mzamane. **Po**

WOLE SOYINKA, *The Interpreters*, Introduction by Eldred Jones, Heinemann (African Writers Series 76), 1970.
Five graduates return from abroad and attempt to integrate the old and the new. A difficult but rewarding novel.
Season of Anomy, Rex Collings, 1973, Nelson Panafrica Library, 1980.
A fictional account of the Nigerian civil war.
The Lion and the Jewel See Unit 10. **D**
Opera Wonyosi, Rex Collings, 1981.
A Nigerian version of Gay's *The Beggar's Opera* and Brecht's *Threepenny Opera*. Fiercely critical of present-day Nigeria. **D**

Background references

Art, religion, philosophy, mythology

ALIYU M. GANI, *The Story of Islam*, Nigerian edition, Edward Arnold and Son/Dinosaur, 1979.
DENNIS DUERDEN, *African Art: An Introduction*, Hamlyn, 1974.
RONALD EYRE, *Ronald Eyre on the Long Search*, BBC Publications, 1979. Illustrated.
ROBIN HORTON, *The Gods as Guests: An Aspect of Kalabari Religious Life*, Nigeria Magazine Publications, Nigeria Magazine, Lagos, 1960.
J.S. MBITI, *African Religions and Philosophy*, Heinemann, 1969.
M. MCLEOD, *Asanti, King of Gold*, British Museum, 1980.
G. PARRINDER, *African Mythology*, Hamlyn, 1967.
R. TAMES, *Approaches to World Religions: Islam*, John Murray, 1982.
R.F. THOMPSON, *Black Gods and Kings: Yoruba Art at UCLA*, Los Angeles, 1971.
R.F. THOMPSON, *African Art in Motion*, University of California Press, 1979.
H.W. TURNER, *Living Tribal Religions*, Ward Lock, 1971.
F. WILLETT, *African Art*, Thames and Hudson, 1971.

Geography, history and pre-history, languages

J. ADDISON, *Traditional Africa*, Harrap World History Programme, 1974.
P. ALEXANDRE, *An Introduction to Languages and Language in Africa*, Heinemann, 1972.
A. ATMORE and G. STACEY, *Black Kingdoms, Black Peoples*, Orbis Publishing, 1979. Photographs by Werner Forman.
M. CROWDER and G. ABDULLAHI, *Nigeria: An Introduction to its History*, Longman, 1979.
T. DAVENPORT, *South Africa: A Modern History*, second ed., Toronto, University of Toronto Press, 1977.
B. DAVIDSON, *Old Africa Rediscovered*, Gollancz, 1965. *The Africans*, Longman, 1969. *Discovering Africa's Past*, Longman, 1978.
N.E. DAVIS, *A History of Southern Africa*, Longman, 1972. New edition, 1978.
R. ELPHICK and H. GILIOMEE, *The Shaping of South Africa, 1652–1820*, Longman, 1980.
P. GARLAKE, *The Kingdoms of Africa*, Elsevier/Phaidon, 1978.
GLADYS HICKMAN, *The New Africa*, Hodder and Stoughton, 1973, second ed., 1976.
H.R. JARRETT, *A Geography of West Africa*, Evans, 1976.
S. MARKS, 'South Africa, the myth of the empty land', *History Today*, January 1980, pp.1–13.
B. OGOT and J. KIERAN (eds), *Zamani: A Survey of East African History*, East African Publishing House and Longman (Nairobi), second ed., 1974.
R. OLIVER and A. ATMORE, *Africa since 1800*, CUP, 1967, second ed., 1972.
R. OLIVER and R. FAGE, *A Short History of Africa*, Penguin, second ed., 1966.
D. WILSON, *A History of South and Central Africa*, CUP, 1975.

Biography, politics and social change, general

G. ARNOLD, *Modern Nigeria*, Longman, 1977.
O. AWOLOWO, *Path to Nigerian Freedom*, Faber, 1947.
E.O. AYISI, *An Introduction to the Study of African Culture*, Heinemann, second ed., 1979.
N. BHEBE, *Lobengula of Zimbabwe*, Heinemann (African Historical Biographies), 1977.
P. BOHANNAN, *African Outline: A General Introduction*, Penguin African Library, 1964.
P. BOHANNAN and P. CURTIN, *Africa and Africans*, New York: Natural History Press, 1971.
J. BOOTH, *Writers and Politics in Nigeria*, Hodder and Stoughton, 1981.
BRANDT COMMISSION, *North–South: A Programme for Survival*, Pan, 1980.

K. YEBOA DAAKU, *Ose: Tutu of Asante*, Heinemann (African Historical Biographies), 1976.

A.J. DACHS, *Khama of Botswana*, Heinemann (African Historical Biographies), 1971.

B. DAVIDSON, *The People's Cause: A History of Guerrillas in Africa*, Longman, 1982.

B. DAVIDSON, S. SLOVO and A. WILKINSON, *Southern Africa*, Pelican, 1963.

DEVELOPMENT EDUCATION CENTRE, *Priorities for Development: A Teachers' Handbook for Development Education*, Selly Oak Colleges, Birmingham, 1980.

K. ELLIOTT, *An African School – A Record of Experience*, CUP, 1970.

OLAUDAH EQUIANO, *Equiano's Travels: His Autobiography*, ed. Paul Edwards, Heinemann (African Writers Series 10), 1967.

W.B. FAGG, *Nigerian Images*, Lund Humphries, 1963.

W.B. FAGG and M. WEBSTER PLASS, *African Sculpture: An Anthology*, 1964.

F. FANON, *Black Skin White Masks*, trans. C. Markmann, Paladin, 1970.

PETER FORDHAM, *A Geography of African Affairs*, Pelican, 1971.

J. FRIEDMAN, *Jomo Kenyatta*, Wayland, 1975.

R. MUGO GATHERU, *Child of Two Worlds*, Routledge and Kegan Paul, 1964.

R. HALLETT, *People and Progress in West Africa. An Introduction to the Problems of Development*, Pergamon, 1966.

P. HARRISON, *Inside the Third World: The Anatomy of Poverty*, Penguin, second ed. 1981.

B.W. HODDER, *Africa Today: A Short Introduction to African Affairs*, Methuen, 1978.

JILL HOLLINGS, *African Nationalism*, Rupert Hart Davis, 1971.

R.W. HULL, *Modern Africa: Change and Continuity*, Prentice Hall, 1980.

O. IKIME, *Chief Dogho of Warri*, Heinemann (African Historical Biographies), 1976.

R. JEFFCOATE, *Positive Image: Towards a Multicultural Curriculum*, Chameleon, 1979.

P.C. LLOYD, *Africa in Social Change*, Penguin African Library, 1971.

A. LUTHULI, *Let My People Go*, Fontana, 1963; Fontana (Fount), 1982. The Autobiography of the winner of the 1961 Nobel Peace Prize.

J. MCNEAL and M. ROGERS, *The Multi-Racial School*, Penguin Education Specials, 1971, repr. 1972.

A. MAZRUI, *The African Condition*, The BBC Reith Lectures, 1979; Heinemann, 1980.

G. OAKLEY, *The Devil's Music – a History of the Blues*, BBC Publications, 1976.

O. ODINGA, *Not Yet Uhuru*, Heinemann (African Writers Series 38), 1967.

M. OMINDE, *Mary Ominde's African Cookery Book*, Heinemann, Nairobi, 1975.

M. PEIL, *Nigerian Politics: The People's View*, Cassell, 1976.

L. VAN DER POST, *African Cooking*, Time/Life Books, 1970.

R.K. RASMUSSEN, *Mzilikazi of the Ndebele*, Heinemann (African Historical Biographies), 1977.

W. RODNEY, *How Europe Undeveloped Africa*, Bogle-L'Ouverture, 1972.

B.E.A. SANDLER, *The African Cook Book*, World Publishing, 1972.

M. SMITH, *Baba of Koro, A Woman of the Muslim Hausa*, Faber, 1954.

R.W. STRAYER, *Kenya: Focus on Nationalism*, Prentice Hall, 1975.

R.O. WILLIAMS, *Miss Williams' Cookery Book*, Longman, Nigeria, 1975.

Critical works

MARTIN BANHAM, *The Lion and the Jewel*, Nexus Books, British Council/Rex Collings, 1981.

ULLI BEIER, *Introduction to African Literature: An Anthology of Critical Writing on African and Afro-American Literature and Oral Tradition*, Longman, 1967, repr. 1980.

DOROTHY S. BLAIR, *African Literature in French: A History of Creative Writing in French from West and Equatorial Africa*, CUP, 1976 (paperback 1981). Includes a comprehensive annotated bibliography.

D. BURNESS (ed.), *Critical Perspectives on Lusophone Literature from Africa*, Three Continents Press, 1981.

DAVID CARROLL, *Chinua Achebe*, Macmillan (Commonwealth Series), 1979.

MICHAEL CHAPMAN, (ed.), *Soweto Poetry*, McGraw-Hill (Southern Africa Literature Series), 1981. A selection of critical articles, reviews, background material.

DAVID COOK, *African Literature: A Critical View*, Longman, 1977.

ROMANUS EGUDU, *Modern African Poetry and the African Predicament*, Macmillan, 1978.

RUTH FINNEGAN, *Oral Literature in Africa*, Oxford University Press, 1970.

ROBERT FRASER, *The Novels of Ayi Kwei Armah*, Heinemann, 1979.

JAMES GIBBS (ed.), *Critical Perspectives on Wole Soyinka*, Heinemann, 1981. Includes an extensive bibliography.

STEPHEN GRAY, *Southern African Literature: An Introduction*, David Philip/Rex Collings, 1979.

GARETH GRIFFITHS, *A Double Exile: African and Caribbean Writing Between Two Cultures*, Marion Boyars, 1978.

TEMPLE HAUPTFLEISCH, *Athol Fugard: A Source Guide*, Ad Donker, Johannesburg, 1982.

GEORGE HERON, *The Poetry of Okot p'Bitek*, Heinemann, 1976.

CHRISTOPHER HEYWOOD (ed.), *Perspectives on African Literature*, Heinemann, 1971.

CHRISTOPHER HEYWOOD (ed.), *Aspects of South African Literature*, Heinemann, 1976.

C.L. INNES and B. LINDFORS (eds), *Critical Perspectives on Chinua Achebe*, Heinemann, 1979.

ABIOLA IRELE, *African Literature and Ideology*, Heinemann, 1981. Includes chapter on African writing in French and the Negritude movement.

ELDRED D. JONES, *The Writings of Wole Soyinka*, Heinemann, 1973, second ed. 1982.

G.D. KILLAM, *An Introduction to the Writings of Ngugi*, Heinemann, 1980.

ADELE KING, *The Writings of Camara Laye*, Heinemann, 1981.

B. KING and K. OGUNGBESAN, *A Celebration of Black and African Writing*, Ahmadu Bello University Press/OUP, 1975, repr. 1977.

H.L.B. MOODY, *Literary Appreciation: A Practical Guide to the Understanding and Enjoyment of Literature in English*, Longman, 1968. Includes African material.

GERALD MOORE, *Twelve African Writers*, Hutchinson, 1980. Includes an annotated bibliography.

ALASTAIR NIVEN, *The Concubine*, Nexus Books, British Council/Rex Collings, 1981.

LEWIS NKOSI, *Tasks and Masks: Themes and Styles of African Literature*, Longman, 1982.

EMMANUEL OBIECHINA, *Tradition and Society in the West African Novel*, CUP, 1975.

OYIN OGUNBA, *The Movement of Transition: A Study of the Plays of Wole Soyinka*, Ibadan University Press, 1975.

OYIN OGUNBA and ABIOLA IRELE (eds), *Theatre in Africa*, Ibadan University Press, 1978.

KOLAWOLE OGUNGBESAN, *New West African Literature*, Heinemann, 1979.

EUSTACE PALMER, *An Introduction to the African Novel*, Heinemann, 1972.

EUSTACE PALMER, *The Growth of the African Novel*, Heinemann, 1979.

KIRSTEN HOLST PETERSEN, *John Pepper Clark: Selected Poems*, Nexus Books, British Council/Rex Collings, 1981.

ADRIAN ROSCOE, *Mother is Gold: A Study in West African Literature*, CUP, 1971.

ADRIAN ROSCOE, *Uhuru's Fire: African Literature East and South*, CUP, 1977.

ROWLAND SMITH (ed.), *Exile and Tradition: Studies in African and Caribbean Literature*, Longman, 1976.

MICHAEL THORPE, *Doris Lessing's Africa*, Evans, 1978.

CHRIS WANJALA (ed.), *Standpoints on African Literature: A Critical Anthology*, East Africa Literature Bureau, 1973.

EDGAR WRIGHT, *The Critical Evaluation of African Literature*, Heinemann, 1973.

HANS ZELL with C. BUNDY and V. COULON, *A New Reader's Guide to New African Literature*, Heinemann, second ed. 1983.

Journals and periodicals

Africa Articles on topical political and economic matters. Useful for contemporary information. Published in London.

African Literature Today ed. Eldred D. Jones. An annual journal of explanatory criticism. Published by Heinemann Educational Books.

Africa Now Lively and well-informed articles on politics and the arts. Published in London.

Index on Censorship ed. George Theiner, 21 Russell Street, Covent Garden, London WC2B 5HP.
Covers position of writers in African countries where censorship is practised: includes South Africa, Kenya, Zambia; articles, interviews, book reviews, poetry, facts. Note the special issue on Africa and Argentina, Vol. 9 No. 3, 1980: includes an interview with Camara Laye, Ngugi on himself, article on African theatre. £11 for 6 issues a year.

Journal of Commonwealth Literature eds Alastair Niven and Angus Calder. Invaluable source of critical articles, also annual bibliographies.

Multi-ethnic Education Produced by the ILEA Multi-ethic Inspectorate. Useful for its articles, reviews and resources.

Network A quarterly publication of USPG (United Society for the Propagation of the Gospel), ed. A. Richmond, 15 Tufton Street, London SW1P 3QQ (Tel: 01-222-4222). Includes excellent articles on matters of topical importance in Zimbabwe, Lesotho, Zambia, South Africa and other countries. Also book reviews, illustrations, maps, photographs. Excellent value. Cost £1.50 per annum.

New African Articles on contemporary affairs in Africa and the arts. Published in London.

Okike ed. Chinua Achebe. An African journal of new writing. Critical articles and poetry. UK representative, C.L. Innes, University of Kent, Canterbury.

Pan African Book World ed. Jane M. Nwankwo. A new magazine aimed at publishers, authors, booksellers, teachers and librarians. Published in Nigeria by Fourth Dimension Publishing Co. 179 Zik Avenue, PMB 01164, Enugu, Nigeria.

South Magazine A monthly Third World magazine with very general coverage and an excellent book review section. Published in London.

Staffrider A new journal of critical writing, prose and poetry. Includes work from writers' groups in Johannesburg and elsewhere in South Africa. In forefront of the present renaissance in South African writing. Available: Staffrider, Box 31910, Braamfontein 2017, Johannesburg.

Wasafiri eds Susheila Nasta and Robert Fraser. The journal of the Association for the Teaching of Caribbean and African Literature (ATCAL). Concentrates on articles on teaching as well as criticism, interviews and reviews. Subscriptions from Christine Archer, 130 Ferme Park Road, London N8 9SD. Cost: personal £3.50; institutional £7 per annum.

West Africa Covers current affairs in Anglophone and Francophone West Africa. Frequent high quality review articles on literature; some poetry. Also articles on African and Caribbean affairs. Published in London.

Index